TRANSFORMATION

TRANSFORMATION

Jung's Legacy and Clinical Work Today

Edited by
Alessandra Cavalli, Lucinda Hawkins,
and Martha Stevns

KARNAC

First published in 2014 by
Karnac Books Ltd
118 Finchley Road, London NW3 5HT

British Library Cataloguing in Publication Data

A C.I.P. for this book is available from the British Library

ISBN 978 1 78049 160 8

Edited, designed and produced by The Studio Publishing Services Ltd
www.publishingservicesuk.co.uk
e-mail: studio@publishingservicesuk.co.uk

Printed in Great Britain

www.karnacbooks.com

CONTENTS

PART VI: THE FUTURE

ACKNOWLEDGEMENTS

Introduction: The epigraph from C. G. Jung, *C.W.*, *V*, par. 685 (Routledge & Kegan Paul, 1956) is used by permission of the publisher.

Chapter Three (Godsil): The epigraph from C. G. Jung, *C.W.*, *11*, par. 391 (Routledge & Kegan Paul, 1958) is used by permission of the publisher.

The epigraph by Michael Fordham from "A critical note of Meltzer's *The Kleinian Development*" in R. Hobdell (Ed.), *Freud, Jung, Klein: The Fenceless Field* (Routledge, 1995) is used by permission of the publisher.

Chapter Five (Wiener): The epigraph by Carol Ann Duffy from "Mrs. Midas" in *The World's Wife* (London: Picador, 1999) is used by permission of the publisher.

Chapter Six (West) The epigraph by C. G. Jung, *C.W.*, *8*, par. 210 (Routledge & Kegan Paul, 1934) is used by permission of the publisher.

Chapter Ten (Carta): An earlier version of this chapter, titled, "Narcissism, solitude, friendship: notes on the therapeutic alliance in the context of the Freud–Jung relationship", was published in the *Journal of Analytical Psychology*, 57(4), 2012: 483–499.

George Bright is a training analyst of the Society of Analytical Psychology and works in private practice in London. He has published in French and German journals as well as in English, and his essay on "Synchronicity as a basis of analytic attitude" was awarded the Michael Fordham Prize by the *Journal of Analytical Psychology*.

Stefano Carta is Professor of Dynamic Psychology at the University of Cagliari, Italy. A graduate of the Jung Institute in Zurich, he is a member of the Associazione Italiana di Psicologia Analitica (AIPA), of which he was President from 2000–2004. He is Deputy Editor for Europe of the *Journal of Analytical Psychology* and has a private practice in Rome. He has published over eighty works on clinical and analytical psychology.

Richard Carvalho is a Fellow of the Royal College of Psychiatrists, a training analyst with the Society of Analytical Psychology and a psychoanalytic psychotherapist (Tavistock Society). He was formerly Consultant Psychotherapist at St Mary's Hospital, Paddington, in London, and is now in private analytic practice.

Alessandra Cavalli, PhD, is a professional member of the Society of Analytical Psychology, trained as a child and adult analyst, who is in private practice in London. She teaches at various institutions and supervises work with children in care in Mexico and Italy.

Brian Feldman, PhD, is a clinical psychologist, child, adolescent, and adult Jungian psychoanalyst and infant observation seminar leader with a private practice in Palo Alto, California. He trained in clinical psychology at the University of California, Berkeley, and served as chief psychologist in the Department of Child Psychiatry at Stanford University Medical Center, where he received the outstanding teaching award. He has been a visiting scholar in the Department of Psychiatry, University of Campinas, São Paulo, Brazil, and is visiting professor at the Russian Academy of Science's Institute of Psychology in Moscow. In 2013, his research on infancy and the psychic skin was honoured by the Psychoanalytic Consortium of Washington, DC. Trained in Jungian psychoanalysis in San Francisco and in London with Michael Fordham, he is on the training faculties of the Jung Institute of San Francisco and the Inter-Regional Society of Jungian Analysts.

Geraldine Godsil is a training analyst and supervisor for the British Psychotherapy Foundation and a training therapist for the Northern School of Child and Adolescent Psychotherapy. She teaches and supervises in Estonia and has published several papers in books and journals. She is on the editorial board of the *British Journal of Psychotherapy*. Her current research interest is the transgenerational transmission of trauma, and she is a doctoral candidate in this area at the University of Essex.

Lucinda Hawkins is a professional member of the Society of Analytical Psychology in private practice in London. She is on the editorial board of the *Journal of Analytical Psychology* and is currently Book Review Editor. Co-author of *Michelangelo* (1991), she was an editor of the Grove Dictionary of Art.

Maggie McAlister is a member of the Society of Analytical Psychology, an HPCP-registered arts therapist, and a forensic psychotherapist within an NHS medium secure unit. She has published many papers, the most recent include "From transitional object to symbol" in *Drama Therapy and Destructiveness* (Jessica Kingsley, 2012) and "Boundaries and homicide", in *Professional and Therapeutic Boundaries in Forensic Mental Health Practice* (Jessica Kingsley, 2012). She is a senior lecturer at Bucks New University and has a private practice in North London.

William Meredith-Owen is a training analyst of the Society of Analytical Psychology and teaches and supervises at the West Midlands Institute of Psychotherapy. He is the Joint Editor-in-Chief of the *Journal of Analytical Psychology*, to which he has contributed papers addressing the interface of Jungian and Kleinian practice and the particular difficulties besetting training analyses. He is in private practice in Stratford-upon-Avon and London. His most recent publications are "The hero, the anima and the claustrum: anality and idealization" (*Journal of Analytical Psychology*, April 2012) and "Jung's shadow: negation and narcissism of the self" (*Journal of Analytical Psychology*, November 2011).

Martha Stevns is a member of the Society of Analytical Psychology in private practice in Cambridge, and she also teaches and supervises. She was an editor of the Swiss art magazine *du*.

Marcus West is a professional member of the Society of Analytical Psychology. He is a member of the editorial board of the *Journal of Analytical Psychology* and a previous Book Review Editor. He has published a number of papers in the Journal and was joint winner of its Michael Fordham Prize in 2004. He is the author of two books: *Feeling, Being, and the Sense of Self* (2007) and *Understanding Dreams in Clinical Practice* (2011), both published by Karnac. He is in private practice in Sussex.

Jan Wiener is a training analyst for the Society of Analytical Psychology (SAP) and the British Psychotherapy Foundation (BPF) and past Director of Training at the SAP. She is Vice President of the International Association of Analytical Psychology (IAAP) and Co-Chair of the Education Committee. She has taught and supervised in Russia for the past fifteen years. She was Consultant Adult Psychotherapist at Forest House Psychotherapy Clinic for twenty-five years and is now in private practice in London. An Assistant Editor of the *Journal of Analytical Psychology*, she has written many papers and chapters. Her most recent publications include *Supervising and Being Supervised* (Palgrave Macmillan, 2003), edited with Richard Mizen and Jenny Duckham, and *The Therapeutic Relationship: Transference, Countertransference and the Making of Meaning* (Texas A and M University Press, 2009).

Introduction

"... the man who comes to us for treatment confronts us with unforeseeable problems and expects us to fulfill a therapeutic task for which we cannot but feel inadequate. The strongest incentive to unceasing research has always come to me from my practice, and it consisted in the simple question which no man can ignore: 'How can you treat something that you don't understand?' ... anyone who wants to practice psychotherapy ... needs a science of the psyche, not a theory about it"

(Jung, *C.W., V*, par. 685)

As clinicians today, we are faced with both the richness and the lacunae of Jung's legacy, and how to use it with patients. To understand where we are in this process, we wanted to bring together the thinking of those who approach their work from the lived experience in the consulting room, rather than adherence to a particular theory. To relinquish the authority of a theoretical position requires courage, but to do so frees us to find the theory relevant to a particular patient at a particular time. Such an approach can help to overcome the rigidity of theoretical positions, since, through this experience, theory can be changed, expanded, and developed.

The book begins with a re-reading of Jung's autobiographical writing in *Memories, Dreams, Reflections* and describes how his inability to integrate his own early trauma influenced his thinking. Despite this, Jung developed many useful clinical concepts, emphasising the importance of learning from experience. Some of the ideas he wrote about, such as the psyche–soma unit and the relevance of affect, are increasingly recognised as central in contemporary practice. Building on this legacy, our contributors discuss in detail technique and the ongoing process of learning. We hope that future clinicians will continue thinking, changing, and relinquishing, in order to transform our work, our patients, and ourselves.

Creating this book has been a surprisingly rich and challenging experience, as it developed a life of its own that we both followed and shaped. We would like to thank all the contributors, especially Jan Wiener and Richard Carvalho, who have supported the book from the very beginning, and through its many transformations.

Alessandra Cavalli, Lucinda Hawkins, Martha Stevns
Editors

PART I
RE-READING JUNG

CHAPTER ONE

On revisiting the opening chapters of *Memories, Dreams, Reflections*

William Meredith-Owen

Introduction

The most vivid impression of my first encounter with *Memories, Dreams, Reflections* (Jung, 1963), during my student years, was its aesthetic impact. In those opening passages one stunning image of the natural world succeeds another: the sunlight through the leaves, the sunset on the Alps, the sand and pebbles on the lake shore lapped by the seemingly infinite expanse of calm water. By contrast, when I returned to it in the early days of my analytic training, I was much more struck by the frequent referencing of the childhood Jung to his alienation from the human world, albeit set alongside this profound sense of connectedness to nature. Thus, we read,

> Dim intimations of trouble in my parents' marriage hovered around me. My illness, severe eczema, must have been connected with a temporary separation of my parents. My mother spent several months in a hospital in Basle, and presumably her illness had something to do with the difficulty in the marriage. I was deeply troubled by my mother being away. From then on, I always felt mistrustful when the word 'love' was spoken. (Jung, 1963, p. 23)

Winnicott (1964), whose review of Jung's autobiography for the *International Journal of Psychoanalysis* remains an inexhaustible source of insight into both men (Meredith-Owen, 2011a), noted the ambivalence in this curious combination of intimate estrangement on the one hand and absorption in the natural world on the other, and writes,

> Jung's early memories are of a consciousness of beauty but there is a negative to this sort of positive feeling experience . . . it will turn out to be a distortion of integrative tendencies secondary to the mother's maternal failure due to her own illness. (Winnicott, 1964, p. 451)

At first glance this assertion looks enigmatic: why should such a capacity for the apprehension of beauty be consequent on this "distortion of integrative tendencies"? What I think Winnicott means by this is that the containment Jung missed from his mother (and perhaps from the parental marriage) he sought for instead through his immersion in nature and his absorption in his own inner world of vision. As Winnicott put it with succinct, earthy irony, 'he went down under and found subjective life' (Winnicott, 1964, p. 453).

For Jung did feel held by his sense of the profound correlation of the natural world with what he was eventually to call the "objective psyche" (Jung, 1953, par. 103). His belief in the intrinsic mutuality of their origins is dramatically evoked in Section 6 of "On the nature of the psyche", where, quoting the alchemist Khunrath, he describes creation as arising from "the arcane substance – the watery earth, (the mud) . . . of the world essence – 'universally animated' by the 'fiery spark (scintillae) of the soul of the world'. . ." (Jung, 1960, par. 388). One can well imagine Jung assuming the stone and mortar with which he constructed his tower at Bollingen to be infused with just such a spirit; a spirit shared by an earlier compatriot, the sixteenth-century physician Paracelsus, of whom Jung wrote admiringly for affirming how

> the characteristic alchemical vision of sparks scintillating in the blackness of the arcane substance could change into the spectacle of the interior firmament and its stars. He beholds the darksome psyche as a star strewn night sky, whose planets and fixed constellations represent the archetypes in all their luminosity and numinosity. (1960, par. 392)

The elevated tone of such a passage has inspired some but left others wary, if not antagonised. For instance, Edward Glover, one of the most influential figures in the British Psychoanalytical Society before the war, dismissed this sort of thing as Jung "vaporising". I find it impressive but a little distant; by contrast, although the opening pages of *Memories, Dreams, Reflections* are equally dramatic, their raw immediacy is also inescapable.

Winnicott fully appreciated this; he commented,

> these first three chapters are genuine autobiography. Here is an autobiography to take its place with the other really convincing autobiographies; one has no doubt about the value of these chapters as a truly self-revealing statement. (Winnicott, 1964, p. 450)

Despite the reservations, compounded by Shamdasani's (2005) scrupulous research, about the status of the remaining chapters as a true autobiographical record, Winnicott's appreciation of the implicit authenticity of these opening passages is surely not misplaced. Neither, it must be acknowledged, is his appraisal of much of it as evidence of Jung's marked pathology. If previously my attention (Meredith-Owen, 2011b) had focused on these difficulties, most notably the self-proclaimed tension between Jung's No. 1 and No. 2 personalities (Jung, 1963, p. 91), what I now noticed was the remarkable degree of integration and coherence that ran, seemingly spontaneously, through the imagery of the memories, dreams, and reflections that Jung had here assembled. And yes, they do indeed include frequent descriptions of borderline states, alienation, and inflation, but let us not forget that Jung's original ground-breaking clinical insight during his early psychiatric work at the Burghölzli was to realise that such material in his patients might yet contain "a germ of meaning". And he elaborated on what this intriguing organic metaphor might imply: "a personality, a life history, a pattern of hopes and desires lie behind the psychosis. The fault is ours if we do not understand them" (Jung, 1963, p. 148). Although it may be pertinent that this insight was born out of his confrontation with pathology, he was later to affirm (using the same analogy) that a similar dynamic sustained the process of individuation which he defined as "the realisation, in all its aspects, of the personality originally hidden away in the embryonic germ plasm; the production and unfolding of the original potential wholeness" (Jung, 1953, par. 186).

The rhizome

Jung's prologue to *Memories, Dreams, Reflections* makes it quite clear that finally now, in his advanced old age, he has taken up the challenge to understand the "germ of meaning" in his own autobiographical raw material:

> My life is the story of the self realisation of the unconscious. Every-thing in the unconscious seeks outward manifestation, and the person-ality too desires to evolve out of its unconscious conditions and to experience itself as a whole. I cannot employ the language of science to trace this process of growth in myself . . . thus it is that I have now undertaken, in my 83rd year, to tell my personal myth. I can only make direct statements, only 'tell stories'. Whether or not the stories are 'true' is not the problem. The only question is whether what I tell is *my* fable, *my* truth. (Jung, 1963, p. 17)

Gone is his characteristic insistence on a stance of scientific objec-tivity; instead, that repeated italicised "*my*" emphasises an unabashed subjectivity. On the following page, Jung goes on to compare "this process of growth" to a plant that draws on its hidden rhizome, a metaphor anticipated in those phrases a "germ of meaning" and "embryonic germ plasm". This becomes a key motif that is revisited and elaborated in the second chapter:

> To this day, writing down my memories at the age of 83, I have never fully unwound the tangle of my earliest memories. They are like indi-vidual fruits of a single underground rhizome, like stations on a road of unconscious development. (Jung, 1963, p. 43)

This modest ("I have never fully unwound the tangle . . .") acknowledgement is something of an open invitation to subsequent commentators to attempt just that, and, from a critical perspective (albeit constructively so), we have already noted that Winnicott (1964) most certainly took up this challenge with some style. His lead was followed by important papers from Atwood and Stolorow (1977), Homans (1979), and Satinover (1985, 1986). Contemporaneously, Michael Fordham, a close associate of Winnicott's, was initiating Jung-ian child analysis and establishing a metapsychological basis for the clinical integration of Jungian perspectives with a more developmen-tal psychoanalytic approach. The extent to which all this background can now illuminate our reading of *Memories, Dreams, Reflections* is well illustrated by Feldman's (1992, 2004) contributions: yet the influence of this "rhizome" running through these opening chapters may reward still further consideration. As we become more familiar with this extraordinarily rich material we realise that the working of this rhizome is manifest not just in its outer form—the apparently spontaneous consistency and coherence of the imagery—but also in its implicit content. Once alert to the thread, we can trace through a series of dramatic vignettes Jung's ongoing ambivalent struggle to establish a satisfactory relationship with the parental couple, while at the same time being powerfully drawn to the defence of omnipotent phallic independence. Within a neo-Kleinian vertex, this material strongly suggests the structuring activity of unconscious phantasy predicated on intimations of a primal scene: I suggest this influence extends from the part-object drama of Jung's first recorded dream all the way through to the principles of his mature metapsychology.

This is what Hinshelwood (1989) has to say in *A Dictionary of Kleinian Thought* about the origins of unconscious phantasy:

> Unconscious phantasies underlie every mental process ... erupting from their biological instigation, unconscious phantasies are slowly converted in two ways; (i) by change through the development of the organs for distant perception of external reality; and (ii) by emergence into the symbolic world of culture from the primary world of the body. Phantasies can be elaborated for the alleviation of internal states of mind by either manipulation of the body and its sensations or direct phantasising. Phantasy is the mental expression of the instinctual impulses and also of defence mechanisms against instinctual impulses. (Hinshelwood, 1989, p. 32)

Thus, the Kleinian view is that unconscious phantasies, originating from the "primary world of the body" (immediate apprehension of one's physical actuality and all its processes), develop a capacity for articulation that both draws on and informs a growing awareness of external reality. A constant interaction between the environment and the innate is implied here as unconscious phantasy strives towards "emergence into the symbolic world of culture". A spectacular instance of one such eruption of "instinctual impulses" must surely be Jung's initiatory dream of the giant tree-trunk phallus in the underground cavern. Yet, Winnicott concludes his commentary on this passage with the dry remark that "the thing an analyst would find lacking (in this account) is any attempt to relate this with the four-year-old Jung's *instinctual* life" (Winnicott, 1964, p. 454, my italics). Certainly, Jung does not record this experience as if it were part of an ongoing emergence of intimate personal awareness; we could say, rather, that Jung presents it as something that happened *to* him rather than *out of* him. Indeed, this hint of something split off is augmented by Jung's own concluding rhetorical flourish:

> Who spoke to me then? Who talked of problems far beyond my know-ledge? Who brought the Above and Below together, and laid the foun-dation for everything that was to fill the second half of my life with stormiest passion? (Jung, 1963, p. 30)

It is so characteristic of Jung to personify the unconscious in this way, to treat it as an "other", albeit one with whom a relationship of "stormiest passion" might then ensue: this became in effect the epis-temological basis that underlay *The Red Book* (2009).

Accordingly, these opening chapters of the autobiography can easily be construed to substantiate Winnicott's assertions that "Jung's . . . concept of the collective unconscious was part of his attempt to deal with his lack of contact with what could now be called the uncon-scious-according-to-Freud" (Winnicott, 1964, p. 453). The implication here is that Jung's "lack of contact" with his personal (Freudian) unconscious, which we might well argue derived from his wary distance from the maternal embrace, drove him to reach for the arms of the (collective) earth mother instead. If this be so, it will be no sur-prise to find that in *Memories, Dreams, Reflections* we have a dramatic account of unconscious phantasy emerging full of the ambivalence that Hinshelwood anticipates and serving as defence against, as well as expression of, instinctual impulses.

However, there is a danger that these valuable (Winnicottian) insights into the compensatory structure in Jung might lead to relative neglect of the creative expressive elements. Although, in these open-ing chapters, Jung may be diffusing his intimate anguish within a grander, more universal archetypal frame, the cumulative effect acquires a distinctive aesthetic coherence that assumes a markedly individual character. If Jung had coined the term "individuation" to refer to such a spontaneous interweaving of the personal and the collective, I would have found it an apt and useful term; that, in fact, he meant something rather different by it is an issue that has troubled and, I would say, hampered analytical psychology ever since.

The theme of the disunited man

This is a controversial assertion that requires us to be as honest about Jung's constraints as we are admiring of his achievements. The title of this section is taken directly from Atwood and Stolorow's (1977) still valuable elaboration of Winnicott's original critique, in which they track Jung's struggle to achieve a stable self-representation. However, here Jung took the lead himself, writing with disarming openness about the painful disunity of his childhood experience. The dominant concern to which Jung repeatedly returns is the troubled relationship between his No. 1 personality and his No. 2 personality: the theme is first explicitly introduced on page 62, and recurs with increasing frequency thereafter (e.g., pp. 75, 81, 84, 87, 91). This first passage must suffice as a representative example:

> The play and counterplay between personalities No. 1 and No. 2, which has run through my whole life, has nothing to do with a "split" or dissociation in the ordinary medical sense. On the contrary, it is played out in every individual. In my life No. 2 has been of prime importance, and I have always tried to make room for anything that wanted to come to me from within. He is a typical figure, but he is perceived only by the very few. Most people's conscious understanding is not sufficient to realise that he is also what they are. (Jung, 1963, p. 62)

Note the measured tone of "*also* what they are" (my emphasis), which turns out to be uncharacteristic of the subsequent descriptions of "the play and counterplay" which do not describe a gradual integration so much as an ongoing bewilderment at remaining torn between basing his identity in either No. 1 or No. 2.

The mature Jung attempted to resolve this tension by elevating it into a metapsychological principle:

> We have to distinguish between a personal unconscious and an impersonal or transpersonal unconscious. We speak of the latter also as the

collective unconscious, because it is detached from anything personal and is entirely universal, and because its contents can be found everywhere, which is naturally not the case with the personal contents. (Jung, 1956, p. 76)

The anticipations of this universality of the collective unconscious, omnipresent through time and space, are certainly to be traced in this description—so redolent of that earlier praise of Paracelsus's vision—of his No. 2 personality:

It was as though a breath of the great world of stars and endless space had touched me or as if a spirit had invisibly entered the room – the spirit of one who had long been dead and yet was perpetually present in timelessness until far into the future. Denouements of this sort were wreathed with the halo of a *numen*. (Jung, 1963, p. 84)

This invisible spirit is also presented in more palpable terms, as, for instance, belonging to "the sphere of the 'old man', who belonged to the centuries" (Jung, 1963, p. 87). Such a figure is felt to have been embodied in Goethe, for whom Jung felt passionate allegiance, even entertaining the fantasy of being his illegitimate offspring (Bair, 2004, pp. 35, 48). Moreover, this hint of something/someone benign and accessible—as might be an admired father—about the collective unconscious/No. 2 personality is sometimes explicit:

The unconscious then gives us all the encouragement and help that a bountiful nature can shower upon man. It holds possibilities which are locked away from the conscious mind, for it has at its disposal all subliminal psychic contents, all those things which have been forgotten or overlooked, as well as the wisdom and experience of uncounted centuries which are laid down in its archetypal organs . . . For these reasons the unconscious could serve man as a unique guide . . . (Jung, 1956, p. 126)

These evocations of the collective unconscious as a wise mentor are complemented by those presenting it as the nurturing mother:

Therefore all those who do not want to dismiss the great treasures that lie buried in the collective psyche will strive, in one way or another, to maintain the newly won union with the fundamental sources of life . . . This piece of mysticism . . . is just as innate in every individual as the 'longing for the mother', the nostalgia for the source from which we sprang. (Jung, 1956, p. 179)

Actually, Jung's self-deprecating description of this as regressive mysticism does these passages scant justice: there are, indeed, some parallels in the mainstream psychoanalytic literature, notably Money-Kyrle's (1971) reference to our hard-won capacity to recognise "the supreme creativity of the parental intercourse", to which these evocations of Jung could read as an extended gloss. Albeit Jung's cosmic primal couple are more distant, perhaps more ethereal (though he was later to explore more embodied exemplars in the King and Queen of the alchemical tradition), nevertheless, the stance he adopts towards them of humility and gratitude is surely markedly similar to Money-Kyrle's.

However, what must also be recognised is that his earliest intimations of the presence of such a couple were far from reassuring. What we, via the childhood Jung, encounter in these opening chapters are starkly brutal encounters with their ambivalent power, as likely to overwhelm or terrify as to console or inspire. More prominent than her nurturing are the devouring aspects of this archetypal mother, while the avuncular Goethe father peels back into the terrifying Jesuit, or, worse, the man-eating phallus (the "subliminal . . . archetypal organ") of the underground cavern dream which also displayed this "halo of a *numen*". This is a picture of a distinctly uncontained part-object world in which projection and introjection abound and polarised states of idealisation and inflation alternate with denigration and repudiation.

I suggested earlier that Jung, missing a secure maternal link, necessarily resorted to other means of securing some containment in the face of such pressures. Hanna Segal elaborates on the possible fates that await the infant/child's emergent raw material "erupting from their biological instigation" (Hinshelwood, 1989):

> Bion extends Klein's concept of projective identification to include a primitive mental communication and interchange. The infant projects into the breast his anxiety and inchoate primitive concrete elements (beta elements). A mother capable of containing projective identification unconsciously processes those projections and responds adequately to the infant's needs. When this happens, the infant can reintroject his projections, modified by understanding, and he also

introjects the breast as a container capable of containing and dealing with anxiety. This forms the basis of his own ability to deal with anxiety [and in Winnicott's terms form a 'unit self']. This modification by understanding transforms the beta elements into alpha elements—a higher level of mental functioning. According to Bion, a good relationship between container and contained is the basis of such later capacities as symbolizing and thinking. When the relation is severely disturbed by mother's adverse response or the infant's envy—usually a combination of both—it lays the basis for later psychotic disturbance. (Segal, in Britton, Feldman, & O'Shaughnessy, 1989, p. 5)

This background would certainly account for Winnicott's assertion that Jung's self-portrait "gives us a picture of childhood schizophrenia" (Winnicott, 1964, p. 450), although the consensus of later commentators has been that "psychotic structure" (Satinover, 1985) might be a fairer designation. Yet, there is a paradox here: although Jung himself makes no bones about his suffering overwhelming waves of anxiety and "psychotic disturbance" (Jung, 1963, p. 109), he does so within a text evidently composed by someone with exceptional capacity for "symbolizing and thinking". Following the Segal model, we would expect such features to be mutually excluding, but in Jung both are writ large: this suggests that there might be other shaping factors involved that Segal's account does not quite accommodate. I find a similar anomaly in Winnicott's acknowledgment of the cultural achievements of Jung while rather scorning the value of his contribution to psychoanalysis (Rodman, 2003, p. 287).

I would suggest that there are two elements that these critiques overlook, or, at least, underestimate. The first is the degree to which Jung was able to fashion an alternative sense of containment from his immersion in nature and certain aspects of culture: in relation to both he evidently enjoyed experiences of reciprocal recognition—aesthetic moments in the parlance of Donald Meltzer (Meltzer & Williams, 1998)—that allowed transformations of beta into alpha elements despite his earlier deprivations. The second element is the role played by Jung's own notion of a teleological energy implicitly informing the emergent self. Although difficult to conceptualise such a force without lapsing into portentous claims that recent neuroscience has challenged, I feel this appeal to some nuclear shaping core to unconscious phantasy might be justified retrospectively: by its fruits shall it be known. In these opening chapters, we can track the evidence for such unfoldings—these manifestations of the rhizome—at first hand. So, I would share Bisagni's (2012) view that the recent theoretical debate around this issue (Knox, 2009, among others) leaves open the retention of such a premise as, at the very least, a useful clinical assumption.

If indeed present, such a process also would have reparative implications; as we noted earlier Winnicott does recognise the healing that Jung's work on his childhood memories must have wrought, but he frames this in rather a particular way: "In old age he appears to have dropped his No. 1 personality to a large extent and to have lived by his true self, and in this way he found a self that he could call his own" (Winnicott, 1964, p. 454). I wonder if this comment does not implicitly perpetuate the very split that was the fundamental structural problem for both men (Meredith-Owen, 2011a; Sedgwick, 2008). For Winnicott's metapsychology incorporated its own split—that between the False and True self—that has marked parallels with Jung's denigration of his No. 1 personality and valorisation of his No. 2 personality. However, is this issue really resolved by just overriding or "dropping" the flawed, False/No. 1 self? From a humbler perspective is there not something too grand(iose) and essentially impersonal about the True/No. 2 self? As an aspirational identity, it can feel ungrounded, divorced from its human feet of clay. That could not be said of those opening chapters whose hallmark is their visceral immediacy: as Winnicott notes, they feel "genuine", "really convincing". Jung achieves this by allowing himself to write in an idiom whose coherence is essentially poetic rather than philosophic: he reaches towards meaning through clusters of affect and image rather than through defining concept. Jung's amanuensis, Aniela Jaffé, reports Jung having said at the time, "The way I am and the way I write are a unity" (Bair, 2004, p. 777).

This is entirely consistent with the spirit of those passages from the prologue quoted earlier, in which Jung invokes his "personal myth", and concludes with reference to "my fable, my truth". The import of these phrases, sustained by the aesthetic of these opening chapters, suggests just that integration of the personal and collective that had previously eluded Jung. Their testimony stands as a powerful quasi-clinical example of the way in which (archetypal) unconscious phantasy seeks (individual) expression: instead of being presumed to be antithetical impediments, the personal and collective are now allowed to interweave and interact. This is a valuable antidote to that tendency in Jung to prefer "being lifted above the personal and into the supra-personal" (Brome, 1978, p. 305). Thus, we can now read the ageing Jung's revisiting of his developmental years as offering (implicitly) a new paradigm for individuation, and beyond that a model for the creative integration of analytical psychology with the psychoanalytic mainstream.

Let us now look at the most prominent examples in more detail. The three vignettes that have received the most attention from later commentators are first, that earliest dream of the erect phallus in the underground cavern; second, Jung's story of hiding his manikin and soul-stone in the attic; and third, his vision of God shitting on Basle Cathedral. To these I would like to add a fourth: his fantasies about living in a lake-bound castle, which he describes as his first experience of immersing himself in what he would later call an extended active imagination. I will argue that, throughout these scenarios, certain key images and affects recur, and that their interweaving testifies to the workings of that "rhizome" that Jung seemed so gratified to have retrospectively recognised in the process of responding to the autobi-ographical challenge that he eventually took up with such enthusiasm so late in life.

The underground cavern dream

Jung is quite clear that it was this dream that was nuclear:

> . . . the earliest dream I can remember, a dream which was to preoc-cupy me all my life. I was then between three and four years old.

> . . . in the dream I was in this meadow. Suddenly I discovered a dark, rectangular, stone lined hole in the ground. I had never seen it before. I ran forward curiously and peered down into it. Then I saw a stone stairway leading down. Hesitantly and fearfully, I descended. At the bottom was a doorway with a round arch, closed off by a green curtain. It was a big, heavy curtain of worked stuff like brocade, and it looked very sumptuous. Curious to see what might be hidden behind, I brushed it aside. I saw before me in the dim light a rectan-gular chamber about 30 feet long. The ceiling was arched and of hewn stone. The floor was laid with flagstones, and in the centre a red carpet ran from the entrance to a low platform. On this platform stood a wonderfully rich golden throne. I am not certain, but perhaps a red

cushion lay on the seat. It was magnificent, a real king's throne in a fairytale. Something was standing on it which I thought at first was a tree trunk twelve to fifteen feet high and about one and a half to two feet thick. It was a huge thing, reaching almost to the ceiling. But it was of a curious composition: it was made of skin and naked flesh, and on top there was something like a rounded head with no face and no hair. On the very top of the head was a single eye, gazing motionlessly upward.

It was fairly light in the room, although there were no windows and no apparent source of light. Above the head, however, was an aura of brightness. The thing did not move, yet I had the feeling it might at any moment crawl off the throne and creep towards me. I was paralysed with terror. At that moment I heard from outside and above my mother's voice. She called out, "Yes, just look at him. That is the man-eater!" That intensified my terror still more, and I awoke sweating and scared to death . . . (Jung, 1963, p. 27)

Feldman shares Winnicott's appreciation of the impact of Jung's writing—"the dream's intense vividness and sensory quality, as well as the emotional terror it evokes, are impressive" (Feldman, 1992, p. 266). He offers a broadly Kleinian perspective on what "the dream might convey of Jung's anxiety about what is going on inside mother's body" (p. 266), particularly his possible fear of the (father's) phallus in proprietarily castrating ("man-eating") mode. He contrasts this with an archetypal (Dionysian) standpoint that might regard the discovery of the regal phallus as a symbol of Jung's first experience of the profound potential of his own mind; certainly Jung records positive associations to the etymology of the word phallus as "shining" or "bright" (Jung, 1963, p. 28), concluding that his dream vision was an initiation into the "secrets of the Earth" (p. 30). Finally, mindful of the background of Jung's parents' evidently dysfunctional sexual relationship, Feldman wonders about the impact on Jung's emerging sexuality of his mother's alarmed reaction to the penis/phallus.

Atwood and Stolorow, though, stay closer to the context of this passage, particularly the preceding pages in which Jung describes his emerging doubts about Lord Jesus. Their summary could not be bettered:

Jung's account of the development of his secret childhood preoccupations begins with some early reflections on the nature of Jesus Christ.

At the age of three, he had been taught to say the following prayer (Jung, 1963, p. 10) each night before going to sleep:

> Spread out thy wings, Lord Jesus mild,
> And take to thee thy chick, thy child,
> If Satan would devour it,
> No harm shall overpower it,
> So let the angels sing.

The prayer pictures Jesus as a protecting and child-loving figure, and Jung at first envisioned him as a nice, benevolent gentleman sitting on a throne in the sky. But the phrase, 'take to thee thy chick, thy child' ('nimm dein Küchlein ein') was confusing; one 'takes' medicine, i.e. swallows it. He thought the prayer meant that Jesus swallows children in order to keep the devil from eating them. The rather ominous connotations of the word 'take' in this connexion were reinforced by Jung's observations of funerals and burials. He witnessed several scenes in which men, dressed in frock coats, top hats and shiny black boots, gathered about a hole in the ground and lowered a mysterious black box into it. (Atwood & Stolorow, 1977, p. 132)

Worthy of particular note is Jung's first envisagement of Jesus "sitting on a throne" and the association of being "taken" with being swallowed up by the ground in burial. This cluster of associations (manifestations of the rhizome) is expanded by the account, which immediately follows the dream, of his "first conscious trauma" at the sight of a figure in a broad hat and strange (androgynous) black garment coming down the hill toward him, inducing "a deadly terror as the frightful recognition shot through my mind: 'That is a Jesuit'" (Jung, 1963, p. 25). Although he had overheard his father referring to them disparagingly, Jung acknowledges that "Actually I had no idea who Jesuits were, but I was familiar with the word Jesus from my little prayer" (1963, p. 26). This further vignette draws on and expands the core imagery through expressing his ambivalence towards Lord Jesus by associating him now not only with comforting prayers and impressive thrones, but also with the devouring worm phallus and the threatening black clad figure of his presumed cohort, both of whom threaten to "take" him. This disturbing conflation is compounded by hearing that internal voice crying out a warning in the very same phrasing he had just heard in the dream: "That is a Jesuit" so closely echoes "That is the man-eater".

Jung's own deliberations on his dream centre on just what interpretation to give to this cry of his mother's: did she mean that "the dark Lord Jesus, the Jesuit, and the phallus were identical", or, by stressing the "That", did she imply that it was the phallus alone that was the man-eater? He seems inclined to the former, for he continues,

> At all events, the phallus of the dream seems to be a subterranean God 'not be named' . . . and such it remained throughout my youth, reappearing whenever anyone spoke too emphatically about Lord Jesus. Lord Jesus never became quite real for me, never quite acceptable, never quite lovable, for again and again I would think of his underground counterpart, a frightful revelation which had been accorded me without my seeking it. (Jung, 1963, p. 28)

This passage ends with a telling phrase: "I could never succeed in overcoming my secret distrust" (p. 29). The echo here is of the chilling conclusion to his earlier reference to the separation of his parents and his mother's subsequent hospitalisation: "I was deeply troubled by my mother's being away. From then on, I always felt mistrustful when the word 'love' was spoken" (p. 23).

These quotations speak of the profound anxiety generated by Jung's conflicting experiences of his mother:

> she was a very good mother to me. She had a hearty animal warmth, cooked wonderfully, and was most companionable and pleasant . . . but the unconscious personality would suddenly put in an appearance . . . a sombre, imposing figure possessed of unassailable authority . . . uncanny. (Jung, 1963, p. 65)

The ambivalent feelings towards Lord Jesus parallel these towards his mother and, by extension, towards the unconscious: can he surrender to their protective care or must he warily protect himself from their ruthless, potentially devouring power? Small wonder, then, at his frustration with his actual father's lack of authority, a weakness that must have left the childhood Jung feeling so exposed to the unmitigated, because unmediated, power of the archetypal. A familiar defence against such a threat is to ally oneself with it: I wonder if this is what Winnicott had in mind when he wrote of "the unconscious of Jung's which I would call: all those things that go on in underground caves, or (in other words) the world's mythologies, in which there is collusion between the individual and the maternal inner psychic realities" (Winnicott, 1989, p. 90). This issue of adequate separation from the maternal matrix in all its symbolic extension may be regarded as the Achilles heel of Jungian thought (Meredith-Owen, 2012; Redfearn, 1979), but we must also consider how experiences of reciprocal recognition within the context of the "world's mythologies" might offer valuable alternative containment in the wake of maternal failure.

Nevertheless, if we look closely at the detail, the texture of the writing, just at the point when Jung begins his reflective commentary on the dream and might well have explored the personal intimate implications of this uprush of instinctual life, we can track how he appears to sidestep and slip into mythological exposition mode. The dramatic immediacy is replaced by a more measured distance, occasioning in turn a more laboured rhythm in the writing:

> The dream haunted me for years; only much later did I realise that what I had seen was a phallus and it was decades before I understood that it was a ritual phallus. . . . The abstract significance of the phallus is shown by the fact that it was enthroned by itself, 'ithyphallically'. The hole in the meadow probably represented a grave. The grave itself was an underground temple whose green curtains symbolised the meadow, in other words the mystery of the Earth. (Jung, 1963, p. 34)

Now these retrospective interpretations of a collective nature are interesting enough, but in the direction his account takes you can feel the vividness of his own childish terror receding into the distance, together, of course, with any substantive recognition that what he had dreamt was the most extraordinary evocation of a primal scene embedded in this organic architecture. It is really quite difficult not to notice the remarkable intuitive detail with which his dream work depicts the "very sumptuous" texture of the curtains (the lips of the labia) opening on to the receding arched chamber (the vagina) with its flash of red from the carpet and the cushion on the throne seating the tree-trunk phallus (the erect penis). We are met instead with Jung's curiously partial insistence that the dream phallus was enthroned by itself, "ithyphallically", in apparent self-sufficient, albeit disconcerting, splendour: any sense of its relatedness or of the heat of sexuality, or, indeed, of the personal, appear to have been left behind.

The manikin and stone

This makes a pointed contrast to our next scenario: Jung's spontaneous creation of a more approachable and connected couple that he
could turn to for reassurance—the manikin and stone:

> My disunion with myself and uncertainty in the world at large led me
> to an action which at the time was quite incomprehensible to me. I had
> in those days a yellow, varnished pencil case of a kind commonly used
> by primary school pupils, with a little lock and the customary ruler.
> At the end of this ruler I now carved a little manikin, about two inches
> long, with frock coat, top hat, and shiny black boots. I coloured him
> black with ink, sawed off the ruler, and put him in a pencil case, where
> I made him a little bed. I even made a coat for him out of a bit of wool.
> In the case I also placed a smooth oblong blackish stone from the
> Rhine, which I had painted with water colours to look as if it were
> divided into an upper and lower half, and had long carried around in
> my trouser pocket. This was his stone. All this was a great secret.
> Secretly I took the case to the forbidden attic at the top of the house
> . . . and hid it with great satisfaction on one of the beams under the
> roof – for no one must ever see it! . . . No one could discover my secret
> and destroy it. I felt safe, and the tormenting sense of being at odds
> with myself was gone. In all difficult situations . . . I thought of my
> carefully bedded-down and wrapped-up manikin and his smooth,
> prettily coloured stone.
>
> Similarly, I never told anyone about the dream phallus; and the
> Jesuits, too, belonged to that mysterious realm which I knew I must
> not talk about. The little wooden figure with the stone was the first
> attempt, still unconscious and childish, to give shape to the secret. I
> was always absorbed by it and had the feeling I ought to fathom it;
> and yet I did not know what it was trying to express. I always hoped
> I might be able to find something – perhaps in nature – that would
> give me the clue . . . (Jung, 1963, p. 36)

Let us recall that the clue was one Jung derived from nature, returning to these mysteries in his old age, the metaphor of the rhizome:
indicative of something buried but nevertheless generative. That the
creation and function of these symbolic objects should be somehow
hidden from view, protected by a penumbra of secrecy, is a feature
repeatedly stressed in that passage.

Picking up on Jung's later remark that "there is no better means of
intensifying the treasured feeling of individuality than the possession

of a secret which the individual is pledged to guard" (Jung, 1963, p. 352), Atwood and Stolorow (1977) comment that this "ritual reflects a partial internalisation which served to gain mastery over the omnipotence of objects and ensure the stability and integrity of the self representation" (p. 209). Indeed, how poignant it is that the secret artefact Jung chose to fashion, the carved black manikin, derived from those very same threatening objects—the underground phallus, the Jesuit, the graveyard figures—that he most feared. Yet, recreated as this little totem, these forces were now rendered accessible and human, *and* provided with a partner in the form of his favourite oblong stone, with whom the manikin is "carefully bedded down" in the pencil-box bed. I would suggest that what we have here is Jung's spontaneous creation of a benign primal scene in which he *could* trust, the antidote to the raw unmediated part-object power of the underground cavern dream or the distress occasioned by his parents' alienation from each other. Jung was not a child who, on waking from a nightmare, might run to his parents' shared bed for comfort; thus, he hid his self-created emblematic couple in their containing pencil box in the safest place he knew—the attic where he had sought refuge from the Jesuit—so he could flee there to his secret source of reassurance whenever anxious fears pressed too close.

Jung relates how he completely forgot about his manikin after about a year, only for it to return to his mind "with pristine clarity" while he was researching *Symbols of Transformation* (1956) and chanced across a reference to "soul-stones" that triggered "the conviction that there are archaic psychic components which have entered the individual psyche without any direct line of tradition" (Jung, 1963, p. 38). Later still, "When I was in England in 1920, I carved out of wood two similar figures, without having the slightest recollection of that childhood experience" and spontaneously realised that "it was a further development of that fearful tree of my childhood dream, which was now revealed as (Atamavictu), "the breath of life", the creative impulse . . . with a supply of life force, the oblong black stone" (1963, p. 39). Thus, Jung explicitly links the ominous phallic tree with the carved wooden manikin and associates both with inspiration (breath): conjoined with the life-force of the soul-stone, this couple is now presented—in terms which echo Genesis—as evidence of the autonomous (impersonal) operation of the collective unconscious. I see this scenario as encapsulating the contemporary Jungian dilemma. Can we admire Jung's chain of association as an impressive archetypal extrapolation, while still remaining mindful of Winnicott's concern that Jung's intimate instinctual components could end up dispersed, dissolved even, in collective considerations?

The cathedral

This tension suffuses our next example. The Kleinian resonance—psyche expressed in the visceral language of bodily process—grows even stronger in the extraordinarily intense and sustained passage in Jung's autobiography where he describes the culmination of his childhood spiritual angst. Some days earlier, walking through Basle, as he admired the freshly restored glazed blue tiles of the cathedral roof, he felt the premonition of a sinful thought. He had guiltily pushed it away, but now

> I gathered all my courage, as though I were about to leap forthwith into hellfire, and let the thought come. I saw before me the cathedral, the blue sky; God sits on his golden throne, high above the world – and from under the throne an enormous turd falls upon the sparkling new roof, shatters it, and breaks the walls of the cathedral asunder. So that was it! I felt an enormous, an indescribable relief. Instead of the expected damnation, Grace had come upon me . . . I had yielded to His inexorable command.

> [Jung goes on to compare his blissful liberation to the depressed ongoing servitude of his father who] . . . did not know the immediate living God who stands, omnipotent and free, above His Bible and His Church, who calls upon man to partake of His freedom . . . in His trial of human courage God refuses to abide by traditions, no matter how sacred. (Jung 1963, p. 56)

Winnicott comments, "We could not expect to find Jung feeling God to be a projection of his own infantile omnipotence and the shitting as a projection of his own hate of the father in the mother" (Winnicott, 1964, p. 454), and certainly Jung does appear to dissociate himself from his own exclusion and helplessness by grandly attributing his consequent retaliatory destructiveness to the will of God. More radically, Winnicott continues, "or at a more primitive level, his own destruction of the good object because of its being real in the sense of being outside the area of his omnipotence" (1964, p. 454). The "good object" here alluded to is the actuality of the primal scene (the parental intercourse), the attack on which is tantamount to a fierce declaration of independence (anticipated by the "ithyphallic" element in Jung's underground cavern dream) which rejects any sense of indebtedness. Money-Kyrle's ingenious punning term for this is the "partheno-genetic fallacy": this implicit phantasy of being born of a virgin (in Greek, *parthenon*) would, of course, pre-empt any "ability to recognize the supreme creativity of the parental intercourse" (Money-Kyrle, 1971). This is a trajectory that might well lead to that over-investment in introversion (Redfearn, 1979, p. 202) for which Britton has coined the term "epistemic narcissism" (Britton, Feldman, & O'Shaughnessy, 1989, pp. 178–196).

Although we noted earlier how, on a collective level, this inter-course, graphically illustrated in the alchemical Rosarium, appears to be the very thing Jung seeks to celebrate, here, in Winnicott's construal ("hate of the father in the mother") on a personal level, this is the very thing that Jung defies and destroys. What might be the wider implications of this? Jung frequently alludes to his phan-tasies/fantasies as feeling more real than his everyday reality, and this is reflected in the continuing tension between his No. 2 & No. 1 personalities, which, as we have traced earlier, was eventually to generate Jung's metapsychological differentiation of the collective from the personal unconscious. However, for Winnicott, as the title of his last great paper "The use of an object" (1969) implies, the crucial issue remained the integration of subjective omnipotence with objec-tive reality, the instigation of a working relationship between them. Winnicott's contention was that this favourable outcome hinged on whether the child's primary assertive aggression could be absorbed and mediated by its environment: if not, the child was forced into either a compliant or else defiant stance toward its objects. So, we find Winnicott asserting in a letter to Fordham that

> Jung seems to have no contact with his own primitive destructive impulses, and he gives support to this in his writing (*Memories, Dreams, Reflections*). When playing as a small child Jung built and then destroyed, over and over again; he does not describe himself playing constructively in relation to having (in unconscious fantasy) des-troyed. In my review I had related this to a difficulty Jung may have

had being cared for by a depressed mother (if this be true). (Winnicott, 1989, p. 229)

What Winnicott alludes to here is Jung's childhood game of constructing model towers from bricks only to triumphantly topple them with simulated earthquakes. Winnicott sees this as Jung parading his insistence, enacting rather than assimilating his necessarily aggressive assertion; certainly, such a construal would be in keeping with both the concreteness and the projected ("I had yielded to his inexorable command") omnipotence of Jung's cathedral destruction fantasy (Meredith-Owen, 2011a). But could it not also be read as Jung spontaneously bringing his phallic constructions back to earth?

The keep

My last vignette is taken from the closing pages of the second chapter, "School years", when Jung is sixteen and he experiences "the first systematic fantasy of my life", the prototype of what he was later to term an exercise in active imagination. It is triggered on his walk to school by the sight of a sailing barge on the Rhine running before a gathering storm. Jung's envisages Basle becoming a port on a great lake, while he lives in a castle built upon a rocky isthmus:

> The nerve centre and raison d'être of this whole arrangement was the secret of the keep, which I alone knew. The thought had come to me like a shock. For, inside the tower, extending from the battlements to the vaulted cellar, was a copper column or heavy wire cable as thick as a man's arm, which ramified at the top into the finest branches, like the crown of the tree or – better still – like a taproot with all its tiny rootlets turned upside down and reaching into the air. From the air they drew a certain inconceivable something which was conducted down the copper column into the cellar. Here I had an equally inconceivable apparatus, a kind of laboratory in which I made gold out of the mysterious substance which the copper roots drew from the air.

> What the roots absorbed and transmitted to the copper trunk was a kind of spiritual essence which became visible down in the cellar as finished gold coins. This was certainly no mere conjuring trick, but a venerable and vitally important secret of nature which had come to me I know not how and which I had to conceal . . . (Jung, 1963, p. 101)

The echoes of the phallus in the cavern dream are several: the coins in the cellar reflect the gold of the throne around its base, the penumbra of rootlets reaching into the air recall the halo of light around its head, the comparison of the erect structure with both human anatomy (as in man's arm or penis) and tree, the geometric (mandala-esque) architecture of the setting, and the reiterated importance of keeping it all secret. We noted earlier how Atwood and Stolorow (1977) suggest that this last motif—the secrecy is a feature of all four vignettes—is a quasi-enacted attempt to establish a secure sense of integrity (integration) as a prophylactic against the threat of identity dissolution, but we might also note its creatively compensatory function. Secrecy is also associated with intimacy (as in sharing a secret), and I would imagine Jung found some significant sense of containment in maintaining his inner world within a cocoon of secrecy. Yet, it had its cost: consequences of this unilateral security are the noticeable absence of any intimate company in Jung's fantasy and the investment in the apparent self-sufficiency (the spontaneous "alchemical" coinage) of its set-up. However, such reservations must be balanced against the evident animation, indeed joy, which also informs the fantasy. Jung's particular genius was to convert a defence into a wondrous thing, and to do so using the very same raw materials of imagery that had previously bodied forth his deepest fears.

Conclusion

> The symbolism of my childhood experiences and the violence of the imagery upset me terribly. I asked myself: "*Who* talks like that? Who has the impudence to exhibit a phallus so nakedly, and in a shrine? Who makes me think that God destroys his church in this abominable manner?" At last I asked myself whether it was not the devil's doing. For that it must have been God or the devil who spoke and acted in this way was something I never doubted. *I felt absolutely sure that it was not myself who had invented these thoughts and images.* (Jung, 1964, p. 64, my emphasis)

Jung is adamant that the imagery (phantasy articulating as fantasy) that threatened to overwhelm (devour) him as a child did not originate in himself: yet, we might well feel that this was essentially a defensive belief, intended to keep at arm's length those "primitive destructive impulses" (Winnicott, 1964, Meredith-Owen, 2011)—oral, anal, and genital aggression—that he intuitively felt his intimate environment could not cope with. Consequently dissociated, these became the driver of inflated phantasies structured around expulsion and destruction (the turd bomb, the toppled towers) and incorporation or its phobic counterpart (being devoured, "man-eaten").

Hinshelwood again:

> Unconscious phantasies about incorporation or expulsion therefore have an influence on the experience of what the subject contains, and what he or she identifies with and actually becomes like. In this sense the phantasy is felt to be actual reality and in fact its effects are real enough. Unconscious phantasy in this sense is omnipotent. (Hinshelwood, 1989, p. 38)

These opening chapters are a remarkable record of Jung's courageous endeavour to fashion some individual coherence out of his wrestling with the projections and introjections generated by these instinctual, and, as yet, still impersonal, forces of unconscious phantasy. Still impersonal (collective) because, owing to the fragility of his early environment, they had not been brought, via adequate containment, within what Winnicott refers to—appropriately enough in a letter to Michael Fordham—as "the sphere of personal omnipotence" (Winnicott, 1989, p. 230).

As Jung says in his prologue "the personality too desires to evolve out of its unconscious conditions and to experience itself as a whole" (Jung, 1963, p. 17). This use of the term "whole" here is interestingly ambiguous: it could either imply something simply undivided, or it could evoke something rather grander, more universal. I have suggested that Jung's metaphor of the unfolding promise of the rhizome, presented in his preface and so amply fulfilled in the pages that followed, suggest he was finally conceiving of "wholeness" in the former, more modest sense. Bair (2004), in her biography of Jung, well conveys the feel of this access of fresh energy in her subject:

> On January 10, 1958, everything changed when Jaffé (his secretary) told Wolff (his publisher) that "something so wonderful and meaningful happened ... *Jung himself is writing his autobiography all over again*" (Jaffé's emphasis). He had begun to write early in November, but not until the end of the month did she allow herself to believe he

would sustain the momentum. She told Wolff "so much had become clear to Jung, and especially the meaning of his life which he had apparently not seen to its full extent." She pronounced what he wrote "splendid, simple and deep like a fairytale." She offered Jung a transcript of their conversations to refer to, but he declined, wanting "to write it entirely new." He had begun at the beginning, with his birth, and was now into "his 9th year (before the experience with the Basle Cathedral)." Jung wanted their biography hours to continue, as he did not know "where it all [his writing] will lead." (Bair, 2004, p. 595)

Returning to this text now, what springs off the page for me is the compelling and deeply poignant evidence of a re-energised Jung setting about the completion of the task that Winnicott refers to as the need to "spend his life looking for his own self, which he never really found since he remained to some extent split (*except in so far as this split was healed in his work on his autobiography*)" (Winnicott 1964, p. 454, my emphasis).

Let me conclude with Hinshelwood's own reflection on the epistemological basis of Kleinian theory:

> . . . the philosophical problem of how a biological entity can transform from a world of bodily gratifications and needs to a world of symbolic gratifications and meanings remains unsolved. The key position of unconscious phantasy on the borderline between the physiological instinct and the psychological representation has led Kleinians to search with confidence for a greater understanding of symbols in their clinical work. (Hinshelwood, 1989, p. 38)

It is a shame that this search has only just begun, almost half a century after Winnicott's lead, to bring an appreciative as well as a critical eye to this marvellous record of the childhood Jung's spontaneous engagement with the raw instinctual elements of the primal scene. It is a resource whose intrinsic value has remained somewhat masked by the impressive edifice his later conceptualisations overlaid it with. Although close consideration of his early imagery suggests an element of "ithyphallic" triumphing over Oedipal anxieties in his valorisation of the collective, we can only admire the courage with which he revisited his formative years with an open heart and mind in his eighty-third year. I have argued that he fashioned through this imagery an impressive amalgam of the intimate and the archetypal, the personal and the collective. The autobiographical Jung may yet prove as rich a source as the metapsychological Jung, and, indeed, allow the reparative and creative aspects of that metapsychological edifice, its defensive components duly acknowledged, to be better appreciated by the psychoanalytic mainstream.

References

Atwood, G., & Stolorow, R. (1977). Metapsychology, reification and the representational world of C. G. Jung. *International Review of Psychoanalysis, 4*: 197–213.

Bair, D. (2004). *Jung: A Biography.* London: Little Brown.

Bisagni, F. (2012). Delusional developments in child autism at the onset of puberty: vicissitudes of psychic dimensionality between disintegration and development. *International Journal of Psychoanalysis, 93*: 667–692.

Britton, R., Feldman, M., & O'Shaughnessy, E. (1989). *The Oedipus Complex Today: Clinical Implications.* London: Karnac.

Brome, V. (1978). *Jung: Man and Myth.* London: Stratus.

Feldman, B. (1992). Jung's infancy and childhood and its influence upon the development of analytical psychology. *Journal of Analytical Psychology, 37*: 255–274.

Feldman, B. (2004). A skin for the imaginal. *Journal of Analytical Psychology, 49*: 285–311.

Hinshelwood, R. D. (1989). *A Dictionary of Kleinian Thought.* London: Free Association Books.

Homans, P. (1979). *Jung in Context: Modernity and the Making of a Psychology.* London: University of Chicago Press.

Jung, C. G. (1953). *Two Essays in Analytical Psychology, C.W. 7.* London: Routledge.

Jung, C. G. (1956). *Symbols of Transformation, C.W. 5.* London: Routledge.

Jung, C. G. (1960). *The Structure and Dynamics of the Psyche, C.W. 8.* London: Routledge.

Jung C. G. (1963). *Memories, Dreams, Reflections*, A. Jaffé (Ed.). London: Collins.

Jung, C. G. (2009). *The Red Book.* New York: Norton.

Knox, J. (2009). Mirror neurons and embodied simulation in the development of archetypes and self-agency. *Journal of Analytical Psychology, 55*: 522–549.

Meltzer, D., & Williams, M. H. (1998). *The Apprehension of Beauty*. Perthshire: Clunie Press.

Meredith-Owen, W. (2011a). Winnicott on Jung: destruction, creativity and the unrepressed unconscious. *Journal of Analytical Psychology, 56*: 56–75.

Meredith-Owen, W. (2011b). Jung's shadow: negation and narcissism of the self. *Journal of Analytical Psychology, 56*: 674–691.

Meredith-Owen, W. (2012). The hero, the anima and the claustrum: anality and idealisation. *Journal of Analytical Psychology, 57*: 167–186.

Money-Kyrle, R. (1971). The aims of psycho-analysis. *International Journal of Psychoanalysis, 52*: 10–106.

Redfearn, J. (1979). The captive, the treasure, the hero and the anal stage of development. *Journal of Analytical Psychology, 24*(3): 185–205.

Rodman, F. R. (2003). *Winnicott: The Life and Work*. Cambridge, MA: Da Capo Lifelong.

Satinover, J. (1985). At the mercy of another: abandonment and restitution in psychotic character. *Chiron*, 47–86.

Satinover, J. (1986). Jung's lost contribution to the dilemma of narcissism. *Journal of the American Psychoanalytic Association, 34*: 401–38.

Sedgwick, D. (2008). Winnicott's dream: some reflections on D. W. Winnicott and C. G. Jung. *Journal of Analytical Psychology, 53*: 543–60.

Shamdasani, S. (2005). *Jung Stripped Bare*. London: Karnac.

Winnicott, D. W. (1964). *Memories, dreams, reflections* by C. G. Jung. *International Journal of Psychoanalysis, 45*: 450–455. Also in: *Psychoanalytic Explorations* (pp. 482–492). London: Karnac, 1989.

Winnicott, D. W. (1969). The use of an object. *International Journal of Psychoanalysis, 50*: 711–716.

Winnicott, D. W. (1989). *Psychoanalytic Explorations*, C. Winnicott (Ed.). London: Karnac.

PART II
AFFECT

A vindication of Jung's unconscious and its archetypal expression: Jung, Bion, and Matte Blanco

Richard Carvalho

Introduction

In this chapter, I want to take up one aspect of Jung's legacy that is in danger of being assimilated seamlessly and without acknowledgement into psychoanalysis as the latter has developed, particularly with the thinking of Bion in the 1960s. This legacy is that of an *unrepressed unconscious* which could only find expression through symbols. These symbols, rather than expressing contents already known and rejected by an experiencing ego, were the only means available of communication between two aspects of the psyche which, in Jung's conception, were utterly alien to one another, and otherwise incapable of traffic.

This intuition was the result of Jung's exposure to psychotic and dissociative phenomenology and, arguably, of his own dissociative psychology, which arose from a very troubled development (Meredith-Owen (2011), which Freud, according to Winnicott (1964) was probably not equipped to understand. It is, however, a phenomenon that is hard to validate theoretically, especially against Freud's more positivistic psychology; accordingly, perhaps, psychoanalysis found it hard to engage for some decades with psychotic and borderline states with which analytical psychology had an easier tradition. Several psychoanalytic thinkers of the late twentieth century offer obvious bridges between the two traditions of psychoanalysis and analytical psychology, the most obvious being Bion (especially in conjunction with attachment theory and neuroscientists such as Panksepp (1998), and Schore (2001)), Matte Blanco (1975), and Ferrari (1992), as well as various forms of intersubjectivism. Bion offers a way of thinking about how it is that infantile affective states that do not meet adequate and consistent attunement should remain dissociated and beyond mental operation, while Matte Blanco provides a logical explanation derived from Freud's phenomenology of the unconscious as to why this should be, and why it should be that the unconscious should be unconscious for *structural* reasons in the first place. Matte Blanco also explains how it is that affect is indistinguishable on logical grounds from emotion, and why it is, therefore, that uncontained affective states, whether in infants or adults, but especially in the former, are potentially disabling because they are dysregulating (Schore, 2001).

One of the difficulties in addressing an unconscious that is unrepressed, and which is unconscious for structural reasons rather than repression, is that it can only be inferred. It is only with Matte Blanco's 1975 reformulation of the unconscious as a logical concomitant of displacement and condensation that this inference gains validity. *Validity* suggests that a theory can be related to the reality it purports to treat, whereas *reliability* suggests internal consistency without any necessary relation to reality. The concept of validity is very important in a field such as depth psychology, but particularly in the case of Jung's psychology, which has often been accused of mysticism, as, indeed, has been Bion's (e.g., O'Shaughnessy, 2005; Taylor's (2011) criticism of Vermote, 2011).

Jung called this unconscious "the collective unconscious", Bion, "O", and Matte Blanco, "the symmetric mode". If this region is totally alien to consciousness, the problem is to demonstrate how there can be any intercourse between the two. Jung's solution is to postulate the manifestation of the archetype in its various symbolic forms. Bion's is to postulate the conversion of emergent beta elements, which are unavailable for use by the psyche, into alpha elements, which can be made use of. This conversion is via the maternal reverie of the alpha function. Matte Blanco postulates a different solution, which is, none the less, compatible. This is that while the symmetric mode and its conscious counterpart, the asymmetric mode, are mutually alien and uncomprehending, the logics that they promulgate intertwine to form an amalgam, bi-logic, with different ratios of symmetric logic to asymmetric logic, the degree of consciousness of any given psychic phenomenon being in proportion to the degree of asymmetric logic present within them. In addition, he demonstrates that the logic of the unconscious is indistinguishable from that of emotion, so that the link between unconscious and conscious is via emotion; this, in turn, relates back to Bion, whose beta elements are essentially affective, and to Jung's archetypes, which, at core, are affective.

In order to illustrate these ideas and links, I will take some rather ordinary clinical material from a patient whose development was marked by emotional privation. This had resulted in a considerable degree of dissociation in which a central complex remained inaccessible. The session in question marks the moment in which, in retrospect, this complex was made available by the chance emergence of a countertransference experience that effectively constellated the archetype. It was what Bion would have called a "selected fact" (Bion, 1992), and it resulted in and marked what he would have called a "transformation in O", beyond knowledge, memory, and desire, because inaccessible to all three in an inaccessible, dissociated unconscious. Taylor (2011) warns us of the dangers of both the concept of O and of interpretations aiming at transformations in O (cf. Vermote, 2011). He warns us of the dangers of what he calls "inspirational interpretation". I think, however, that the logic of Matte Blanco allows us, as I have suggested, the possibility of exploring the validity of such an interpretation, whether we understand it as a transformation in O or as an "archetypal" interpretation leading to what Jung would have termed "individuation".

A clinical example

Wanting to communicate and express a self

This is a patient I had seen for several years.[1] Her original presentation had not been dramatic. She was not especially "ill" or problematic when she first arrived, but she was unaccountably angry, unhappy, and very driven, sometimes to the point of exhaustion, by work she thought essentially was futile, and to the point of having once had a potentially life threatening accident. This was not just because of being so tired, but also because of how cut off she was from herself and, therefore, her environment. Early in her analysis, particularly the first year or two, she had seemed curiously absent from the sessions. She seemed very lost, despite her competence in life, and her many achievements and accomplishments. Yet, despite all these achievements, she felt cut off from her creativity. It was an ambition of hers to write, though this seemed an impossible aim until much later in the analysis.

Several years later, and shortly before the session in question, she had started to discuss the idea of finishing her analysis. This was something we had been wondering about for some months. The session was quiet and unremarkable; however, she said that she found herself *not* anxious about a lecture she had to give in a few days' time. Previously, she had felt she had had to use other people's words and was terrified of being demolished by criticism. Now, however, she was quietly writing her lecture and enjoying using her own words. She seemed confident. She described finding herself in conversation with a prominent editor, who had assumed that she would want to publish and was surprised when my patient was not interested. She had said, rather, that all she wanted to do was to "communicate and to express herself".

I was very struck by this wish "to communicate and express herself", because some months before she had been horrified when a colleague asked to video another of her talks. My patient had refused, telling me that she could not stand the sound of her voice, her accent, or the sight of her ash-blond hair. I felt extremely shocked, and we were able to link this with an occasion when, as a little girl, a friendly elderly neighbour whom she knew to be fond of her had greeted her with "Hello Blondie!", which she had received as if it were sneering, sarcastic, and rejecting.

Some background issues

I will return to the wish to "communicate and express herself" in a moment. First, I need to explain some of the background that informed the way in which I heard this wish "to communicate and to express herself" in my countertransference.

We had been puzzled by the lack of sexual material in the analysis. It was not that this woman had not been sexual; she was a mother, and there had been a great deal of explicit Oedipal material: her father had had to be absent for much of her childhood, and, as the practical member of her family, she felt she largely replaced him as husband to her mother, whom she felt rather contemptuously to be incompetent, and then there were circumstances that allowed her to feel preferred by her father as an intellectual and emotional partner to her mother, as well as to the other children. This had enhanced the development of a rather phallic self: it would not be correct to say that she was mannish, though her femininity was not to the fore, but it was more that she was impatiently competent and impervious to external or internal vulnerability. By the time of the session in question, all this had softened beyond recognition, but it had seemed difficult to get her body explicitly in the room, and the dreams she had had about it tended to disappear rather than create a dynamic trail. One of these dreams had been striking for a person who was still rather physically self-loathing at the time: in it, she had been strolling casually and seductively, completely naked, through a hotel lobby. Another dream, several months later, had involved withdrawing money from a cash dispenser which had somehow presented itself as the vagina of an alluring, naked, dancing girl.

So, there was something elusive about her physicality and her sexual self in the analysis so far.

As I have already indicated, when my patient had first arrived in analysis, she could be quite extraordinarily absent, though physically present, and this was particularly marked on the sessions before weekend breaks, or when we resumed the following week. My feeling was of her being in some very distant universe where I would have to search for her over stratospheric distances. There seemed no point in waiting for her to come back and I felt she needed me to find her. Much later in her analysis she was able to tell me that her experience of her mother was of mutual absence: she said that it was a relationship that could not be said to exist because it could not be said to *not* exist. *À propos*, she told me a story about running away at the age of eight or so. She stayed with a neighbour. When the neighbour sent her home early next morning, she met her mother coming home from church where she had been praying all night. It is interesting, in relation to my countertransference compulsion to go to find her, that it had not occurred to the mother to look for her daughter. It was only much later that my patient was able to understand at last that by praying, her mother had been caring for her desperately, caring deeply *about* her, but ineffectually.

My patient was aware of her "absences" in the sessions, but was unable to do anything about them. She could see intellectually that they happened particularly around breaks, but could not *feel* it. Similarly, she could sometimes recognise that there might be material suggestive of the longer breaks mattering in some way, but again this was not *felt*. Then, one break some years into the analysis, she put her back out catastrophically to the point of being immobilised. She was helped to associate this affliction, at least intellectually, to my absence over the break by a dream about me as a cruel female doctor whose assistant she was, and who left her patients to die experimentally. Her habitual demeanour, however, was of impatient independence, and she was contemptuous of the anxiety that her partner openly showed on occasions whenever he had to leave the house, whether for a holiday or on business. She was finally able to register her own anxiety on an occasion when she herself had to go away on business. She was suddenly very anxious and realised that she missed her partner in a way she had never allowed herself to in the past. On a later occasion when her partner was obliged to go abroad on business, she had an anaphylaxis, an allergic reaction that, if severe enough, can result in collapse and death. She was able to link this potential "collapse" with her partner's absence and also with her "collapse" due to back problems over my earlier break.

This dawning realisation of her reaction to absence culminated in an experience some years later when she came to her first session after the summer break in a state that she experienced as almost literal paralysis: it was as if she were unable to think, to talk, to move. It was an experience of intense and painful physicality together with emotional pain. Clearly, at the same time she was not paralysed, and had got herself to the session, while she was also able to let me know, however minimally, what she was experiencing. None the less, the intense anguish of the experience was of waking nightmare.

This experience made sense to her as a somatic memory of an otherwise inaccessible infantile state beyond memory. She felt tiny and utterly helpless. She knew that she had been born to a grieving mother who had lost a baby girl shortly before she had conceived my patient. Her mother was, therefore, devastated, quite unable to welcome her infant into the world. She was also burdened by more children than she could cope with, and so it was that my patient felt that there had been "no place for her" in the family. She assumed that she only survived because her grandmother looked after her. So, in this way, she was not so much de-prived as "prived". It was as if, in returning from the summer break, she was rehearsing a memory of being born to a mother who might have no mind for her.

It had seemed that my patient had had no way of knowing about this infant self and this very early experience which lay far beyond any possibility of explicit memory other than in such manifestations of implicit memory. At the same time, she had no intention of knowing about it either. It was both dissociated and also kept split from her awareness. This seemed to be expressed in a dream in which she found herself in the company of a little girl who has no shoes on. Mary Warnock, whom the patient associated with her famous work on ethics, is upbraiding her for neglecting this child, whose feet must be very cold, but who, as far as my patient is concerned, has nothing whatsoever to do with her. There was another dream, close in time to this, of a little boy with ash-blond hair, like herself, burdened by a heavy stone of which she, the patient, could easily have relieved him, but did not. In the background of the earlier dream, there is an image of a normally docile, timorous animal tearing out the throat of another innocent animal, as if the message might be that to be conjoined with her feeling self would be violently fatal. Certainly, the subsequent somatic experiences of paralysis had felt deadly, the collapse from her back had felt dramatically violent, and the anaphylaxis could have been, literally, fatal.

Back to communication and a self to express

I want to return to the quiet and, on the face of it, rather inconsequential-seeming session to which this is the background. My response to hearing my patient say that all she wished was "to communicate and to express herself" was to be suddenly struck by the word "communicate" and to think simultaneously that communication implied an "intercourse", and that an intercourse involved eros. In the same instant, I found myself with a strong visual image of two paintings, one of which was Titian's *Sacred and Profane Love*, and the other his[2] *Concert Champêtre*, both of which feature voluptuous nudes. Part of this countertransference reverie was to remember having read that these nudes corresponded to sacred love in the first, and to "divine figures"—muses—in the second.[3]

Although I felt unable to justify this with direct evidence, none the less I shared my tentative idea that what my patient had said about the wish to communicate had suggested a very powerful impression of its implication of the erotic, a wish, as it were, for an intercourse with her audience, but that this in turn strongly implied her assumption that she would be enjoyed. I shared with her the strange visitation of the Titian nudes as seemingly the embodiments of the idea of love and inspiration, saying I felt them to be the counterpart of the erotic dreams we had failed to understand in the past (which included the dream of her nude self in the hotel lobby, and the vagina cash dispenser), and I finally added that it was also important that she now felt she had an emotional self to express and to enjoy.

What I said made immediate and vivid sense to my patient. Her response was to talk about her previous sense of non-existence—that is, of not having a sense of a self. It was not so much that she had suffered a sense of what might be called "negative narcissism", an investment in a negative view of herself, though this also featured, as I shall mention later. This experience was more that she had *no* view of herself, a sort of minus-narcissism (the analogy is with Bion's $-K$, there being a space where K ought to be) of a child who had been born to a mother who was virtually out of action emotionally. Happily, though, it seems, as I have said, that her grandmother must have cared for her before she died when my patient was four, an event which might well have contributed to her sense of absence. Such absence led to a corresponding sense of "minus eros", an absence of connection. Indeed, her very sense of her *relationship* with her mother was one of absence. There was no early sense of her mother as an audience with whom to be connected and who might enjoy her. She had not felt that she had "her own words", partly because she had not been helped to put her sensations and feelings into words (Ferrari, 1992), and this experience had been painfully present in the experience of wordless paralysis in the session following a summer break. Access to her own feelings was, therefore, somewhat curtailed, though shame was only too painfully and readily imminent. So, although she had a powerful intellect, she did not feel she had an available feeling self to express; neither had she any expectation that there would be anyone to receive her eros.

In addition to this minus narcissism, she was, as I have indicated, also afflicted by "negative narcissism", but this was, in my view, a later development. It involved her recruiting the contempt of her older siblings into a self-contempt which was an identification with a "repulsive"—in the sense of pushing away—object, repulsing a repulsive infant whose voice and accent and looks became disgusting to her. This sense of being repulsed, or being repulsive, had left my patient with the powerful sense of shame which I have mentioned, and which became the expression of a self whose body, with its needs and desires, was shameful to her. Nakedness could never be gloriously Titian-like: it could only be connoted as being stripped naked and exposed, exposed to derision and left for dead, of which her anaphylactic reaction to her partner's absence, her catastrophic back condition during my absence, and her experience of paralysis after the later one had been echoes.

While initially it had seemed that I had, in my absences, hurled her into an abyss and broken her back etc., other material—her expression of self-disgust, her dream rejection of the little girl without shoes, her refusal to help the little blond boy—made it clear that these catastrophes were, in fact, latterly at least, self-destructively inflicted out of this identification with the repulsing other.

Titian's nudes, voluptuous but not salacious, are the diametric opposite: they were the personification of wholesome eros, of love out of which she could draw her value,[4] as she had perhaps in the dream about the alluring vagina cash dispenser or, indeed, of being naked in the hotel lobby.

Commentary

While clearly significant emotionally to both of us, and indicating a shift of great moment to my patient, my intervention about communication implying eros also seemed curiously obvious after the event. In trying to account for this, I was struck by Bion's observation that any formulation is but one aspect of a multi-dimensional experience which, once interpreted, "ceases to be of moment" (Bion, 1970, p. 71), while, once such a "truth" has been expressed, "the thinker [or the thinkers, here, both analyst and analysand] become redundant" (Bion,

1970, p. 104). On reflection, it was also a noticing of something that had happened without our quite having noticed it: it had evidently occurred since the relatively recent event where my patient had expressed disgust at her accent, voice, and hair. What we were now noticing represented a dramatic *change of sign* from negative to positive. The negative was first in terms of what had hitherto been absent—the sense of a reflecting other and a sense of self—and second in terms of a sense of self-disgust which had arisen out of the perception of this absence as an act of repulsion.

This I think we could call a *complex*, in Jung's terms, and in Matte Blanco's, a *non-vital structure*. It meant that my patient not only had a consistently negative view of herself, which had not changed with changing circumstances (she had been unable to "learn from experience"), but it severely restricted her availability to herself and her creativity—her self-expression.

What replaced this non-vital structure was a *vital structure* whereby she was able to perceive and react in ways which were no longer constrained into the inevitable funnel of this complex, but which allowed her access to a self which she could express, and to creative thought.

One way of thinking of this is that it was a change from something hateful to something which admitted love, or that it was a change from a negative mother to a positive one.

I shall now turn to a commentary in terms of Matte Blanco's logic—or more properly, "bi-logic"—before turning to a Jungian commentary. This will require a brief exposition of Matte Blanco's thinking.

Matte Blanco

Symmetry and the unspeakable, infinite, multi-dimensional unconscious

In order to think about complexes, archetypes, archetypal representations, and the legitimacy (or not) of intuitive interventions from a vantage point outside Jung's phenomenology, an "Archimedean point" as Jung would have called it (1947, par. 421), I am going to describe the thought of Matte Blanco, who, like Jung, describes an unconscious which is unrepressed. This is in contrast to a repressed unconscious, which Jung would have termed a personal unconscious. Matte Blanco's description is in terms of a logic that he derived from the characteristics of the unconscious described by Freud. He argued as well that Freud's original concept of the unconscious was also of one that was unrepressed. I shall not give an account of this here, but refer the reader to Chapter Five of Matte Blanco's *The Unconscious as Infinite Sets* (1975).

The five characteristics and infinity

Matte Blanco's logic demonstrates a psychic *mode* that is multi-dimensional, timeless, and spaceless. It cannot be a process—a *primary process* as Freud dubbed it—because without time or space process is impossible: whence the coinage, "mode". These phenomena are explained as follows. *Displacement* and *condensation* imply that all contents of the psyche are ultimately interchangeable. This is because the unconscious treats totally disparate objects as identical on the basis of a single similarity, however trivial. I might dream, for instance, of Bill, who has a beard, in order to represent Bob, who also has a beard, and in doing so I am treating them as interchangeable on the basis of this single and rather trivial similarity. This is an example of displacement. If I use Bill to represent not only Bob, but Tom (who also has a beard), as well as Bill himself, as in condensation, then the three of them are being treated interchangeably. Where this psychic mode is treating contents like Bill, Bob, and Tom interchangeably, it can also treat the points which might otherwise define space and time interchangeably, so, for this mode, *space and time do not exist*, or, at least, not in the way we think of them. In addition, if Bill is interchangeable with Bob, then it cannot be said that Bill is not Bob (*non-negation*) while Bob and Bill remain themselves as well (*non-contradiction*). These characteristics, *condensation, displacement, non-negation* (non-contradiction was not part of the original list), *timelessness*, and the absence of distinction between inner (fantasy) and outer (reality) (i.e., *the absence of space*) are the five characteristics of the unconscious as originally described by Freud.

The interchangeability of contents in this mode also means that the psyche can reverse any proposition, so that "Mary is Bob's mother" can be reversed to yield "Bob is Mary's mother". Similarly, the proposition, "the breast is part of Mary" can be reversed to yield "Mary is part of the breast", a statement of a part-object (Jung spoke of *pars pro toto*). So, this psychic mode treats all propositions as if they can be reversed to their symmetric opposites according to the *principle of symmetry*,[5] which leads Matte Blanco to call it the *symmetric mode*.

Multi-dimensionality and infinity

Importantly, though, there is another corollary of symmetry, which is that the reversibility of what can contain what—a mother a breast, a drawer a chest, etc.—can only happen in more spatial dimensions than three, as indeed can condensation, which requires that two or more three-dimensional bodies occupy the same three-dimensional space. Thus, the symmetric mode is *multi-dimensional*.

In addition, the reversibility of content and container is also a feature of what is known in mathematics as an *infinite set*, one in which a proper subset can be substituted for what is called the propositional function. The obvious example is of all whole numbers: this is an infinite series which one could count literally "for ever and ever" without ever coming to an end, but then, so are the proper subsets of all even whole numbers, all odd ones, square roots, and so on: each is an infinite series within the original infinite set, and, therefore, numerically interchangeable with it. When the symmetric mode reverses content with container, then it is containing the propositional function within the proper subset, or is treating the propositional function as interchangeable with the contents of the set it contains. If we return to our part-object example, all of this will become obvious. The symmetric mode treats "mother", which is the propositional function of the set of everything mother contains, as interchangeable with one of its functions or contents, in this case "breast". There are other similar examples when we employ symbols metaphorically to represent, say, our country: people "fight for the flag", "for the king", "for the crown",[6] "for their mother-land", and so on, all representatives as well as members of the set defined by the propositional function, which, in this case, is "country".

The consequences of all these features of symmetry are as follows: first, it is literally *unspeakable* because it defies the conditions which would allow it to be spoken (there are no distinguishable objects, no negation, etc.). Second, it is *inconceivable* to our conscious minds because it is infinite, and, as multi-dimensional, it is *unimaginable* to a mind whose imagination is three-dimensional. This, says Matte Blanco, is why the symmetric mode—the unconscious—is unconscious in its very nature: it is structurally unconscious. It is a realm that coexists with its antinomian opposite mode of *asymmetry* as if they were inert (therefore unreactive) gases, just as Jung described conscious and unconscious as behaving like immiscible fluids, utterly alien to one another. So, crudely, *the unconscious is the symmetric mode*, while *consciousness is the asymmetric mode*. In contrast to the symmetric mode, in the asymmetric mode, the proposition, "Mary is Bob's mother" cannot be symmetrically reversed.

Generalisation

The symmetric mode also operates according to another principle, that of *generalisation*. This means that the unconscious tends to group things into wider and wider sets: a man, for example, is part of the set of humans, part of the set of animals, part of the organic kingdom; the crown is part of the set of the king which is part of the country, which is part of the planet earth, and this in turn is part of the solar system, the universe . . . etc. Obviously, all these sets are likely to be interlocking, so that metal objects may include the set of tin cans, of motor cars, of moving vehicles, and it might intersect with the set of shiny, glittering things, which may in turn contain gold rings and tinsel, and intersect with the set of sparklers and fireworks, whence bombs . . . and so on. More crucially, however, they appear to be defined by affect. Indeed, according to Matte Blanco, the logic of emotions is indistinguishable from that of the unconscious, so that, for instance, the affect of a patient confronted by a break might fail to distinguish between the analyst in the present, the mother who abandoned him at birth, and the girlfriend who left him last week. Matte Blanco explores this extensively in his first book (1975), but perhaps one way of demonstrating that affects are infinite sets is as follows: in the proposition, Bob loves Mary, the propositional function is "love" and, within it, Bob and Mary are reversible as well as interchangeable, as indeed they are with the propositional function itself. Mary and Bob become the embodiment to one another of all things lovable; they are both intensive infinities, in every possible way to the maximum degree, and their love knows no bounds: they will love one another to the ends of the earth and for eternity, and they knew the instant they met that they had known one another for ever before that. All this assumes that Bob's and Mary's love is mutual, but even if it is not, then the emotional state of the one will bear all these imprints: think of Dante or of Petrarch, who each extolled one woman (Beatrice and Laura, respectively) as the epitome of all love, or of Cesare Pavese, who wrote cycles of poetry which were almost indistinguishable from one another to his different muses as if they were each interchangeable.

The unconscious, then, is defined by hugely diverse sets (principle of generalisation) in which all contents are mutually interchangeable (principle of symmetry) so that everything is "everything else"; there are, none the less, what he called "packets of asymmetry" (Matte Blanco, 1975), lines of potential fission between affects, and so on.

Bi-modality, affect and thought, conscious and unconscious

What we have is a sort of binocular psyche: one lens, the asymmetric, is digital and laborious and associated with the sort of thinking that is possible in conditions where everything is *not* everything else, and where there are discrete and well-defined objects not blurred by displacement and condensation. Without this mode, thinking is impossible. The other mode is like a quantum computer in which every particle is simultaneously in both up and down positions and all states in between until a single observation "collapses" it into a solution. It functions at states of high emotional intensity. If you have been keyed up for a *viva voce* examination and are faced with a seemingly impossible question, recondite knowledge of whose existence you were barely aware can surge out in the most unexpected manner; the glimpse of a leaf will have you up a tree in a split second before you realise that it is not a predator's ear; a borderline patient will *know* that you are rejecting her as you glance at the clock, even though you are concerned to contain her within the time constraints of the session. Symmetry–affect will give you an answer in a microsecond, but it might be wrong and needs to be quality controlled by asymmetric thought.

The logics of the modes and bi-logic

So, if there is no traffic between the modes, how can anything come into consciousness? What we might call the expressive tools of the modes are their respective logics. We are familiar with the sort of logic we use every day in normal speech or thought or working out our grocery bills. This is so-called Aristotelian logic, sometimes called "bivalent logic" because it has two values, true or false. Matte Blanco calls this *asymmetric logic*. Strictly speaking, there is no *symmetric logic*, but, rather, violations of normal logic[7] involving the sorts of mechanisms we have already discussed, and Matte Blanco calls this *symmetric logic*. He suggests that all psychic phenomena manifest a mixture of these two logics, which allows the symmetric mode to "unfold" its multi-dimensionality and simultaneity into the three-dimensional constraints of the asymmetric mode in the single dimension of time. A dream would be an example of a three-dimensional pictorial representation of the multi-dimensional structure underlying it.

The constitutive stratified bi-logical structure

Matte Blanco further suggests that the psyche falls into roughly five different regions, according to the ratio of symmetry to asymmetry, each with a rather different sort of affectivity. At one pole, there is the stratum, *stratum one*, of pure asymmetry, containing well-delineated and defined objects, where an object is what it is and nothing else, the region in which pure mathematical thought is possible. At the other extreme, there is *stratum five*—which can only be inferred—of pure symmetry. Here, everything is everything else, and so all emotion cancels out. *Stratum four* is the stratum in which affect and objects are beginning to emerge. This is the stratum of drives and beta elements, of bizarre objects. In *stratum three*, emotions are highly polarised and most violent, as in the idealisations and rages of toddlers or of borderline patients. This is the region of symbolic equations (Segal, 1957) or of psychic equivalence (Target & Fonagy, 1996), where if I *feel* or imagine something to be the case, it *is* the case; whereas, in *stratum two*, I can feel it to be the case and simultaneously know it not to be: this is the stratum, therefore, where play is possible, where I can pretend to be a tiger or know that my playmate is pretending to be one without getting frightened; it is the region in which simile is possible.

The important thing is that, in health, this five-layered structure, which Matte Blanco calls the *constitutive stratified bi-logical structure*, is immensely fluid and it is "lived as a unity". All the strata coexist simultaneously, while the two modes, like binocular microscopes, function in parallel, focusing through whatever situation is at hand in the way I suggested earlier: the idea of stratification is merely a spatial metaphor and misleading, since all the modes are nested and implicit within one another. There can, for instance, be no single isolated object at stratum one without its being implicit in (etymologically, "folded into") the several classes to which it inevitably belongs, and all the infinite potential classes with which these intersect in turn; however highly symmetrised the infinite sets of stratum five, these, nevertheless, contain particular individuals which remain simultaneously distinct according to the principle of generalisation.

A clinical example of someone living this structure as a unity is a man who came in to his session reporting that he had just been "cut up" by a motorist. He felt literally murderous. He felt very uncomfortable, rather trapped and cut off. Initially, it seemed to have no relevance to the session he was trying to settle into, but then he became aware of an image in which he was "cutting up" a photograph of me. He then realised that the motorist had put him in touch with a rage that already existed within him. This went back to circumstances in childhood, and he was in a rage with me for putting him in touch with it. It then came to him that he was feeling very sad, "cut up" himself, which enabled him to realise that as well as feeling literally murderous towards me, he did not want me to die. As the session proceeded, he started to become circumstantial and diffuse. This allowed him to think that he was running away, which, in turn, allowed him to get in touch with the fantasy of my murderous retaliation. Notice in this a continuous movement from affect to thought: there is a movement from a vague state of *being* (discomfort or trappedness, circumstantiality, and diffuseness—stratum 5–4) to powerful *feeling* (rage and images of cutting up—stratum 3, where equivalence makes him sad because I really will die, and frightened because I will also really be vengeful), to coming into *thought* (being able to observe his feelings, to realise that he is having fantasies, that an image of cutting up a photo is not the same as cutting *me* up, that he does not want me dead as well as wanting me dead, playing with the idea—stratum 2–1).

The importance of the stratified structure, lived as a unity, is also important in terms of the limitations of Aristotelian logic. This is because Aristotelian, asymmetric logic is tautologous, and tautology can only deliver truths implicit in its premises. It is incapable of novelty, so novelty, innovation, and imagination depend on symmetric logic and emotion (Bomford, 1999).

Jung

Individuation: from affect to thought

This relationship between being, feeling, and thinking in Matte Blanco is striking (the title of his second book (1988) was *Thinking, Feeling and Being*, strangely, in reverse order) because it almost exactly reflects that imagistic version of the idea of individuation which Jung found in alchemy and described in the last chapter of *Mysterium Coniunctionis* (Jung, 1963). In that book, Jung describes the first *coniunctio* as being between soul and spirit, making it quite explicit that, in modern parlance, soul is the equivalent of feeling, and spirit the equivalent of thought. There is a second *coniunctio*, the preparation of the balsam, which will be the binding for the third and final one, this being between the product of the first coniunctio (feeling–thinking) and what Jung calls the ground of our being. This becomes more comprehensible if we think of what Matte Blanco says of symmetry: that, being devoid of process, it can only be described as *being*. This *coniunctio*, which unites being, feeling, and thinking, is in line with Jung's idea of the archetype having what he calls an "instinctual pole" and a "spiritual pole" (Jung, 1947), the latter referring, again, to thought. I would replace "instinctual" here with affective, because, as Matte Blanco demonstrates, instinct as *process* is precluded in timeless, spaceless *being*. However, the important issue is that, for Jung, as for Matte Blanco, thought arises out of an affective unconscious,[8] out of affective archetypes which, until they can be thought are collective and impersonal—not individual, not *individuated*.

Jung's collective unconscious, archetypes, and the archetypal

Matte Blanco does not use the term collective, but he talks about the state of affairs (the basic matrix) where symmetry is highly prevalent so that space is effectively absent: there are, therefore, no spaces, internal or external, into or out of which or across which anything might be "projected", projection as a process being precluded in any case. In this state of affairs, primitive affects are simply shared, as with the mother who, in a state of primary maternal preoccupation has her feet on the floor, out of bed, moments before her newborn cries (some weeks later, she will not waken until her infant cries, and will then indicate that it is the father's turn).

This is, I think, equivalent to Jung's use of Lévy-Bruhl's concept of *participation mystique*. And it is in these sorts of states of high levels of symmetry, especially in states of intense emotion, that synchronistic phenomena occur. Jung's unconscious is timeless and spaceless, and is collective in the sense that the anatomy of the brain in which it arises, as well as the inevitability of shared common experiences, means that the symbolic phenomena are collective rather than individual. Jung called these experiences archetypal. The *repressed unconscious* is the product of individual experiences and contents which have to have attained sufficient contact with asymmetric processes to have been rejected—to be, for instance, *not* acceptable, subject to the law of negation and of non-contradiction, and so be subject to the laws of symmetric logic.

I will not discuss the idea of the archetype beyond suggesting that it is likely to be based on the affective "packets of symmetry" I mentioned earlier. I suspect, for instance, that the "good mother" has a lot to do with anything that promotes the secretion of oxytocin and attachment/attunement, which for an infant will be mother, mother's body, her breast, its milk, her gaze, her voice, her presence, her contact and warmth, and so on; I imagine that a "terrible mother" is likely to be most of the things that lead to difficulty of attachment and, for instance, the secretion of cortisol. It is these latter sorts of negative experience that are more likely to become the core of *complexes* in Jung's parlance, of *non-vital structures* in Matte Blanco's, which, unlike the constitutive stratified bi-logical structure or the *coniunctio*, will not permit the free to and fro between sensation, emotion, and thought characteristic of individuation or of the constitutive stratified bi-logical structure "lived as a unity" (Matte Blanco, 1988).

As to the archetypal image or phenomenon, pragmatically speaking, it is whatever evokes the archetype, that is, whatever for the individual substitutes the propositional function. If it does so, it will be a more or less numinous, powerful experience. Very powerful experiences of the numen are probably due to the fact that, as Matte Blanco says, the psyche has a tendency to personify infinite sets, so they easily become gods. An example is the idea of the unconscious (an infinite set *par excellence*) as Mercurius, or, indeed, the self as Christ,[9] of Bion's O as "godhead",[10] or of love, or the muses as depicted by Titian and Giorgione.

It is easy to see how inevitable the charges of vagueness and mysticism are against both Jung and Bion (O'Shaughnessy, 2005; Taylor, 20011), both in the light of Matte Blanco's revelation of how the symmetric mode, indistinguishable from Freud's original unconscious, is, like the godhead, "formless and infinite", and in the light of its inevitable personification as an infinite set.

On a more mundane level, a child in boarding school might comfort himself by snuggling down in bed with his teddy bear. "Tucking up in bed" is a function of Mummy, an infinite set which includes the proposition "Mummy tucks me and teddy up in bed" (MTme,t) as something that Mummy does to me. Here, the proposition, Mummy tucks me up, MTme,t,[11] becomes an infinite set in which the propositional function is Tucks up. So, this can be expressed as T[Mummy, me,t . . .], in which I ("me") become interchangeable with Mummy as a member of the set: it is not merely reversible. Mummy tucks me up; I tuck me up; I am Mummy: the activity, in Winnicott's language, becomes a "me-not-me" experience,[12] as does the teddy bear. In a secure child, the teddy evokes the mother archetype and comforts the child. In an insecurely attached child, whose experience is of an absent mother, it will more likely evoke the absent mother, the bad mother archetype, and make him more distressed.

Propositional functions and intensive infinities

I will make one final theoretical observation before returning to my patient's material and discussing the nature of my intervention. This is that anything which the psyche uses as a substitute for the propositional function also functions as what is called an *intensive infinity*. This idea becomes obvious when we think of it in opposition to its antithesis, which is an *extensive infinity*. An extensive infinity is when we count for ever and ever and ever . . . (and this sort of repetition is a way of evoking an extensive infinity in rhetoric). An extensive infinity never ends. An intensive infinity, on the other hand, is one element that "contains" the extensive infinity within it. The most obvious example is Blake's "To see the world in a grain of sand": the whole world is contained in a tiny grain of sand, an example, of course, of an infinite set where part contains whole. As I said above, there is no isolated object, even at stratum one, that does not "contain" the infinite intermeshing classes that invisibly contain it. A stratum is just a point of view, one of infinite convergence, as is a zero-dimensional point.

The zero-dimensional point, such as the single word, "communicate", is an example of an intensive infinity; and it is also an example of what Bion (after Poincaré) would call a "selected fact" (Bion, 1962, p. 72[13]).

With these two concepts (the idea of the *propositional function* and that of the *intensive infinity*), I think we can understand how it is that the asymmetric ego can access the unknown world across the caesura which separates conscious/asymmetry from unconscious/symmetry, K from O, the asymmetric mode from the symmetric mode, and that it does this by means of a "translation" or "unfolding" (Matte Blanco, 1975) of more dimensions into fewer.

Back to my patient and to my intervention

I think that it is helpful to start with the fact that the complex from which my patient suffered was dissociated. That is to say that the affects associated with it seemed to have had hardly any access to what Bion would refer to as alpha function, that is, to containment or reverie. The idea that she might be loved or that she might love was non-existent for her, and, indeed, she had always rejected her husband's protestations of love as nonsense, not out of malice so much as simple incomprehension. As she said of her mother, the relation with her was an "empty space", and this was what she brought to me, as well as, no doubt, to her husband.

In the absences I have described during her earlier sessions, it would not be possible to say who was absent from or abandoning whom, and if we look at this in terms of the propositional function *is absent from/abandons* ("A"), we might write it as *Someone* (S) *Abandons* (A) *Someone Else* (SE), A[S,SE] (another example of SRSE, referred to in footnote 12, above). As we have seen, the someone and the someone else are entirely interchangeable: she, her mother, I, her husband, and she was for a very long time, at least three years, completely unable to recognise absence/abandonment as an issue even when she was confronted with the most compelling evidence. I do not think that this was denial. The complex essentially consisted of the notion that intimacy was abandonment, or, more fundamentally, absence, and the affect involved when it did begin to surface was entirely somatically expressed in catastrophic and even potentially fatal form (*vide* the anaphylaxis). It is true that her husband expressed some of the anxiety she might have been expected to have felt, but the ideas of splitting and projective identification were expressed most clearly, if they were present, in the dream about the little girl without shoes and the little burdened ash-blond boy, that is, into discarded aspects of herself. It was only much later in the analysis that she started to become more aware of separation as an issue. Then affects could begin to emerge as feelings rather than symptoms. All this is suggestive to me of a set that is highly symmetrised within itself, unconscious and dissociated.

In the context where relationship was an empty space, the idea that she could love or be loved, or that she might need anyone, was incomprehensible, because it had never been reflected in reverie. When she started to get in touch with need, it was again somatic to start with, and experienced as appalling shame. Need, desire, and her body were shameful to her, so that even love as an affect could not be differentiated from something hateful, which is, again, suggestive of a high degree of symmetrisation in the region of the fourth, even the fifth, stratum of the stratified structure, and we would expect this to be accompanied by a deep inaccessibility to conscious awareness.

It would seem, therefore, that both the complex and its potential remedy lay, dissociated, some way beyond the caesura, beyond obvious means of communication, especially as projection was not a significant source of communication in this case: Bion argues that beta elements tend to be used in the service of projection, but I wonder if this is possible with such high degrees of symmetry.[14]

It will be apparent from what I have written that, by the time of the session I have described, there had been an enormous softening of this complex: we were not, by this stage, absences to one another; she was aware of her need, of an appropriate dependency through which she had grown, so that she could now consider leaving, albeit with sadness, and she had been able to experience this as need that was not shameful, as well as to express and experience affection. Nevertheless, there seemed to be a persistent puzzle around her sexual body which I continued to be predisposed to understand in terms of shame regarding her body with its need and desire.

As I have said, it seems that the word "communicate" struck me with the force of an intensive infinity, a selected fact, which in a moment unfolded a class of objects in a completely different and unexpected way—memory and desire could not have anticipated them. The class is infinite in the sense of its elements being interchangeable, which is what made the "election" of one of its elements as the propositional function possible in the first place because, as we have seen above, the characteristic of an infinite set is that any of its members can substitute for the propositional function. Its multi-dimensionality, however, made it inaccessible until it could "unfold" into consciousness as a single, zero-dimensional point. This is, I think, how symbols function, as a single point, a piece of the original multi-dimensional object of which it can be shown to be a part when reconnected.

The eros that the class includes obviously belongs to a related class that intersects with the one in question but is also different. This seems in retrospect the class in which "Hello Blondie" is the expression of affectionate appreciation rather than a sneer, a class in which she can be gazed on lovingly, where she is a joy to hear, and where there is a mother's loving touch: in short, a version of the loving mother archetype which she had previously been unable to constellate, but which we were now able to notice was available to her. It was not primarily about a sexual body, but about a body that could only become sexual if it had first been in touch with maternal eros and so constellate her femininity. I am struck, in retrospect, that I saw Titian's *Sacred and Profane Love* in my mind's eye as personifications of this set. The fact that her emotional self was no longer shameful and this meant that it was now available as a self to express was part of this and, I think, informed my "seeing" the Titian/Giorgione muses of the *Concert Champêtre*.

Conclusion and summary

I hope that this exercise in triangulation between Jung, Bion, and Matte Blanco offers some validation for all three, but, in the context of the present book, above all for some of Jung's conceptual equipment. The topic of his psychology is much too vast to reduce to a single chapter (and I have, of course, merely alluded to Bion's), but there is, I think, convincing evidence that vindicates several of those aspects of

Jung's work which have hitherto been held to be contentious, at least in certain quarters.

First, there is the notion of an unrepressed unconscious. This manifests itself in ways that are collective, and predictably so, in virtue both of the underlying brain functions which subserve it and of the commonality of experiences that we all undergo in living. It is less obviously collective in the sense that Matte Blanco's symmetry predicts, but which suggests the dissolution of individuality at high levels of symmetry and a situation where we would expect *participation mystique*.

I think, second, that it also offers some support for the notion of affective dispositions, which we increasingly understand to be dependent on appropriate environmental mirroring in order to be realised. Unmirrored, they remain, as do Bion's beta elements, unusable by mind, and, thus, dissociated nameless dreads, undifferentiated as things-in-themselves from the background O or unconscious out of which they arise.

Such affective processes, like the symmetric mode, which I am suggesting is synonymous with O, or Jung's collective unconscious, are highly symmetric, and, as such, inaccessible to asymmetric consciousness without being furnished with a propositional function via maternal reverie, which allows them to become alpha elements. This, I think, is consonant with Jung's notion of archetypes and archetypal images: there are affective dispositional cores—archetypes—which can generate a series of imagistic forms which is infinite in that each is interchangeable with the other as the propositional function. As we have seen in the clinical material, just one of these can serve as the selected fact, as the archetypal image that can make the rest of the series available to awareness, but, more importantly, lead to a transformation in O. This is my third "vindication".

Fourth, a complex can be understood to be a highly asymmetric structure that always construes new perceptual material in its terms, so that learning from experience is impossible. Its gradual dissolution is, therefore, of paramount importance in order to permit the novelty of such a transformation in O and to promote the *coniunctionis* which make individuation possible, individuation understood in terms of the free and constant interchange between being, feeling, and thinking. This is my fifth point. Thinking divorced from being and feeling remains tethered to knowledge, memory, and desire, and, thus, tautologous, but sixth, our thinking, positivistic selves are always suspicious of being as if it were "mystical". Matte Blanco's derivation of a logic of being as infinite sets frees us from that anxiety, and the notions both of the interchangeability of the members of an infinite set with the propositional function and of that of the intensive infinity enable us to see how symbols may arise out of an otherwise inaccessible unconscious and legitimately represent it.

I think that Matte Blanco's tripartite *constitutive stratified bi-logical structure*, which we have seen is reminiscent of Jung's final *coniunctio*, offers another instructive parallel: this is with the models of development of Ogden (1989) and, later, Hinshelwood (1997). Independently, they suggest that as well as the paranoid–schizoid and the depressive positions, there was also a stage anterior to these, which Ogden (1989) (adopting Grotstein's term from an unpublished paper) refers to as the autistic–contiguous phase. Its task is to "build a house out of which something might be thrown" before projection is possible (to adopt Alvarez's (2010) use of something which Anna Freud said in relation to Klein's concept of projective identification and the paranoid–schizoid position). Ogden and Hinshelwood favour Tustin and Bick, respectively, but the sense in all three papers is that uncontained affective life needs to be gathered into a sense of continuous self with interiority before the sort of ego that Klein's structure assumes can operate or relate. The Ogden–Hinshelwood scheme corresponds well to Matte Blanco's structure, in that the upper reaches of the model that correspond to "thinking" relate to the depressive position, the middle reaches, or "feeling", to the paranoid–schizoid position, while the earlier, undifferentiated phase relates to what Matte Blanco would call "being". My seventh point is that it was this stage, anterior, as I have said, to the paranoid–schizoid, that Jung was forced by his own development to realise and which, according to Winnicott, Freud was not equipped to understand (Meredith-Owen, 2011; Winnicott, 1964).

Finally, and eighth, what is of further interest here is that in this work of relating the individual to their bodily-affective selves (Carvalho, 2012; Ferrari, 1992), the transference to the analyst, like the relationship to the mother, while clearly paramount and never absent, is, none the less, secondary in a clinical sense to the focus of the relationship between the individual—infant or patient—and their affective selves (see Lombardi, 2003 and subsequent discussion in Bonaminio, 2004, Grotstein, 2004, and Lombardi, 2004). This puts

Jung's very ambivalent relationship to the idea of the transference, one that he expressed in the Tavistock Lectures (Jung, 1935), into a light that has, to my knowledge, remained unexplored hitherto. He was clear that the transference always existed, but also clear that sometimes to insist on it was obstructive.

Notes

1. I am most grateful to my patient for having not only given her consent to my using her material, but for having read it and endorsed my account.
2. There is argument about who painted *Concert Champêtre*, Titian or Giorgione, which is irrelevant to the present discussion, though Filippo Pedroccho includes it firmly in his *Titian: The Complete Paintings* (2001), in which can be read the arguments for and against this inclusion.
3. Pedrocco (2001) is dismissive of this iconographic interpretation, but see Edgar Wind (1958) for the argument for it. Again, it is irrelevant to the clinical argument, which rests upon the *affective* (rather than intellectual) significance of the figures in my countertransference experience.
4. The eros here is interesting in that it is not simply about eros—connection with other—but with connection with self. If we think of *Fête Champêtre*, the nude figures here symbolise (divine) inspiration, that is, connection with the somatic–emotional which Ferrari (1992) describes as the vertical axis (Carvalho, 2012).
5. Symmetry is another way of explaining the absence of space and time: the proposition, A preceded B (in time or space) is also reversible in symmetry, yielding B precedes A.
6. "The crown" is an interesting example here: "the crown" is a reversible sub-set of the reversible sub-set "king".
7. As a matter of fact, whereas Aristotle did define the logic we attribute to him, which he called "dialectical logic", in which things are either this or that, he also wrote about *rhetoric*, in which things were much more fuzzy (i.e., symmetric and emotional), somewhat this and somewhat the other, an art that was the art of persuasion via the manipulation of the audience's emotions. By extension, to learn how to resist such false logic, one had to learn how to recognise how it operates, both in terms of its violations of logic and in terms of the emotions to which it is appealing (Leith, 2011).
8. Matte Blanco is fond of quoting Freud's dictum that "Emotion is the mother of thought".
9. Bomford (1999) points out that the characteristics of the unconscious—unspeakable, timeless, and spaceless—correspond precisely with the

attributes of the apophatic god of the mystics of whom nothing which might be said can be said (ineffable), and who is eternal and ubiquitous.

10. The godhead is "formless and infinite", like the symmetric mode. Trying to extract definitions of O from Bion's writings of many of his concepts is a difficult task which faces the reader with the contradictions and paradoxes that are inevitable in trying to translate symmetry into asymmetric thought, but the page from which this phrase is taken (1970, p, 88, and, indeed, the whole Chapter Nine) make the equation difficult to avoid. Still on the theme of personification, in the same chapter, on p. 85, Bion refers to the affect (symmetry) to be "contained" as the Dionysian, and to its (asymmetric) "container" (asymmetric) expression as Apollonian. It is a short step to the personifications, Dionysos and Apollo.

11. Those familiar with Matte Blanco will recognise this as a variant of SRSE, Something Relates to Something Else, the triadic *non plus ultra* beyond which no logic can go, but of which the unconscious—symmetry— renders each term an infinite set, defined by the propositional function of the verb. This is the logic behind the explanation in a passage above of how affects can be shown to be infinite sets. The notation, R[S,SE], or, in the example above, T[Mummy, me], or, by extension, T[Mummy, me, teddy . . .] we owe to Bomford (1999) as an extension of Matte Blanco's thinking.

12. Me-not-me is an interesting example of non-negation, in which I, mummy, and the object (teddy, etc.) that might represent mummy cannot be said not to be one another, and of non-contradiction, where teddy is both me and not-me.

13. Selected facts, according to Poincaré, "unite elements long since known, but till then scattered and seemingly foreign to each other, and suddenly introduce order where the appearance of disorder reigned" (quoted in Bion, 1962, p. 72), and "The selected fact is the name of an emotional experience" (Bion, 1962, p. 72—that is, in Matte Blanco's terms, a propositional function).

14. I would suggest that if we consider every psychic content to exist simultaneously at every level of symmetry to asymmetry, though the presence of maternal reverie is essential in order to obtain self-reflective awareness, then, where such reverie has been deficient, such contents exist predominantly in stratum 5, where they are absolutely symmetric, and in stratum 4, where projection may start to become possible. I think that this observation might suggest that we need to revise our notion of beta elements as process rather than element, movement from O towards K via intensive infinities. Interestingly, in the only paper in which Matte Blanco extensively discusses Bion ("Reflecting with Bion", in Grotstein's

festschrift, Do I Dare Disturb the Universe (1981)), Matte Blanco confesses that he is unable to understand the concept of beta elements, but suggests elsewhere in the same paper that the function of the alpha function is *to confer a value* on the propositional function of the set *and thus subject it to asymmetric operation*. I think that this would make sense of what I am suggesting here, that "beta elements" are not available as mental contents because insufficiently "asymmetrised" and, therefore, condemned to dissociation because unavailable for "mental operation".

References

Alvarez, A. (2010). Levels of analytic work and levels of pathology: the work of calibration. *International Journal of Psychoanalysis, 91*: 859–676.

Bion, W. R. (1962). *Learning from Experience*. London: Karnac.

Bion, W. R. (1970). *Attention and Interpretation*. London, Tavistock.

Bion, W. R. (1992). *Cogitations*. London, Karnac.

Bomford, R. (1999). *The Symmetry of God*. London: Free Association Press.

Bonaminio, V. (2004). Commentary on Dr. Riccardo Lombardi's "Three analytic sessions". *Psychoanalytic Quarterly, LXXIII*: 793–799.

Carvalho, R. (2012). A brief introduction to the thought of Armando B. Ferrari. *British Journal of Psychotherapy, 28*: 409–434.

Ferrari, A. B. (1992). *L'Eclissi del Corpo*. Rome: Borla.

Grotstein, J. (2004). Commentary on Dr. Riccardo Lombardi's "three analytic sessions". *Psychoanalytic Quarterly, LXXIII*: 787–792.

Hinshelwood, R. (1997). Catastrophe, objects and representation: three levels of interpretation. *British Journal of Psychotherapy, 13*: 307–317.

Jung, C. G. (1935). *Tavistock Lectures. The Symbolic Life, C.W., 18*, R. F. C. Hull (Trans.). London: Routledge & Kegan Paul.

Jung, C. G. (1947). On the nature of the psyche. In: *The Structure and Dynamics of the Psyche. C.W., 8*, R. F. C. Hull (Trans.). London: Routledge & Kegan Paul.

Jung, C. G. (1963). *Mysterium coniunctionis. C.W., 14*, R. F. C. Hull (Trans.). London: Routledge & Kegan Paul.

Leith, S. (2011). *You Talkin' to Me: Rhetoric from Aristotle to Obama*. London: Profile Books.

Lombardi, R. (2003). Catalyzing the dialogue between the body and the mind in a psychotic analysand. *Psychoanalytic Quarterly, 2*: 1017–1041.

Lombardi, R. (2004). Response to commentaries on "Three analytic sessions". *Psychoanalytic Quarterly, LXXIII*: 807–814.

Matte Blanco, I. (1975). *The Unconscious as Infinite Sets*. London: Butterworth.

Matte Blanco, I. (1981). Reflecting with Bion. In: J. Grotstein (Ed.), *Do I Dare Disturb the Universe* (pp. 489–528). London: Routledge.

Matte Blanco, I. (1988). *Thinking, Feeling and Being*. London: Routledge.

Meredith-Owen, W. (2011). Winnicott on Jung: destruction, creativity and the unrepressed unconscious. *Journal of Analytical Psychology, 56*: 56–75.

Ogden, T. (1989). On the concept of an autistic–contiguous position. *International Journal of Psychoanalysis, 70*: 127–140.

O'Shaughnessy, E. (2005). Whose Bion. *International Journal of Psychoanalysis, 86*: 1523–1528.

Panksepp, J. (1998). *Affective Neuroscience*. New York: Oxford University Press.

Pedrocco, F. (2001). *Titian: The Complete Paintings*. London: Thames & Hudson.

Schore, A. (2001). Minds in the making: attachment, the self-organized brain and developmentally oriented psychoanalytic psychotherapy. *British Journal of Psychotherapy, 17*: 229–321.

Segal, H. (1957). Notes on symbol formation. *International Journal of Psychoanalysis, 38*: 391–397

Target, M., & Fonagy, P. (1996). Playing with reality: II. The development of psychic reality from a theoretical perspective. *International Journal of Psychoanalysis, 77*: 459–479.

Taylor, D. (2011). Commentary on Vermote's "On the value of 'late Bion' to analytic theory and practice". *International Journal of Psychoanalysis, 92*: 1099–1112.

Vermote, R. (2011). On the value of "late Bion" to analytic theory and practice. *International Journal of Psychoanalysis, 92*: 1089–1098.

Wind, E. E. (1958). *Pagan Mysteries in the Renaissance*. London: Faber and Faber.

Winnicott, D. W. (1964). *Memories, Dreams, Reflections* by C. G. Jung. *International Journal of Psychoanalysis, 45*: 450–455. Also in: *Psycho-Analytic Explorations*, C. Winnicott (Ed.). Cambridge, MA: Harvard University Press, 1989.

CHAPTER THREE

Reversal and recovery in trauma: unrepresentability in Bion, Jung, and Fordham

Geraldine Godsil

"It is not I who create myself, rather I happen to myself"

(Jung, 1958)

"The primary self . . . [is] . . . indestructible"

(Fordham, 1995)

My aim in this chapter is first to locate Wilfred Bion in the context of his history as a war veteran and to explore whether the theory of thinking that emerges from this history offers a way of better understanding the impact of trauma at the micro level of process. Second, and much more tentatively, I want to explore through three clinical examples whether his concept of reversal of alpha function might be relevant in thinking about the consequences of the particular kind of trauma experienced under totalitarian systems, where attacks on the mind are aimed at distortion of the truth. My hypothesis is that a double environmental deprivation might then exist, in the state itself and in its intrusions into, and consequences for, the family culture. This exploration is motivated by a sense of something missing in Jung's and Fordham's theories of representation as they currently stand.

In 2003, a volume of the *Journal of Analytical Psychology* was devoted to clinical and theoretical aspects of trauma. I shall take this as my starting point because it introduces not a unified theory, but an explosion of new knowledge and new integrations in the field. The previous year, Bovensiepen (2002) had used Bion's concept of reverie, which assumed mature development in the mind, to add a dimension that he felt was missing in the classical concept of transcendent function. Through his work with the child Tom, Bovensiepen stresses the importance of a process towards symbolising within the matrix of the transference–countertransference relationship. He redefines the prospective function of the symbol as the experience of restoring hope and imagination. This is the precursor to any possibility of mourning. If something cannot be represented, it cannot be mourned, and the complexity of symbolising processes is a central topic currently in a range of psychoanalytic and Jungian analytic work (Botella & Botella, 2005; Cambray, 2009; Colman, 2007, 2010; Green, 1999, 2000; Hogenson, 2005, 2009; Knox, 2011a; Martin-Vallas, 2006, 2008, 2009).

In the 2003 Journal volume, Bion's work is implicit and explicit in several accounts. In Kalsched's account of daimonic objects, Bion's bizarre object is seen as an equivalent construct (p. 147). My argument is that Bion has more to contribute to Jungian theory at a micro-level of process but first needs to be restored to his particular context as the survivor of severe trauma himself. The contact barrier, its reversal, and the production of bizarre objects and beta screen may provide tools for understanding the disturbed thinking that results from trauma. This is a more subtle attack on the mind than the gross attacks coming from the psychotic part of the personality described in his work of the psychotic period (1984). His development of a theory of constant dreaming, awake and asleep, so that conscious experience is being worked on continuously, might have something to offer in clarifying the detailed processes (the micro level) underlying the "natural process" of the transcendent function (Jung, 1957[1916]). I suggest that the stress in the Jungian tradition on the psyche's self-healing properties can be extended and enriched through Bion's concept of alpha function and its reversal. What is implicit in Jung's use of alchemical metaphors (1946) needs to be spelled out.

Bion's work, like Jung's, is not simply determinist. He views the mind as layered like an onion with different caesuras constantly being negotiated as new unprocessed material stored in an unsymbolised area emerges (Bion, 1989, 1990, 2000). The beta element as raw sensory data that is meaningless and the beta element as the harbinger of the unknown in his later formulation can open up new ways of observing clinical material in those unrepresentable areas called "psychoid" by Jung (1952).

André Green had found conversations with Bion a great help when he was writing his book on blank psychosis with Donnet (Donnet & Green, 1973, p. 109). Green's account of one of the dimensions of blank psychosis seems to resonate with Bion's interest in −K phenomena, particularly the consequences of reversal of alpha function. If the symbolising processes of the mind are themselves attacked, then a malignant disarticulation can be established:

> If projective identification is not possible because it may itself cause a threat of annihilation through the emptying of the mind another mechanism is still at hand: a process of erasure, an activity of effacing or deletion that has nothing to do with repression as a censorship but, rather, with a radical suppression of what happens to the mind. This is what happens, I believe, in blank psychosis or to a lesser degree in states of blankness. The result is a "blank hole" in the mind, which not only acts as an inner void but also has a power of attracting all mental contents or thoughts that are linked with the main topic in the centre of the blank hole. An extremely powerful −K activity, a sort of negative linking, is here in action. (Green, 2000, p. 114)

Fordham was himself aware of what Bion had to offer in making more specific what was implicit in Jung. He refers to Jung's definition of the symbol "as the best possible expression of an otherwise unknown datum" (1995, p. 229) and that, in Bion's terms, this unknown datum is "capable of experience". By this, I think he means that this is the locus where Bion's theory of thinking can usefully operate in Jungian territory. However, Fordham's hunch is not fully integrated into his theory of representation, although he can see that several of Jung's later alchemical texts might benefit from such treatment (1995, p. 224). Fordham does not develop a negative grid for identifying how trauma both early and late might lead the mind to reverse its symbolising capacities, although the concept is implicit in Jung, as I discuss elsewhere (Godsil, 2005), and also in Fordham's concept of a failed deintegrate that is split off (Urban, 1996).

What I aim to do first in this chapter is to re-read Bion's theory of thinking through the lens of his *War Memoirs* (1997) and his notebooks *Cogitations* (1992) with a view to establishing the usefulness of the concept of reversal phenomena when working with traumatised populations. I am taking this line of enquiry because I think that reversal of alpha function and the resulting bizarre objects and beta elements contribute to a further understanding of "nameless" experience which is impossible to represent. Bion called this "nameless dread" (1984, p. 116), but it occupies the same space as Green's "blank psychosis" (Donnet & Green, 1973) and the Botellas' interest in unrepresentable states (2005). The distress caused by an experience that cannot be represented introduces a layer of communication that is not accessible unless the analyst can tolerate regression and unconscious identification with archaic states. This area has, I think, consequences for how we understand countertransference. Bion's "becoming" (1970), the Botellas' "double" (2005), and Jung's "unconscious identity" (1946) all have something in common and imply a regression in the analyst so that a new awareness can emerge.

The War Memoirs *and* Learning from Experience

Bion's first account of the war (1997, pp. 5–72), written in his early twenties before he went up to Oxford, was sent to his parents to compensate for not writing to them during the war. Dissociated states were part of his experience, and his wife, Francesca Bion, describes how he talked about the war on the first occasion they dined together and how he still had nightmares. He did not write about the war again until he was sixty, when travelling through Amiens on the train stirred up memories (1997, pp. 215–308). This remembering was the account that was written contemporaneously (1958–1960) with the development of his theory of beta and alpha elements in his notebooks (1992, pp. 1–113). Parthenope Bion, his daughter from his first marriage, makes the link between the war writings and the primitive elements of mind that Bion's theory of thinking describes.

> This vision of the mind as a palimpsest with a continual potentiality
> for an almost instant regression can be seen to tie up to the theory of
> beta-elements, a continuous flow of unprocessed pre-mental sensory

data, which then have to be subjected to alpha function in order to be used for thinking at all, in the sense that these two theories deal with the rock bottom of mental and pre-mental life. (1992, p. 310)

In his seventies, looking back on his war experiences in *Commentary*, Bion says the most awful thing about them was that they were forgotten, but he also adds, "I don't remember it but my gut does" (1992, p. 209). These sensory elements, which are never forgotten but cannot be given meaning, contribute towards Bion's theory of beta elements. In his notebooks, he envisages them as existing within an envelope of sensory experience in an atmosphere of persecution, but still searching for meaning as "communicating particles" that have not yet been understood (1992, p. 36).

In Amiens, Bion dramatises the functioning of his theory in relation to the death of his young runner, Sweeting, who has been fatally wounded by shell fire. In a complex autobiographical construction, he enacts the dilemma faced in trauma. He is both Sweeting and the rejecting object unable to take in Sweeting's repeated call for his mother. Bion is repelled, vomits, and wants the terrifying agony of Sweeting removed. In one of his last war writings, in the autobiography he wrote in his seventies in Los Angeles (1982), he makes the identification with Sweeting clear. He says, "I died on August 8th 1918" (p. 265), and, when he speaks of Sweeting's death, he writes, "And then I think he died. Or perhaps it was only me" (p. 249). He writes from an insider position as a war veteran, but also as an experienced psychoanalyst who understands annihilating anxieties and their impact on the mind. To survive, you need to project into an object that can tolerate and make sense of the projection. In the later account of Sweeting's death in *The Long Weekend*, where identification with the dead is stressed, he seems to suggest that the working through of his war experiences involved recognising the introjection of experiences of death and horror that continued to need working through. Without that, there will be dead areas to the mind that cannot be represented. Parthenope Bion notes, when she reviews his war writings, that "some episodes are carried over almost unchewed and apparently undigested . . . as though no further working-through were possible" (1997, p. 309).

Sweeting's terrible wound in the thoracic cavity destroys the respiratory system and punctures the skin container, which also conveys the inadequacy of the mind to metabolise such experiences. The inadequate field dressing, like the incapacitated mind after trauma, cannot restore the rupture in representational capacities. As the historian Roper comments on the veterans of the First World War, "They searched for words to express horror, not because their language was inadequate but because the actual emotional experience was not then, and perhaps never would be, capable of being thought" (2009, p. 266).

Bion's use of the words "nameless dread" in his theory of thinking (1962, p. 96, 1984, p. 116) locates him firmly in the context of the war. It was a term in frequent use at the time for post-traumatic states (Roper, 2009, pp. 262–263). In his clinical writing, Bion uses it to describe the state of meaninglessness experienced by the human infant when the mother's alpha function and reverie are not available to receive the infant's experiences. This has long-term consequences for the infant and for future development. There may be a misunderstanding object in the mind that fosters meaningless states, or an actively malignant object in the mind that strips and destroys meaning. This model of the mind has been applied in different contexts: to child development, to psychosis, and to psychosomatic illness. I think it can be applied to post-traumatic states in the area of alteration of self-perception and might be a feature of the complex PTSD discussed by Herman (1997, p. 121). She applies this formulation to the effect of totalitarian systems on the individual, whether these systems arise in a political or domestic context.

In his last reference to Sweeting in his trilogy (1991, p. 256), Bion seems to suggest that mourning for the destructiveness, both intentional and unintentional, of past events is almost impossible to do fully, but is essential to undertake continually. How the wound of unrepresentability might be healed or repaired is the central concern in Bion's writing. Both how we might learn from experience and how this process might be undermined, attacked, or become impossible are essential in his project. Interest in the links between Bion's war experiences and the development of his theoretical work is reflected in recent studies (Grotstein, 2000; Roper, 2009; Souter, 2009; Szykierski, 2010).

An adverse environment and its consequences

Conceptual precision is increasingly hard in an area where an explosion of new thinking is happening. I would differentiate Bion's bizarre object from Kalsched's daimonic object. The bizarre object of *Learning from Experience* is the result of a reversal of alpha function and the destruction of the contact barrier, so that thinking is interfered with in particular ways. What happens to the *process* in which meaningless-ness erases meaning is emphasised. I think this can be useful in under-standing the subtle defences in post-traumatic states. Kalsched's daimonic object belongs to a pathological organisation of the person-ality, and this trauma complex has a rigidity and ineducable quality that makes it very difficult to transform. Bion offers a more detailed commentary in *Learning from Experience* on how this happens and how it involves an alteration of perception that reverses meaning but can also in itself be reversed. A close reading of this might also offer further detailed understanding of the attacks on reflective function described by Knox (2003a,b, 2011a,b) and to the problems described by Urban when a traumatic experience cannot be assimilated (2003). My interest in reversal phenomena and their effect on perception is also rooted in considering how totalitarian systems might affect both object relationships and mental processes. In both the political and the private sphere, it is the mind of the individual that is attacked. "The most potent weapon in the hands of the oppressor is the mind of the oppressed" (Biko, 1987, p. 92).

Bizarre objects and beta screen

Bizarre objects are first named in Bion's account of his work with psychotic patients. They are the result of fragmenting attacks on the perceptual apparatus and projection of these fragments into the out-side world, where a confusional agglomeration of these particles occur. The bizarre objects of the psychotic period are not my focus. It is later, in the context of *Learning from Experience*, that a second type of bizarre object is postulated. It takes on a more subtle presence linked to reversal of alpha function, and I think it can extend our repertoire of understanding defences in studying less obviously disturbed patients and the effects of trauma. Meaning is distorted by the interruption of symbolising processes. Fragments of meaning may still be detected in the ruins of thought, like a structure that has been fragmented or distorted but retains bits of recognisable debris. Meltzer (1986, p. 107) illustrates this phenomenon by the example of smashed-up Lego[(r)] constructions where clumps of Lego[(r)] pieces may still show recognisable features of the original object (the wheel or axle of a car, for example).

The sculptor, Cornelia Parker, provides a consciously playful example of these processes. In her famous sculpture of the exploded shed, *Cold Dark Matter: An Exploded View* (1991), the fragments are suspended and a light, placed in the middle, casts shadows of the fragments on to the wall. Parker was interested in the nature of the physical properties of matter and explored them by suspending, exploding, crushing, and stretching elements. This example from a contemporary sculpture might clarify how Bion's concept of an alteration of the alpha elements brought about by reversal distorts both perception and meaning but, at the same time, by dismantling might also enable new connections. The analyst's clarity of perception can arrest the process of distortion (Meltzer, 1986, p. 121). As alpha elements facilitate narrativisation within a temporal structure, the restoration of these elements would strengthen the capacity to dream new versions of old dilemmas. This has important implications for recovery from traumatic experiences that have never been able to be assimilated.

What triggers reversal?

In his notebooks, Bion (note dated 1958) suggests that the development of thinking—alpha function—can be affected at the point where there is an overload of mental pain. He calls it α-destruction. It might be initiated by hatred of reality, fear of a primitive superego taking shape, or intolerable depression at the threshold of the depressive position (1992, p. 96). Later (1962), he describes how reversal of alpha function affects the contact barrier and produces beta elements, a beta screen, and bizarre objects. This later formulation can be understood as the result of trauma and failures of containment. Brown (2005) considers that it is the impact of an external event that triggers reversal. Tarantelli (2003), in conceptualising how extreme helplessness might bring about psychic death, refers to "the ontological precariousness of the survivor" (p. 926).

In the following clinical vignette, both helplessness and shame are triggers for the reversal of alpha function.

Joseph dreams that he goes into work and finds the aquarium empty and the water very muddy. A very aggressive shark has got into the aquarium and eaten up all the dolphins and the other fish kept there.

He explains that, as a marine biologist, he has been working on the dolphins with a group of colleagues. One of his associations is that sometimes he has a fear that he is drowning. The marine biology project has clear connections with the work of therapy that has been going on but is now interrupted by the break.

During the break, he sends further dreams. In the second dream, his loving feelings and longing for sensuous contact disappear from his awareness and are located in a black girl who longs to kiss him. In the third dream, he is rejected by his students, who do not want to take the course he is running at the university. He decides within the dream that to avoid this unpleasant and embarrassing experience he will stop teaching altogether. Then he will not feel humiliated and the students will not be inconvenienced.

In reality, he is a teacher who is highly valued by his students. I want, at this point, to concentrate on the destruction of the dolphins by the shark, the intense feelings of shame and rejection, and the impact on his capacity to accurately perceive his experience.

Dolphins have a sensory sonar system (echolocation) that they use for communication and locating objects. They emit calls to the environment and listen to the echoes of those calls that return from various objects near them. They use these echoes to locate and identify the objects. This biological sonar system is used for navigating and for foraging in various environments (Whitlaw, 1993). The shark also has sensing capacities. Through electroreception, it can detect fields that all living things produce. The purpose is to hunt and eat prey, so this function has a predatory imperative.

Although the material can be read in object-relation terms as an attack on the good object and good parts of himself, I think the meaning of the dream series gains further depth if it is read as a reversal of alpha function. Having cannibalised the therapist's alpha function, the patient is himself unable to think. The water in the tank becomes muddy. He cannot locate his own feelings of love and need, so they are projected into the black girl, and, finally, his confidence in his own thinking and learning capacities is lost. One of the most interesting features in this reversal of alpha function is that the trigger is the pain of intense shame and powerlessness, not guilt. The shark attacks the dolphin so that these feelings cannot be perceived.

In his history, his family had experienced relocations and starvation under a communist regime. Toughness and survival were emphasised in the family culture, which seemed to verge on abusive. His mother became very depressed and died.

I think work with this patient suggests that the sheer weight of pain and shame to be borne at times when he feels deserted can, in itself, trigger the reversal. The patient, identified with a powerful predator, cannibalises alpha function in order to obscure perception. The muddy water in itself might refer to this process and convey the functioning of a beta screen. The series of dreams shows the consequences for the patient whose capacity to orientate himself is then emotionally damaged temporarily. The distortion of perception does not last, and he finds his way back to a different state of mind in which he can contact his therapist by e-mail and acknowledge his need.

Reversal of alpha function, bizarre object, and beta screen have something to offer in understanding how the mind defends itself from mental pain and mounts an attack on its own symbolising capacities in trauma. In post-Soviet societies where thinking and otherness have been relentlessly attacked, the mind's own self-attacking propensities might be magnified (Paju, 2007; Parktal, 2012; Sebek, 1996, 1998; Solzhenitsyn, 1963, 2002).

The contact barrier, with its constantly renewed alpha elements in the process of dreaming, protects sanity with its permeable membrane and fosters continuous narratives, ordering and sequencing and memory. This formulation of Bion's does away with the ontic significance of the unconscious and is compatible with current interest in the Jungian field in emergence and moments of meeting (Cambray, 2006, 2009; Hogenson, 2005, 2009; Knox, 2003a, 2011b).

In the only two papers that have fully explored these reversal phenomena, the trigger for the process differs. Meltzer's (1986) account focuses on avoidance of mourning and reparation. Brown (2005) argues that the reversal and production of a beta screen is triggered by the traumatic event of a rape. He suggests that the beta screen then becomes the traumatic organisation, alpha function as a symbolic process is arrested, and, instead of being dreamed, aspects of the rape experience are encoded in the body as terrifying "things" available to the analyst only through his bodily countertransference and enactments. There is a different weighting in each account of internal and external factors and different qualities and quantities of mental pain. The interplay between these elements has to be borne in mind.

Meltzer considers that the alpha elements, once constituted, cannot be destroyed, only distorted and covered over with lies. This distortion of the truth has much in common with totalitarian systems where propaganda is insidious and surveillance continual. Hatred of otherness and of independent thought and dreams in the privacy of the mind is attacked and suppressed. Hence, there is a need for intellectual, artistic, and personal expression and memory in the process of recovery. On this point, historians, cultural theorists, artists, and psychoanalysts agree (Bulgakov, 1997; Kadare, 2008; Kurvet-Kaosaar, 2008; Laar, 2007; Laub, 1995; Paju, 2006; Parktal, 2012; Ramphele, 2008; Wieland-Burston, 2012).

A very interesting series of papers by Sebek (1996, 1998), a Czech psychoanalyst, explores whether a vulnerability to introject these totalitarian objects, which already exist in myth, religion, and ancient history, might be increased when there has been a long period of oppression under a totalitarian system. The destructiveness of such systems in their particular and different forms across Eastern Europe are only now beginning to be fully described from a psychoanalytic, historical, political, and cultural perspective.

> The posttotalitarian personality is not a new diagnostic category but a pattern of psychological characteristics shared by the generation of people who had accumulated their major life experiences in totalitarian societies (Central and Eastern Europe). By means of everyday introjections they created internal totalitarian objects that continue to assure their adaptation in the post-totalitarian period. The result is a crisis of identity and authority that is conceived mostly as negative. A search for an identity and a positive authority seems to be a task for the future. (Sebek, 1998, p. 308)

These "adaptations" may permeate the symbolising processes of those who have been touched by such perverse influences in spite of themselves. These areas of the mind represent formidable difficulties in analysis, as both patient and analyst in the matrix of the transference struggle to restore a distorted perception that conceals the nature of the emotional conflicts involved.

Reversal phenomena in the interplay between the double adverse environments of state and family living under totalitarian systems

I am going to give two further examples to illustrate the above reversal phenomena. The three clinical cases in this chapter come from individual work, but each patient inhabited a cultural context where totalitarian regimes in Africa and Eastern Europe had dominated family life. Otherness is punished and exterminated and curiosity is taboo. Even where there is active resistance, there may coexist a vulnerability to influence in such environments so that distortion is accepted as normal and evasion of truthful and emotionally significant experience becomes essential to survival. I stress the tentative nature of this hypothesis, which requires further work.

Elektra and the beta screen

The beta screen does not link, it strips meaning from potentially meaningful elements and its purpose is to perpetuate meaninglessness. It aims to produce emotional involvement in the analyst and, at the same time, block thought. Bion, in an interesting note (1962, p. 101), suggests that a word that had been a highly developed symbol system might be left intact, but all the tissue of linking experiences and associations that give the word its vitality and meaning are stripped away. It can now neither generate new meaning nor remember past meanings. It is a symbolic husk: the place where meaning was. There are highly verbal patients who use words in this way to obstruct meaning, rather than to communicate so that words become things. Words can form a beta screen and so can physical symptoms, as in the example below where the beta screen is encoded in the body.

This example refers to a patient who knowingly reversed alpha function to create a highly purposeful and malignant beta screen encoded in the body. She had experienced extreme adverse circumstances in childhood, since her mother had suffered from post-natal depression and violently rejected her child. It was later revealed that, during the Second World War, her mother had put her first child up for adoption. This event was unknown to Elektra, but, when discovered, it helped her to be able to locate an external circumstance as significant in her illness. It relieved her of the burden of feeling that all the badness was inside her. It was, however, the beta screen encoded in the body that halted work at this point. The beta screen developed as a last-ditch defence at the point where her awareness of a receptive object and her feeling of containment was a reality and where a contact barrier was beginning to form. She was less mad, but more aware, and that was the crucial agony that triggered the reversal of alpha function. With awareness come the feelings related to need, vulnerability, and helplessness, and, in her case, an agonising sense of loss. There was, as a result, not just an attack on an understanding object, there was also an interference with the building blocks of potential thoughts themselves.

In my attempts to stay in contact with her, I was experienced as a dangerous allergen. She reacted with life-threatening symptoms of swelling in the respiratory system. These were diagnosed as angioedema, or an auto-immune disorder, the consequences of which can be fatal as it leads to obstruction of the airways and suffocation.

The beta screen in the body encompassed swelling, burning, asphyxiating elements, like a Cornelia Parker experiment with matter. I felt bombarded by sensations that obliterated thought. At one point, she described herself as a leper, and, at the time, I experienced this in my own bodily response as rot, smell, and decay. I think now there is a further layer of meaning to this experience. It describes an alive contact barrier being reversed into a collection of dead "things". The distress caused by this unconscious defensive manoeuvre is intensely persecuting, as the mind experiences its own fragmentation as "rot". Why she would do this is complex. There was considerable deficit in her background; the failures of containment in her early history meant that she did not have the capacity to tolerate anxieties related to emotional growth. This failure becomes internalised and identified with. However, the purposefulness of the reaction of the lungs at the point where alpha function was established suggested that the complex dialectic between external and internal factors needed to be clarified. Elektra's swollen tissues might have been "a self survival tactic" and an "effort at reorganisation and reconstitution of the self" (Mitrani, 1993, p. 336) in the face of maternal failure. The trigger for reversal might have been the impossibility of metabolising the pain of the mother's rejection so the beta screen gives some stability. Fordham's interest in early defence systems (1974, pp. 192–199) stresses the primitive protective functioning of such early defences. Both perspectives need to be borne in mind. In my work with her, it was only at a late stage that the beta screen became a useful concept for me. The active, purposeful nature of it as a defence is at the point where meaning is beginning to emerge and the picture of the self that is becoming clearer is too unbearable to be tolerated.

One could understand Elektra's auto-immune reaction as the immune system attacking a healthy part of herself because of confusion and panic and difficulty differentiating. However, I think focusing on the micro level of beta element organisation in the beta screen allows another perspective to be formulated where Elektra attacks her own alpha function to avoid the pain of seeing the wound in herself (Urban, 2003). This is a profound structural deficit that, from a Jungian perspective, indicates a need for continuing very careful work in the countertransference and in the analyst's self-analysis. There is a need to dream the patient's material further. Bion, throughout his writing on the war, is involved in a continuing self-analysis of his own war experiences and the difficulty of wounds to the mind ever fully healing (1991, p. 256).

This area of work in the countertransference is the subject of another publication, but I was able to sustain the work with her because I could develop a model, part dream and part myth, about the functioning of the respiratory system. This helped me to stay in contact with her inchoate experience. The symbolising capacities of my own mind accompanied her relinquishment of the beta screen organisation that nearly killed her. I think it is this activity of the analyst that the Botellas are describing in their work with a child, Thomas. The analyst produces the sound of a wolf's growl when other more verbal interpretations have failed. They consider that this helps Thomas out of the distress of non-representation and provides a development towards representation. They write, "Under the effects of the captivating power of the analyst's figurability, we see emerging in the child the rough outline of a world of representation" (2005, p. 34).

Eric and endometriosis. Reversal of alpha function and bizarre objects in the body

Endometriosis is an illness in which the lining of the womb floats out into the cavities of the body, obliterating differentiated elements in the internal organs and sticking them together so that adhesiveness and agglomeration are produced. It is, for me, a very vivid analogy to the operation of reversal of alpha function. The internal organs/alpha elements, because they represent symbolic fields as well as biological functions, are reversed into bizarre objects disrupting representation.

The material in the session I am discussing below relates to Eric's wife's medical problems and her hospitalisation for a hysterectomy. The tone of his presentation was one of nameless dread and the therapist felt horror at the details about the physical state of his wife's body—swollen and suppurating. He thought the patient was using what was going on in his wife's body as an arena for describing his own mental processes. The endometriosis and its operations in the body as an obliterating agent evoked something of the shift from perception, with its linking elements to agglomeration, into bizarre objects clogging up the mind. He seemed to the therapist to be doing something to his own mind which was the equivalent of destroying the contact barrier and its alpha elements so that he did not have to be aware of painful emotional experiences to do with death and separation. His wife had been very ill indeed after the operation.

It is important to know that this man's childhood had been overshadowed by various wars. His father had been posted to many different locations and Eric's life had experienced frequent disruptions. His mother's many pregnancies had resulted in him being sent to alternative carers, and when he returned he would find her depressed and impatient with him.

In the session material, Eric's wife's body had become almost unrecognisable to him, and it was this aspect of loss of recognition and distortion of a familiar form that seemed to provoke horror. Her internal organs had the quality of bizarre objects. His anxiety was located in his fear of what he would see if he looked and investigated. He was afraid of what sight would be revealed if he helped to dress his wife's wound. He was afraid to look and worried about an infection that nobody could see. Unfortunately, he had had to miss two sessions in the middle of the week, so there had been no analytic arena to project into. The therapist thought that his fears about the endometriosis obliterating the live and differentiated aspects of his mind showed he had some perception that his capacity for thinking was being reversed.

Following his intuition that the patient was using his wife's body as an arena into which he could project his own mental processes, the therapist addressed an interpretation to Eric's anxiety about the functioning of his own mind. He thought the experience of damage to alpha function and the alpha elements inside him was the main horror the patient felt and said, "The skin of the week had been ruptured and Eric felt as if his own mind had a hole in it and he might leak out and stop functioning." In the next session, Eric was more depressed, but more in touch again with his feelings.

The reversal of alpha function may allow for a reworking of alpha elements in a new configuration and avoid permanent deterioration in an area of mind. Eric's life had been secure and successful, so the earlier difficulties in his childhood had been kept at bay, but his wife's illness had exposed them. As alpha elements facilitate the development of narratives within a temporal structure, their rearrangement may allow for past experiences to be integrated within present emotional dilemmas. Reversal of alpha function in this case could be a precursor to recovery and growth and a blank area might gradually acquire symbolic meaning. To be without the ability to represent your experience is, in itself, traumatic, as the Botellas indicate. It is from within the relationship "founded on mutual unconsciousness" (Jung, 1946) between patient and analyst that these wounds to the self can be healed. After this material had occupied sessions for several weeks, the analysis entered a new phase.

Conclusion

The reversed alpha element that turns into a beta element screen or a bizarre object might have explanatory power in working with a traumatised population, and further clarification of these concepts might be gained by studying them further in such a context. The opportunity to develop theory further might come from shared work with our colleagues in countries recovering from totalitarian systems, and I am grateful to those colleagues who have let me use their material. Confusion over what is true and what is meaningful might be a particularly painful dimension of such environments. What remains remembered only in the gut and dissociated from the rest of the personality is likely to hinder psychological growth, but the consequence is more extreme than this. It leaves the traumatised person exposed to the "distress of non-representation" (Botella & Botella, 2005, p. 33). The strange entities that Bion describes might create the possibility of representation of experiences that seem to have been consigned to the gut and banished from the mind, or where perception has been so distorted that emotional reality cannot be recognised. The link between the totalitarian objects of a repressive system and the internal domination of beta screen and bizarre objects might be further clarified in the ongoing clinical discussions taking place in many different countries recovering from totalitarian rule. This has to be a process of mutual learning if we are to avoid the unconscious re-enactment of totalitarian attitudes. Otherwise, these will almost certainly reverberate in the group processes of our cross-cultural clinical engagements at many different levels.

References

Biko, S. (1987). *I Write What I Like*. London: Heinemann.

Bion, W. R. (1962). *Learning from Experience*. London: Heineman.

Bion, W. R. (1970). *Attention and Interpretation*. London: Karnac.

Bion, W. R. (1982). *The Long Week-end*. London: Fleetwood Press.

Bion, W. R. (1984). *Second Thoughts*. London: Heinemann.

Bion, W. R. (1989). *Two Papers: the Grid and Caesura*. London: Karnac.

Bion, W. R. (1990). *Brazilian Lectures*. London: Karnac.

Bion, W. R. (1991). *A Memoir of the Future*. London: Karnac.

Bion, W. R. (1992). *Cogitations*. London: Karnac.

Bion, W. R. (1997). *War Memoirs 1917–1919*. London: Karnac.

Bion, W. R. (2000). *Clinical Seminars and Other Works*. London: Karnac.

Botella, C., & Botella, S. (2005). *The Work of Psychic Figurability*. London: Routledge.

Bovensiepen, G. (2002). Symbolic attitude and reverie: problems of symbolization in children and adolescents. *Journal of Analytical Psychology, 47*: 241–257.

Brown, L. (2005). The cognitive effects of trauma: reversal of alpha function and the formation of a beta screen. *Psychoanalytic Quarterly, 74*: 397–420.

Bulgakov, M. (1997). *The Master and Margarita*. London: Penguin Books.

Cambray, J. (2006). Towards the feeling of emergence. *Journal of Analytical Psychology, 51*: 1–20.

Cambray, J. (2009). *Synchronicity*. College Station, TX: Texas A & M University Press.

Colman, W. (2007). Symbolic conceptions: the idea of the third. *Journal of Analytical Psychology*, 52: 565–583.

Colman, W. (2010). Mourning and the symbolic process. *Journal of Analytical Psychology*, 55: 275–279.

Donnet, J., & Green, A. (1973). *L'Enfant de Ça: Psychoanalyse D'un Entretien: La Psychose Blanche*. Paris: Les Editions de Minuit.

Fordham, M. (1974). Defences of the self. *Journal of Analytical Psychology*, 19: 192–199.

Fordham, M. (1995). Critical note of Meltzer's *The Kleinian Development*. In: R. Hobdell (Ed.), *Freud, Jung, Klein – The Fenceless Field: Essays on Psychoanalysis and Analytical Psychology*. London: Routledge.

Godsil, G. (2005). Reflections on death and mourning in relation to Dickens' novel *Our Mutual Friend*. *Journal of Analytical Psychology*, 50: 469–481.

Green, A. (1999). *The Work of the Negative*. London: Free Association Books.

Green, A. (2000). The primordial mind and the work of the negative. In: P. Bion Talamo, F. Borgogno, & S. Merciai (Eds.), *W. R. Bion: Between Past and Future*. London: Karnac.

Grotstein, J. (2000). Bion's "transformations in 'O" and the concept of the "transcendent position". In: P. Bion Talamo, F. Borgogno, & S. Merciai (Eds.), *W. R. Bion: Between Past and Future*. London: Karnac.

Herman, J. (1997). *Trauma and Recovery*. New York: Basic Books.

Hogenson, G. (2005). The self, the symbolic and synchronicity: virtual realities in the emergence of the psyche. *Journal of Analytical Psychology*, 50: 271–284.

Hogenson, G. (2009). Synchronicity and moments of meeting. *Journal of Analytical Psychology*, 54: 183–198.

Jung, C. G. (1946). The psychology of the transference, *C.W.*, *16*, M. Fordham (Ed.). London: Routledge & Kegan Paul.

Jung, C. G. (1952). Synchronicity: an acausal connecting principle, *C.W.*, *8*, M. Fordham (Ed.). London: Routledge & Kegan Paul.

Jung, C. G. (1957[1916]). The transcendent function, *C.W.*, *8*, M. Fordham (Ed.). London: Routledge & Kegan Paul.

Jung, C. G. (1958). *Psychology and Religion*, *C.W.*, *11*, M. Fordham (Ed.). London: Routledge & Kegan Paul.

Kadare, I. (2008). *The Palace of Dreams*. London: Vintage.

Kalsched, D. (2003). Daimonic elements in early trauma. *Journal of Analytical Psychology*, 48: 145–169.

Knox, J. (2003a). *Archetype, Attachment, Analysis*. New York. Brunner-Routledge.

Knox, J. (2003b). Trauma and defences: their roots in relationship. An overview. *Journal of Analytical Psychology, 48*: 207–233.

Knox, J. (2011a). Dissociation and shame: shadow aspects of multiplicity. *Journal of Analytical Psychology, 56*: 341–347.

Knox, J. (2011b). *Self-Agency in Psychotherapy.* New York: W. W. Norton.

Kurvet-Kaosaar, L. (2008). Inquiries into trauma and history in Imbi Paju's Memories Denied. www.imbipaju.wordpress.com/leena-kurvet-kaosaarinquiries into trauma and history. Accessed: 27.7 2011.

Laar, M. (2007). *Estonia in World War II.* Tallinn: Grenader.

Laub, D. (1995). Truth and testimony: the process and the struggle. In: C. Caruth (Ed.), *Trauma: Explorations in Memory.* Baltimore, MD: Johns Hopkins University Press.

Martin-Vallas, F. (2006). The transferential chimera: a clinical approach. *Journal of Analytical Psychology, 51*: 627–641.

Martin-Vallas, F. (2008). The transferential chimera II: some theoretical considerations. *Journal of Analytical Psychology, 53*: 37–59.

Martin-Vallas, F. (2009). From end time to the time of the end: some reflections about the emergence of subjectivity. *Journal of Analytical Psychology, 54*: 441–460.

Meltzer, D. (1986). *Studies in Extended Metapsychology.* London: Karnac.

Mitrani, J. (1993). "Unmentalized" experience in the etiology and treatment of psychosomatic asthma. *Contemporary Psychoanalysis, 29*: 314–342.

Paju, I. (2007). *Memories Denied.* London: Kindle.

Parktal, A. (2012). Lost chances and prosperous present? The traumatic past and Estonian life today. *Journal of Loss and Trauma, 17*: 350–357.

Ramphele, M. (2008). How does one speak of social psychology in a nation in transition? *Journal of Analytical Psychology, 53*: 157–167.

Roper, M. (2009). *The Secret Battle: Emotional Survival in the Great War.* Manchester: Manchester University Press.

Sebek, M. (1996). The fate of the totalitarian object. *International Forum of Psychoanalysis, 5*: 289–294.

Sebek, M. (1998). Post-totalitarian personality-old internal objects in a new situation. *Journal of the American Academy of Psychoanalysis and Dynamic Psychiatry, 26*: 295–309.

Solzhenitsyn, A. (1963). *One Day in the Life of Ivan Denisovic.* London: Penguin.

Solzhenitsyn, A. (2002). *The Gulag Archipelago.* London: Perennial Harper Collins.

Souter, K. (2009). The War Memoirs: some origins of the thought of W. R. Bion. *International Journal of Psychoanalysis, 90*: 795–808.

Szykierski, D. (2010). The traumatic roots of containment: the evolution of Bion's metapsychology. *Psychoanalytic Quarterly, 79*: 935–968.

Tarantelli, C. B. (2003). Life within death: towards a metapsychology of catastrophic psychic trauma. *International Journal of Psychoanalysis, 84*: 915–928.

Urban, E. (1996). 'With healing in her wings . . .': integration and repair in a self-destructive adolescent. *Journal of Child Psychotherapy, 22*: 64–81.

Urban, E. (2003). Developmental aspects of trauma and traumatic aspects of development. *Journal of Analytical Psychology, 48*: 171–190.

Whitlaw, W. (1993). *The Sonar of Dolphins.* New York: Springer-Verlag.

Wieland-Burston, J. (2012). Holocaust victims and perpetrators. *Journal of Analytical Psychology, 57*: 413–424.

PART III

TECHNIQUE: TRANSFERENCE AND COUNTERTRANSFERENCE

CHAPTER FOUR

Jung's concept of psychoid unconsciousness: a clinician's view

George Bright

Introduction

Jung's use of the term "psychoid" in his published work dates, with one outlying exception, to the late period, 1947 to 1958. In these eleven years, there are barely a dozen references, mostly in passing, half of which are in published letters to a variety of correspondents. Jung makes neologistic use of a word imported from Hans Driesch via Eugen Bleuler, and his concept of psychoid unconsciousness amounts, in my view, to an original and clinically important conceptual statement. Addison (2009) has recently set out the historical evolution of the term. Not unusually, Jung introduces a concept for which no contemporary word suffices. He borrows a word from a similar field, gives it a meaning of his own, but nowhere in his published work provides us with a full treatment to define, discuss, or clarify his conceptual neologism. Shamdasani (2012, p. 375) has suggested that Jung cannot be regarded primarily as a theoretician, but rather as a "psychological essayist", and he proposes that Jung's theories are "simply an approximation by which he is trying to translate his insights into a language for a scientific and medical audience". This leaves the contemporary analytical psychologist with a number of possible tasks in developing or commenting on Jung's thought. Some have tried to create a unified and consistent set of theories from Jung's published work. This seems to me neither realistically possible nor consistent with Jung's own approach.

My aim in this chapter is to draw on Jung's own published work to clarify and develop his thought around the concept of psychoid unconsciousness and then to apply the field of ideas so derived to the clinical task to suggest how Jung's original approach might be used to orientate the analyst to his task. My thesis is that his tentative formulation of the concept of psychoid unconsciousness, the unknowable, is the ultimate protection Jung could invoke, and for which he claimed an ontological basis, in order to protect the symbolic from the "psychic murder" of over-interpretation. The symbolic requires such protection because, in Jung's view, symbols are the building blocks of the individuation process but are always prone to attack by the one-sided and often urgent demand of the ego for conscious knowledge.

Jung's project: human existence as the relationship between two worlds

Jung's life-long project might be described in terms of his attempt to establish relationships between two worlds. In *Memories, Dreams, Reflections*, he locates this interest in his perception of himself as two personalities. He clarifies,

> The play and counterplay between personalities No. 1 and No. 2, which has run through my whole life, has nothing to do with a "split" or dissociation in the ordinary medical sense. On the contrary, it is played out in every individual. In my life No. 2 has been of prime importance, and I have always tried to make room for anything that wanted to come from within. He is a typical figure, but he is perceived only by the very few. Most people's conscious understanding is not sufficient to realise that he is also what they are. (Jung, 1983, pp. 62–63)

No. 1 personality refers to Jung the scientist and empiricist; No. 2 connotes Jung's living in

> . . . another realm, like a temple in which anyone who entered was transformed and suddenly overpowered by a vision of the whole

cosmos. . . . Here nothing separated man from God; indeed, it was as
though the human mind looked down upon creation simultaneously
with God. (Jung, 1983, p. 62)

Interplay between these two worlds runs throughout Jung's work.
They appear in his early medical dissertation in the form of a scientific investigatory method applied to spiritualistic phenomena. As a
psychiatrist, he addresses the interface of sanity and madness. As a
Kantian, he investigates the relationship between the phenomenal and
noumenal worlds, which, in the broader tradition of German idealism,
is expressed as the interface between the Real and the Ideal; as a
psychotherapist, his concern is with the interplay of his patient's ratio-
nality and irrationality, which might equally be expressed as the relationship between the conscious and unconscious mind. Theologically,
the pair features as Man and God, or the human and divine, earth and
heaven. Most broadly of all, they are expressed in Jung's writing on
the relationship between matter, including body, on the one hand,
and, on the other, what he variously terms "psyche", "mind", "spirit",
or "soul". Recent discussion of Jung's approach in terms of Max
Weber's concept of "enchantment" and "disenchantment" suggests
that "Jung chooses to locate himself and his work precisely on the
border between the two constellations" (Saban, 2012, p. 23). In 1957,
Jung told Jaffé that "[my works] are fundamentally nothing but
attempts to give answer to the question of the interplay between the
'here' and the 'hereafter'" (Jung, 1983, p. 330).

Jung's interest includes the dynamics of the relationship between
the two. The first term of the pair (phenomenal, Real, rational, conscious, Man, body, matter) is, by definition, accessible to investigation
and measurement, but by what means can we investigate and engage
with the second, whether conceptualised as noumenon, Ideal, irrational, unconscious, God, mind, psyche, or soul? Jung's work emerges
from the matrix of a post-religious situation in which the Christian
programme of revelation, faith, and religious practice is no longer
widely acceptable or workable as the bridge between the two, yet in
which the positivist response is equally unacceptable. The problem, as
posed by Kant, was of an invidious choice between soul-less materi-
alism ("*seelenloser Materialismus*") on the one hand and groundless
spiritualism ("*grundloser Spiritualismus*") on the other (cf. Bishop, 2000,
p. 307). Jung's project was to replace the decayed religious bridge

between the two worlds by a psychological understanding of the same universal myths and symbols used by religion. He sets out his project thus in the work which effectively brought his collaboration with Freud to an end:

> I think *belief should be replaced by understanding*; then we would keep the beauty of the symbol, but still remain free from the depressing results of submission to belief. That would be the psychoanalytic cure for belief and disbelief. (Jung, 1916a, par. 356)

Jung's project is also, I think, the central project of Jungian analysis, whose conceptual starting-point is that the human condition is not merely material, and which must, therefore, work with the dynamic relationship between two worlds. Jung puts it thus:

> By means of active imagination we are in a position of advantage, for we can then make the discovery of the archetype without sinking back into the instinctual sphere, which would only lead to blank unconsciousness, or, worse still, to some kind of intellectual substitute for instinct. (Jung, 1946, par. 414)

Conscious investigation of, and relating to, the unconscious realm is the task of all analysis, and while Jung here singles out active imagination as a method for such analytic work, this is not to exclude the other technical means available to the analyst in his mediatory task, most obviously working with transference and countertransference phenomena and dream analysis. In all of these, analysts have developed workable ways of mediating between the two worlds of conscious and unconscious within the dyad of the analytic relationship.

Psychoid unconsciousness: from the unknown to the unknowable

Jung's revival of the term "psychoid" comes late in his published work and he has not left us any published comprehensive account of the meaning he gives to this concept. My own engagement with it came from a reading of his essay, "Synchronicity: an acausal connecting principle", in which he argues from the observable fact of synchronicities to suggest that they imply an underlying state of meaningfulness which exists objectively in matter as well as subjectively in the human mind of the observer (cf. Bright, 1997). Jung uses the term "psychoid" to denote that this objective underlying meaningfulness is not only unconscious, but also ultimately unknowable. He states that

> . . . chance ideas . . . reveal the structure of that which produces them, namely the unconscious. . . . It is the decisive factors in the unconscious psyche, the archetypes, which constitute the structure of the collective unconscious. The latter represents a psyche that is identical in all individuals. It cannot be perceived or "represented", in contrast to the perceptible psychic phenomena, and on account of its "irrepresentable" nature I have called it "psychoid". (Jung, 1952, par. 840)

This takes up his earlier distinction between the representation of an archetype and the archetype itself: "The archetype as such is a psychoid factor that belongs, as it were, to the invisible, ultra-violet end of the psychic spectrum. It does not appear, in itself, to be capable of reaching consciousness" (Jung, 1946, par. 417).

This is the territory of Jung's reception of Kant, an area which has been the subject of a masterly survey by Bishop (2000). Jung is positing, on the basis of observable synchronicities, ". . . an empirical concept which postulates an intellectually necessary principle" (Jung 1952, par. 960); that is, a meaning which is *a priori* to human consciousness and apparently exists outside man, though "What that factor which appears to us as 'meaning' may be in itself we have no possibility of knowing" (1952, par. 916) . In other words, Jung is suggesting that synchronicities provide evidence of the existence of an underlying world of absolute or transcendent meaning that is independent of the categories of space, time, and causality, the only categories which can be empirically investigated. By terming this meaningful and patterned underlying world "psychoid", he is asserting that it is not only unconscious, but also unknowable. In religious terms, this seems to me to be identical to the concept of a transcendent divinity who has a mind, but the content of whose mind is unknowable, and whose mindful existence is hinted at or partially disclosed by "revelation", which is inherently and necessarily ambiguous. In terms of psychotherapeutic work, I have argued (1997) that this necessary ambiguity also defines the analyst's orientation or attitude towards his task, a theme to which I shall return later in this chapter.

In summary, Jung has argued from the observation of synchronistic phenomena to posit the psychoid nature of meaning, in much the same way as Freud argued from parapraxis to propose the existence of the personal unconscious. By "the psychoid nature of meaning", Jung implies that:

1. Meaning is *a priori*; it has an objective existence, rather than being merely a subjective creation of the human mind. I think that Jung is arguing that it is both objective and subjective, not one or the other.
2. Objective meaning exists in matter as well as in mind.
3. Such meaning is unconscious and ultimately unknowable.

Equally, we could use Jung's concept to refer to the psychoid nature of order or pattern. This would imply that:

1. All things and events are related in an underlying and objective way, rather than subjectively ordered only in the human mind.
2. This underlying order is unknowable, and although some very useful inferences may be made about it, these can only be provisional.
3. Another way of expressing this would be that order is objectively given, as well as subjectively imputed.
4. Hence, meaningful order is to be discovered as well as made.

If I were attempting a systematic exposition of Jung's model of the psyche (and I am not), I would want to suggest that, beneath the familiar levels of the personal unconscious and the collective unconscious, both of which can be investigated and related to by the conscious mind, there subsists a lower level, psychoid unconsciousness, at which the distinction of matter and mind is no longer possible, and which is wholly impenetrable to the conscious mind, which imputes the existence of a psychoid level of unconsciousness from the observable fact of meaningful coincidences.

Bishop suggests that the assertion of underlying, though unknowable, meaning was not only a well-attested preoccupation of Jung's (sometimes dismissively described as his "mysticism"), but also corresponds to a significant contemporary area of concern. He writes,

Jung's yearning to transcend the restrictions of spatio-temporal categories, and his desire to embrace the absolute, represent nothing less
than a modern restatement of the romantic dream of immediacy and
totality. Furthermore, whilst the Jungian notion of the archetypes
licenses the most un-Kantian speculations, such notions as the "mysticism of physics" and the existence of an "implicate order" suggest that
key aspects of Jung's later psychology may well be symptomatic of a
deeper underlying trend in current Western thinking. And this trend
could well, in Kant's terms at least, be called *Schwärmerei*, of the kind
which the philosopher of Königsberg thought he had dispatched for
good. (Bishop, 2000, pp. 58–59)

Schwärmerei was Kant's dismissive term for what he regarded as
unwarranted romantic credence in the irrational and non-observable,
the state into which we fall if we transgress the limits of reason and
claim direct knowledge of the noumenal world. Bishop has cogently
argued that Jung misread Kant (whether deliberately or by what he
terms "misprision") to support his project of bridging from the world
of the No. 1 personality, the rational, consciousness, and matter deep
into the underlying worlds of Spirit and the divine, the world of his
No. 2 personality. In my reading of Jung, the assertion that, at the
psychoid level, unconsciousness is not merely unconscious but also
unknowable guards adequately against any attempt to over-claim
knowledge of what a religious person might term "the mind of God"
or what the analytical psychologist can call "the psychoid unconscious". However, Jung's fascination with the other-worldly undoubt-
edly occasionally tips over into credulity, even though he consistently
guarded against such over-claiming in his published scientific work.
For example, in his 1934 essay, "The soul and death", he suggests,

> Under certain conditions ... [the psyche] could even break through
> the barriers of space and time precisely because of a quality essential
> to it, that is, its relatively trans-spatial and trans-temporal nature. This
> possible transcendence of space–time, for which it seems to me there
> is a good deal of evidence, is of such incalculable import that it should
> spur the spirit of research to the greatest effort. (Jung, 1934, par. 813)

This reads to me like the harbinger of Jung's subsequent research on
synchronicity, and so a root of his concept of psychoid unconsciousness. In his published work, Jung was careful not to over-claim

beyond the assertion that the psychoid is unknowable. In his personal and private intuitions, he may have gone further.

Clinical implications of Jung's concept of psychoid unconsciousness: interpretation and analytic attitude

Jung's project of conceptualising and investigating the working relationships between two worlds is also the clinical terrain of every psychotherapist. All psychodynamic psychotherapeutic approaches speak of making connections between the conscious and unconscious mind. The more positivistic psychoanalytic approach has formulated a number of well-established conceptual models to help the analyst to orientate to the bridging task, in terms of, for example, infantile sexuality (Freud), unconscious phantasy and the achievement of the depressive position (Klein), regression (Winnicott), attachment, and separation (Bowlby) and many more. I do not think it is the main task of the contemporary Jungian analyst to offer yet another model, whether in competition with others or as a counterpoint or supplement. The London school of analytical psychology has, I think, gone as far as it can in offering a Jungian model of the psyche to conjugate or contrast with, or as a supplement to, other psychodynamic models. This has been a useful process, at any rate from the Jungian side, in that it has encouraged the widest possible thinking about how we conceptualise and approach the analytic task, but I think we are now scraping the bottom of the barrel in trying to continue along these lines.

Fortunately, in the past twenty years, help has come from a quarter outside the psychotherapeutic profession of analytical psychology, in the form of a renewed academic interest in Jung's work and, indeed, in the work of the other depth psychologists. This scholarly interest has resulted in a steady stream of important publications from historians of ideas such as Ellenberger, Shamdasani, Makari, Main, McGrath, ffytche, and others, and, for Jung scholarship, from the work of the German scholar Paul Bishop. Further, the publication of *Liber Novus, The Red Book*, has provided us with the key text for a complete reassessment of the development of Jung's thought. Analytical psychologists now have rich new resources upon which to draw in orientating ourselves to the clinical task, in the form of a more understandable and better researched guide to Jung's prolific writing and important but complex ideas.

Rather than looking for clinical orientation mainly through comparing our approaches with those of our psychoanalytic colleagues, we are now, for the first time, able to draw on a serious, scholarly, and independent critique of Jung's thought. I am not suggesting that analysts attempt a kind of imitation in which we try to research and emulate the Master's supposed way of working. Jung himself was quite definite in his rejection of imitators and insisted that every analytic psychologist had to find his own approach, but how? In raising this question, I am not simply raising a question about technique; I am looking for the underlying basis for defining the clinical task of analysis, from a point of view true to Jung's insights, which might help in developing a contemporary clinical approach specific to analytical psychology.

The terrain for such exploration, to my mind, lies in Jung's positioning of himself between two worlds, however these are conceptualised. In Kantian terms, participation in, and research of, the phenomenal world is relatively straightforward, as this is the proper province of the conscious mind. The analyst's task, though, cannot be confined to disciplined consciousness alone. Analysts must also participate in the dynamic world of their own and their patients' unconsciousness. Elaboration of theoretical models of the unconscious has been of unquestionable help in this analytic task, but I agree with the psychoanalyst Vassalli (2001) that the "misleading prominence given to theory" in contemporary psychoanalysis (and in much contemporary analytical psychology) has not greatly advanced clinical work. Vassalli suggests that analysis is better defined in terms of technique than in terms of theoretical orientation. Engaging with the many theoretical approaches to analysis will demonstrate to all but the most credulous that none of these theories amounts to much other than a more or less useful conceptual sketch-map of the field, and that anyone looking in the analytic field for theories in the more formal scientific sense of disprovable hypotheses will be disappointed. I suspect that problems in an analysis very commonly arise when the analyst privileges his theory above listening with an open mind to what his patient is communicating.

Jung postulates psychoid unconsciousness as an underlying ordered and meaningful realm which is inaccessible to consciousness but with which the conscious mind nevertheless has to engage when psychic distress drives us beyond satisfaction with the conscious banalities of life. It is the analyst's task (not dissimilar in another context to the priest's) to mediate between two worlds. I regard the key to analytic training to be in the achievement and maintaining of an "analytic attitude" by the analyst, and I have argued that:

> Analytic attitude, in Jungian analysis, is . . . based on the concept that there is an underlying, psychoid dimension to meaning. We acknowledge this . . . by our attitude of restraint towards explicitly stating the meaning of any aspect of the patient's experience – or, indeed, of our own experiences in the countertransference – as if our grasp of the meaning were absolute. This attitude of restraint is based on the premise that while there is an underlying meaning and pattern in all human experience, it is unconscious, and can therefore only be known indirectly and in a provisional way. 'Psychoid' is Jung's term for this premise. On the basis of the premise of unconscious underlying meaning and pattern we are then relatively free to allow unimpinged space within which patient and analyst together can see what they can make of the experiences of the analysis. (Bright, 1997, p. 633)

In clinical terms, the key to Jungian analytic attitude is the positioning of the analyst between the conscious and unconscious worlds. Both are dynamic in the sense that each is driven by its own quantum of libido, psychic energy, or life-force. Jung conceptualises the unconscious domain as shading from personal, through collective, to psychoid unconsciousness, and I shall try to demonstrate why I value his proposition that meaning and pattern in the unconscious are ultimately unknowable and "psychoid", not merely unknown. The analyst mediates between the two worlds in a role analogous to that of the god Hermes in the Hellenistic pantheon. Jung's exposition of his hermeneutic approach was "never fully and consistently developed" (Smythe & Baydala, 2012). Nevertheless, I think that it is possible to trace in Jung's developing thought after 1912 a clear and definite movement towards a specific hermeneutic and interpretative approach based on an attitude towards meaning which I believe defines Jungian analysis, and of which the development of the concept of psychoid unconsciousness might be regarded as the last-added keystone of Jung's hermeneutic edifice.

Another pair of worlds between which the analyst mediates is the world of the analyst and that of the analyst's Shadow. "Shadow", like "psychoid", is an original concept of Jung's on which he produced no major definitive paper, although hundreds of references to Shadow pepper his published work. In the illustrations of analytic attitude that follow, I want to lay specific emphasis on the analyst's capacity to position himself as mediator between his conscious sense of himself and his Shadow, as this seems to me to be another aspect of the mediatory, or in-between-two-worlds, nature of analytic attitude. The Shadow, like all archetypes, shades off into its own psychoid depths, implying that it is energetic, purposeful, patterned, and meaningful. Ultimately, the meaning and purpose of his Shadow is unknowable to the analyst because its roots are in the psychoid unconscious. In working analytically, the analyst's Shadow is at least as much involved as are the positively connoted conscious and unconscious aspects of his personality. This means that the analyst is obliged to work with its unconsciousness, rather than claim any capacity to know all about his Shadow. Frequently, when something goes badly wrong in an analysis, the cause can be traced with hindsight to the analyst's loss of his mediating and integrating capacity between his ego and his Shadow.

Jung's developing hermeneutic stance on analytic understanding and interpretation[1]

Offering interpretations to the patient is a universal aspect of analytic activity. The history of the development of the concept and practice of interpretation has yet to be written and a study of it would, I think, shed much light on the ways in which both psychoanalysis and analytical psychology have developed during the first century of their existence. Any interpretation is based in the analyst's understanding of what is going on in the analysis (in the patient, in himself, or in the analytic relationship, for example). Interpretations are hermeneutic activities in as far as they attempt to elucidate or impute meaning. In what follows, I am not attempting any comprehensive discussion of Jung's hermeneutic approach, but simply aim to trace a single development between 1912 and 1915 in Jung's thought concerning his clinical approach to understanding the patient, and then to consider how this developed insight might be applied in contemporary analytic practice. Although this development predates his formulation of psychoid unconsciousness by over thirty years, I shall argue that it is consistent with Jung's later theoretical formulation and that, taken together, the two provide for the analyst a uniquely Jungian orientation to the clinical task.

In the closing paragraphs of *Wandlungen und Symbole der Libido*,[2] published in 1912, Jung meditates on the theme of "understanding". He writes,

> The only one who really understands us is the mother. For *verstehen*, "to understand" (Old High German *firstân*), is probably derived from a primitive German prefix *fri*, identical with περὶ, meaning "round-about". The Old High German *antfristôn*, "to interpret", is considered as identical with *firstân*. From that results a fundamental significance of the verb *verstehen*, "to understand", as "standing around something." *Comprehendere* and χατασονλλάμβανειν express a similar idea as the German *erfassen*, "to grasp, to comprehend". The thing common to these expressions is the surrounding, the enfolding. And there is no doubt that there is nothing in the world which so completely enfolds us as the mother. When the neurotic says that the world has no understanding, he says indirectly that he misses his mother. (Jung, 1916a, par. 700)

In November 1915, in a letter to Hans Schmid (Beebe & Falzeder, 2012), Jung returns to the same topic, but with a very different emphasis amounting to a *volte-face*. He writes,

> In the meantime, and after long deliberation, the problem of resistance against *understanding and coming to an agreement* has become clear to me. . . . So the devil is the devourer. To understand = *comprehendere* = χατασονλλάμβανειν, and also to devour. Understanding and agreement are an act of swallowing. One should not let oneself be swallowed, however, unless one is really someone who can overpower the monster from within. . . . In the wish to understand, which seems to be so ethical and all human, there lurks a devil's will. . . . Understanding is a terribly binding power, a veritable soul murder when it levels out vitally important differences. The core of the individual is a mystery of life, which dies when it is "grasped." That is also why *symbols want to keep their secrets*; they are mysterious not only because we are unable to clearly see what is at their bottom. For the symbol wants to prevent Freudian interpretations, which are indeed so

pseudo-correct that they never fail to have an effect. For ill people, "analytical" understanding is as healingly destructive as cauterization or thermocautery, but healthy tissue is banefully destroyed by it. . . . We can commit no greater error, however, than to apply the principles of this technique to an analysed psychology.

But there's still more to this! All understanding as such, being an integration into general viewpoints, contains the devil's element, and kills. It tears another life out from its own peculiar course, and forces it into something foreign in which it cannot live. That is why, in the later stages of analysis, we must help the other to come to those hidden and unopenable symbols, in which the seed of life lies securely hidden like the tender seed in the hard shell. . . . But if understanding and agreement on this have become generally and obviously possible, the symbol is then ripe for destruction, because it no longer covers the seed which is about to outgrow the shell. . . . In this way salvation is given to the unopenable and unsayable symbol, for it protects us by preventing the devil from swallowing the seed of life. The threatening and dangerous thing about analysis is that the individual appears to be understood: the devil takes away and eats up his soul, which has been born into the light as a naked and exposed child, robbed of its protective cover. This is the dragon, the murderer, which always threatens the new-born Son of God. . . . He must be hidden once again from the "understanding" of men.

True understanding, however, seems to be what is not understood, yet is still effective. . . . We should bless our blindness for the others' mysteries, because it prevents us from devilish deeds of violence. (pp. 139–142)

What has happened in three years to account for this about-turn in Jung's attitude to understanding the patient; from regarding analytic understanding as the sought-after and benign motherly matrix of growth to a view that, while of value as an approach to a patient's pathology, more comprehensive understanding by the analyst is tantamount to psychic murder of the patient?

The broadest answer is that, through the process recorded in *Liber Novus*, Jung has rediscovered the Divine and is no longer trying, as he was in *Symbols of Transformation*, to replace religious belief by psychological understanding. More specifically for our understanding of Jung's hermeneutic, I think that *Liber Novus* provides us with a clue to how Jung's view changed on the role of understanding and interpretation in the analytic task. The section of *Liber Primus* entitled "Murder of the hero" recounts Jung's active imagination in which he murders Siegfried, his hero. This fantasy has long been available to commentators in the version presented by Jaffé in *Memories, Dreams, Reflections* (Jung, 1983, pp. 204–205). In the 1925 Seminar (Jung, 2012, p. 53), Jung comments that killing Siegfried represented the killing-off of his superior function of intellect.

In *Symbols of Transformation*, the "sacrifice of the hero" is the longing of the libido to re-enter the mother for rebirth. When, in *Liber Primus*, Jung's soul first speaks to him, after several nights of silence in the face of his impassioned appeal, her first words to him are: "You speak to me as if you were a child complaining to its mother. I am not your mother" (Jung, 2009, p. 236, "Experiences in the desert"). His Soul continues, "Do you still not know that you are not writing a book to feed your vanity, but that you are speaking with me? . . . Do you know, then, who I am? Have you grasped me, defined me, and made me into a dead formula?" The German verb translated in the *Liber Primus* text as "grasped" is again from *erfassen*, thus linking directly to Jung's discussion of understanding in *Symbols of Transformation*, published the previous year. So, it is nothing less than Jung's Soul that reorientates his attitude to understanding, effectively telling his "I" that his very Soul has been damaged by his intellectual understanding attitude towards her. For Jung, this is information from the highest possible authority.

This exchange with his Soul took place on the night of 11 December 1913. The murder of Siegfried in active imagination follows a week later on the night of 18 December. These are recorded in Jung's Black Books. His subsequent commentary in the calligraphic *Liber Primus*, copied from the Draft which he began late in 1914, sheds considerable light on the topic of understanding and meaning and, I think, greatly helps the contemporary Jungian analyst to orientate to Jung's developing insights into analytic stance. Jung writes, "In that night my life was threatened since I had to kill my lord and God . . ." He continues, ". . . [men] do not know that they should kill their Gods in themselves" (Jung, 2009, p. 242). Among other possible readings, this seems to me to sustain a reading that Jung had to kill not only his superior intellectual function, the *sacrificum intellectus*, but also to kill off inherited analytic wisdom and practice (including the insights of his successful 1912 publication) so as to make possible a relationship with what later in the same section he refers to as "the new wheat, the young germinating God" (2009, p. 242). Again, the imagery of seed and germination is taken up a year later in the letter to Schmid. The theme of "meaning" also straddles the two. In a lyrical passage following the murder of Siegfried in *Liber Novus*, Jung writes,

> If the God grows old, he becomes shadow, nonsense, and he goes down. The greatest truth becomes the greatest lie, the brightest day becomes darkest night.
>
> As day requires night and night requires day, so meaning requires absurdity and absurdity requires meaning. . . .
>
> So meaning is a moment and a transition from absurdity to absurdity, and absurdity only a moment and a transition from meaning to meaning. (p. 242)

This is an amplification of the words recorded in the Black Book a year earlier, in which the spirit of the depths speaks to Jung and states, "The highest truth is one and the same with the absurd". Jung notes, "This statement saved me. . . ." (2009, p. 242).

Thus, between 1912 and 1915, Jung moves from a position on understanding in which it is equated with the benign mother to a position in which understanding in analysis is to be used with great caution. It is useful when dealing with evident pathology ("it has a wholesomely destructive effect, like a corrosive or thermocautery"), but it is "banefully destructive" on sound tissue. "Sound tissue" equates with what Jung came to describe as the "symbol", for which he used in his letter to Schmid the analogy of the germ of a seed—that is, something formed and structured which has the potential for growth and development. This implies that the symbol is a living organism, with a life and vitalistic destiny of its own. It requires proper conditions for growth and, when these are provided, will sprout of its own accord. In the period in which Jung was formulating these thoughts, analysis was still mainly regarded as a medical treatment for the psychologically unwell. Without in any way minimising the degree of psychic pain that brings a patient into analysis, it is clear to me that many analysands cannot primarily be described as "unwell", whereas they can convincingly be regarded as relatively robust people driven by psychic distress to pay serious attention to the unmet demands of their lives. To some extent, this is a self-selecting population, as the cost of analysis in terms of money, time, and capacity to engage with a disciplined analytic timetable make it far more readily accessible to those whose ego function is relatively reliable.

"Symbol", for Jung, refers to something that currently holds the dynamic tension of opposites within the psyche and, therefore, that has the potential for growth. In the year after Jung wrote to Schmid on analytic understanding, he stated in *The Transcendent Function* (1916b, par. 176) that "The danger of wanting to understand the meaning is over-valuation of the content, which is subjected to intellectual analysis and interpretation, so that the essentially symbolic character of the product is lost". This clarifies that, in trying to impose understanding on the meaning of what is happening in an analysis, there lies a danger of stymying a symbolic dynamic process. A good example of Jung's concept of the symbol was provided for me by a trainee in a seminar in which we were trying to clarify Jungian uses of the term "symbolic". The discussion had taken us to a point where many clearly felt confused and out of their depth, and one participant said soulfully, "So it's a bottomless pit, then?" She had unwittingly hit on a clear example of the symbolic in Jung's sense, for the image of the bottomless pit can carry equally and simultaneously the negative sense of the destructive pit of Hell as well as the positive sense of that other pit with no lower limit, the Wellspring of Life. A symbol, as defined by Jung, is just such an image or other representation in the conscious mind of a holding-together at a deeper level of unconsciousness of a pair of rationally incompatible opposites in the hope that the transcendent function of opposites can thereby be constellated, moving the psyche on towards a new and more individuated position (see Bright, 2002).

In his essay "The structure of the unconscious", published in 1916, Jung elaborates further on the kind of hermeneutic and interpretative approach that his concept of the symbol requires. He writes,

> The essence of hermeneutics . . . consists in adding further analogies to the one already supplied by the symbol; in the first place, subjective analogies produced at random by the patient, then objective analogies produced by the analyst out of his general knowledge. This procedure widens and enriches the initial symbol, and the final outcome is an infinitely complex and variegated picture . . . (Jung, 1916c, par. 493)

Here is an early statement of what Jung elaborated as "amplification", a technique which has been treated with circumspection in the London school of analytical psychology, partly because it has been regarded as detracting from the focus on the transference situation by intruding too much extraneous material from the analyst's general or expert knowledge. However, Jung's key point here is to encourage the analyst to allow associations to accrete rather than attempting an over-hasty reductive analysis of the patient's material by stating its mean-ing at an early stage and so effectively denying the symbol its possibility of growth and development. In Chapter Twenty of *Liber Secundus* ("The way of the cross"), he writes,

> If one accepts the symbol, it is as if a door opens leading into a new room whose existence one previously did not know. But if one does not accept the symbol, it is as if one carelessly went past this door . . . Salvation is a long road that leads through many gates. These gates are symbols. (Jung, 2009, p. 311)

Also, in *Psychological Types*, his first major publication after the experiment on himself of which *Liber Novus* is the record, he attempts a systematic definition of his concept of the symbol in terms of what can and cannot be understood (Jung, 1921, pars 814–829). Besides stressing the future-orientated potential of the living symbol, Jung here also outlines the "symbolic attitude" required to allow the tran-scendent function of opposites to emerge from engaging with the symbolic. I take this to be one of the earliest of Jung's formulations of the basis of Jungian analytic attitude. This clinical approach to inter-pretation characterises all Jung's subsequent work. For example, twenty years later, in his essay, "The psychology of the child arche-type" he writes, "Not for a moment dare we succumb to the illusion that an archetype can be finally explained and disposed of . . . The most we can do is to *dream the myth onwards* and give it a modern dress" (Jung, 1940, par. 271).

By 1921, then, Jung had moved to a position on meaning and understanding in analysis in which any heroic approach to under-standing risks becoming an act of "psychic murder" in all but the most evident circumstances of psychopathology. In all but evident neuro-sis, such imputing of meaning risks killing off a process which Jung later termed "individuation". This process involves identification and

respect of the symbolic, of which the hallmark is apparent contradiction ("The highest truth is one and the same with the absurd"; "meaning requires absurdity and absurdity requires meaning"). In Jung's
volte-face in his approach to meaning between 1912 and 1915, and in
his clinical application of it to the analytic task, I suggest that we can
detect the early roots of what, thirty years later, he was to elaborate in
his references to the psychoid nature of unconsciousness, a formulation which, I think, defines the very nature of Jungian analysis and
acknowledgement of which constrains the analyst to what I believe to
be a necessary analytic attitude. The letter to Schmid of 1915 might, I
think, be read as a very early statement of Jung's view about how the
analytical psychologist is to orientate himself to the hermeneutic task
of working with meaning and understanding in the clinical situation.
His later psychoid formulation, first mentioned in print in 1947 and
then linked with his work on synchronicity, suggesting that the
unconscious cannot ever be fully comprehended because it shades
into psychoid foundations, thus effectively completes Jung's much
earlier work to provide the analyst with a basis for greatly needed
protection against the potentially destructive heroic wish to understand his patient. I believe that such protection of the living unconscious from the over-zealous ego (whether the analyst's or the
patient's) is a prerequisite of all analytic work. It is not, though. without its practical problems.

Working with psychoid meaning in and beyond analysis

Xandra and Yves are both psychotherapists and they meet regularly
and formally for mutual professional and personal support. This is not
analysis or supervision, but one of the many ways in which psychotherapists meet in a serious and boundaried way to support one
another in work and life. Yves has recently dreamt that he is facing
three people: a friend who has the same first name as he; on one side of
this friend is a woman who is the friend's girl-friend whose name is
"Tango", or "Tangy", or something like that. On the friend's other side
(to the dreamer's left) is another woman. In the dream, Yves notes that
he finds this other woman uninteresting and does not care for her. The
dream is still in his mind when his colleague joins him for their discussion. Xandra says that on the way to meeting Yves, a woman has

stopped her in the street, asking to be directed to a local church. The woman is new to the area, just moved in. Xandra mentions a church nearby, but as she is describing it—that church is quiet, dark, and mysterious—she senses that the woman might not like it, might find it dull. It occurs to Xandra that she might prefer another, different one, which she also describes to her; they play guitars there in the service. "Oh yes," she says, "I like 'low church'." She thanks Xandra, saying she obviously landed on the right person. Xandra laughs, because she is not a church-goer. This interaction feels significant to her.

Later on in the conversation, Yves tells Xandra that, as part of redecoration done to his home, the builder removed some black paint around a fireplace, revealing a beautiful, shiny brass surround. He then goes on to tell Xandra his dream.

This dream has meaning for Xandra because, with Yves, she typically feels at once essential and uninteresting to him: deeply loved and yearned for, but also not cared for. She wonders about being a mother to a newborn baby, for whom the mother is everything, a lifeline, but also does not exist, in the sense that the baby has no interest in the mother as a separate person with a separate mind or a separate history.

At the end of their meeting, Yves tells Xandra, as if it were the first time, about the newly revealed brass surround on the fireplace. "It's a frame," she says. "Yes, for the fire," he says.

Discussion

While the conversation I have reported is not an analytic session, the two psychotherapists involved have consciously and deliberately adopted an analytic attitude in their endeavour. This attitude is marked by their reticence to determine meaning in the hope that more extensive meaning might thereby emerge. There is a clear sense of meaning emerging in the mind of one of them in relation to the previously meaningless dream of the other. Yves had been unable to derive meaning from the dream by pondering it on his own. In recounting it to Xandra, however, meaning began to emerge as, in her experience, the two women in the dream corresponded to how she often found herself feeling in relation to her colleague—both cherished and ignored. If this were an analytic session, one might speak of "meaning emerging in the transference". Xandra added an intellectual (thinking) interpretation to suggest possible further meaning: that her experience in relation to Yves might be analogous to the experience of being the baby of a narcissistic mother, adored but not seen, and related to as if she were a part of her mother. For Yves, this thought brought in the possibility that some aspect of himself comparable to a new birth might be emerging. Neither Yves nor Xandra had any idea about what the content of such a process of birth might be, and neither felt inclined at that moment to investigate. In terms of Jung's letter to Schmid, as understanding the dream in terms of a transference (i.e., unconsciously shared) aspect of the relationship between Yves and Xandra was becoming more possible, "the symbol is then ripe for destruction, because it no longer covers the seed which is about to outgrow the shell". In a subsequent discussion, Xandra questioned Yves's appropriating of her thought about the newborn and its mother to himself, suggesting that in making the reference personal to him he was stymieing the process. Xandra wondered whether this was not an over-determination of the meaning and, thus, an act of "veritable soul murder" of the living symbol. She suggested that it was truer to the symbolic quality of her thought that either or both she and he could be the mother or the baby.

Other symbols remained firmly and properly locked in their shells. The conversation with the stranger about churches seemed pregnant with meaning to both Yves and Xandra, but, despite some discussion, its meaning remained opaque and tantalising, perhaps for elucidation in time. Both agreed about the sense of significance of the conversation, but neither could amplify or interpret it. It had to be held with respect for its possible future growth into consciousness from its currently psychoid roots. In a subsequent discussion, Xandra raised the possibility that the two churches in her encounter with a stranger might have something to do with the two women of Yves's dream: one wanted and familiar, the other unwanted, yet perhaps mysterious, or even potentially numinous. Yves's unconsciously repeated reference to a restored frame, which Xandra noted, might express the importance that both protagonists attach to the frame (the pattern of meeting regularly and formally), which provides a safe hearth for the fire of unconscious dynamic process to smoulder away. These slow-burning processes include discussion of the underlying sexual dynamics of their relationship, and later discussion of Yves's dream drew out some of the erotic implications of the girlfriend, the threesome, and the terms "tangy" and "tango" as they featured in the unconscious or transference working relationship of Xandra and Yves. Restoration of the frame that contains these processes might have been particularly significant, as this was the first meeting Yves and Xandra had had following a long summer break in their work.

Another possible understanding of the story of the woman in the street emerged later when Xandra reminded Yves that, for each of them in previous discussions, "church" had held considerable aspects of the Shadow. She speculated that an overlapping, split-off aspect of them both might have gained so much energy in their mutual repression of it that meaning had become matter, taking physical form in the street before their meeting. This made sense to Yves, and the experience could thus remain in play between the two protagonists as a possible emergence of important content from the shadow of either or both.

I am very grateful to my colleague, who has most generously provided me with the greater part of the text of this illustration and who has also greatly helped me in the development of an approach to this topic.

Two themes of the interaction between Xandra and Yves strike me as important to any consideration of the clinical usefulness of the concept of psychoid unconsciousness: the themes of sexuality and of religion. These two, which I regard as two aspects of the phenomenon of sexuality–spirituality, seem to me to be aspects of human experience which bridge between the worlds of matter and mind, body and spirit, and so might be regarded as typical points of entry into the psychoid level at which the two worlds of phenomenon and noumenon are no longer distinguishable. In the Romantic tradition in which Jung stands, sexual love is often regarded as the most intensely spiritual of all human experiences. Religion, similarly, retains a place in the Romantic universe as a mediator between the two worlds. In *Symbols and Transformations of the Libido*, Jung argued in 1912 that all religion could be understood in terms of symbols of libido. From December of the following year, the experiences recorded in *Liber Novus* show Jung recanting on his reductive work on religion and setting out to re-find the soul he has lost. I regard sexuality and religion as the two major organisers of our experience of the most powerful dynamics of our being.

The psychoanalyst Renik has suggested that

> Instead of the analyst as surgeon or reflecting mirror, our guiding metaphor might be the analyst as skier or surfer—someone who allows himself or herself to be acted upon by powerful forces, knowing that they are to be managed or harnessed, rather than completely controlled. . . . In this sense, perhaps we should think of effective clinical practice as not unlike good sex, in that it is impossible to arrive at the desired outcome without, in some measure, relinquishing self-control as a goal. (Renik, 1993, p. 564)

Sexuality and religion both feature in the reported engagement between Xandra and Yves. When the ego engages with something that it intuitively feels to be utterly beyond its comprehension, it may experience either awe or shame, which I consider to be the shadow of awe. In other words, the conscious aspects of Xandra and Yves know themselves to be engaged with something which will not yield to understanding or knowing and which must be creatively (or maybe destructively) engaged with, rather than reductively "understood". In a more specifically religious context than analysis, the attitude to be adopted at this point would be the attitude of worship rather than of understanding. In analysis, however, understanding is highly valued and sometimes over-valued as analyst and patient (or in my example, Xandra and Yves) attempt to understand as much as possible about what they are experiencing, not least because of the demands that psychic distress impose on the analytic situation in which the patient comes in the urgent hope of relief from mental pain. Hence, when the conscious mind of the two protagonists meets with something that will not yield easily (if at all) to understanding, as is the case with both sexuality and spirituality, an impasse is met. The effect of this on the conscious ego is to induce shame, as the ego must admit that its limits have been reached, at least for the moment. The concept of psychoid unconsciousness adds that these limits are both real and necessary, that the ego cannot grasp everything, and will have to acknowledge that there is a territory of the unknowable which is beyond its comprehension but with which it must, nevertheless, engage.

"Understanding" and "meaning" both tend to be regarded positively by analysts and this forces their opposites into the analyst's Shadow. Conscious awareness of "failing to understand" and "meaninglessness" are, therefore, difficult states of mind for the analyst to bear. However, the analyst's dilemma is not limited to the bearing of difficult states of mind. It is easy to overlook the fact that the analyst's Shadow is *unconscious* to him. He only has indirect hints of it, often with hindsight. I regard analytic attitude as a studied and practised positioning of the analyst between his conscious ego and his unconscious Shadow, in exactly the same way as he balances himself as mediator between the world of consciousness and the unconscious, and between the knowable and the psychoid unknowable.

In another context, religion has, over many millennia, crafted safe and reliable containers ("hard shells") for sexuality and spirituality, which both protect these from the over-comprehending hubris of the ego and also provide a safe-enough containment for human engagement with the powerful forces which Renik likens to the skier's engagement with gravity or the surfer's engagement with the immense power of the breaking wave. The task of analysis is, similarly, to provide a sufficiently strong and reliable container (the ethical analytic relationship and the analytic frame) for two people to engage, in awe, excitement, and with practised skill, with forces that are beyond their comprehension, in the service of the individuation of both.

I conclude with an illustration of what I consider to be an analytic attitude to the psychoid, but drawn not from the context of analysis, but from the much older discipline of religious practice. I attended the funeral of a young man who had met a sudden and violent death. Before the service, the priest officiating pointed out both to his parents and to me that the date of the funeral was exactly eighteen years to the day since the deceased's baptism in the same church and at the same hour—an event which the parents and I had attended. I was very struck that the priest communicated this information, and left it without comment. I could well have imagined another priest milking this meaningful coincidence for significance, perhaps drawing inferences about the death and rebirth symbolism of both baptisms and funerals, either as supporting evidence for a statement of what he might believe to be objective religious truth, or at least to try to offer some comforting sense of meaning to mourners affronted by the apparently meaningless death of a much-loved child and friend. The fact that he did not so do, I think, greatly helped the mourners to confront the archetypally based forces of rage, grief, and death, these being far better mediated by the symbolic situation of containment

within a church and its liturgy than by the bathos of a spoken interpretation.

In juxtaposing this illustration to the foregoing discussion of an
incident involving a church, I am struck by the similarity that has now
spontaneously emerged between an example of containment within
the church and its liturgy, and the woman's request to Xandra for
direction towards a church which might, perhaps, serve for her as a
bridge into another world, replete with psychoid possibilities,
whether we think of that world as the unconscious or as the Divine.

Conclusion

Symbols and symbolic processes are central to a Jungian approach to
analysis. Working with them requires a synthetic and teleological
orientation rather than aiming to reduce them to their causes. In this
chapter, I have traced a small but significant development in Jung's
thinking about how we approach the symbolic in the analytic situation and I have suggested that, in his developing attitude of restraint
towards interpreting the symbolic, he foreshadows his later development of a concept of psychoid unconsciousness. In my view, Jung's
formulation of the psychoid unconscious effectively works as his ultimate safeguarding of the symbolic against the destructive effects of
premature or over-definite interpretative understanding. Such destructive understanding is often strongly motivated by the shame that
both analyst and patient can experience when their wish to know is
thwarted. I have argued that, if we can consider such frustration of the
wish to know as the necessary consequence of our encounter with the
unknowable (which Jung terms the psychoid), then we may, in analysis and in life, be able to engage more constructively and reverently
with the underlying power of existence in ways which can promote
our individuation. Or, as the Anchorite in *Liber Novus* puts it to Jung
(Jung, 2009, p. 268),

> . . . men strive to assign a single meaning to the sequence of words, in
> order to have an unambiguous language. This striving is worldly and
> constricted, and belongs to the deepest layers of the divine creative
> plan. On the higher levels of insight into divine thoughts, you recog-
> nize that the sequence of words has more than one valid meaning.
> Only to the all-knowing is it given to know all the meanings of the
> sequence of words. Increasingly we try to grasp a few more meanings.

Notes

1. The author gratefully acknowledges his debt in relation to the historical section of this chapter to Professor Sonu Shamdasani's seminar on 'Liber Novus'.
2. This reference is taken from Hinckle's translation of Jung's 1912 German text, published under the title *The Psychology of the Unconscious*, rather than from the more familiar but revised 1952 text of *Symbols of Transformation* (*C.W.*, 5).

References

Addison, A. (2009). Jung, vitalism and 'the psychoid': an historical reconstruction. *Journal of Analytical Psychology*, *54*(1): 123–142.

Beebe, J., & Falzeder, E. (Eds.) (2012). *The Question of Psychological Types. The Correspondence of C. G. Jung and Hans Schmid-Guisan, 1915–1916*. Princeton, NJ: Princeton University Press.

Bishop, P. (2000). *Synchronicity and Intellectual Intuition in Kant, Swedenborg and Jung*. Lewiston, NY: Edwin Mellen Press

Bright, G. (1997). Synchronicity as a basis of analytic attitude. *Journal of Analytical Psychology*, *42*(4): 613–635.

Bright, G. (2002). Response to the Nymphea symposium. *Journal of Analytical Psychology*, *47*(4): 563–566.

Jung, C. G. (1916a). *Psychology of the Unconscious: A Study of the Transformations and Symbolisms of the Libido*, *C.W.*, *18*. Princeton, NJ: Princeton University Press.

Jung, C. G. (1916b). *The Transcendent Function*, *C.W.*, *8*. London: Routledge

Jung, C. G. (1916c). The structure of the unconscious, *C.W.*, *7*. London: Routledge.

Jung, C. G. (1921). Psychological types, *C.W.*, *6*. London: Routledge.

Jung, C. G. (1934). The soul and death, *C.W.*, *8*. London: Routledge.

Jung, C. G. (1940). The psychology of the child archetype, *C.W.*, *9(i)*. London: Routledge.

Jung, C. G. (1946). On the nature of the psyche, *C.W.*, *8*. London: Routledge.

Jung, C. G. (1952). Synchronicity: an acausal connecting principle, *C.W.*, *8*. London: Routledge.

Jung, C. G. (1983). *Memories, Dreams, Reflections*, A. Jaffé (Ed.). London: Fontana.

Jung, C. G. (2009). *The Red Book. Liber Novus*, S. Shamdasani (Ed.). New York: W. W. Norton.

Jung, C. G. (2012). *Introduction to Jungian Psychology: Notes of the Seminar on Analytical Psychology given in 1925* (revised edn), S. Shamdasani (Ed.). Princeton, NJ: Princeton University Press.

Renik, O. (1993). Analytic interaction: conceptualizing technique in the light of the analyst's irreducible subjectivity. *Psychoanalytic Quarterly*, 62: 553–571.

Saban, M. (2012). The dis/enchantment of C. G. Jung. *International Journal of Jungian Studies*, 4(1): 21–33.

Shamdasani, S. (2012). After Liber Novus. *Journal of Analytical Psychology*, 57(3): 364–377.

Smythe, W. E., & Baydala, A. (2012). The hermeneutic background of C. G. Jung. *Journal of Analytical Psychology*, 57(1): 57–75.

Vassalli, G. (2001). The birth of psychoanalysis from the spirit of technique. *International Journal of Psychoanalysis*, 82(1): 3–26.

CHAPTER FIVE

The world through blunted sight: money matters and their impact on the transference

Jan Wiener

And who, when it comes to the crunch, can live with a heart of gold?

(Duffy, 1999, from "Mrs Midas")

Introduction

The paucity of literature about the role of money in analysis is startling, particularly since the exchange of money through analytic fees is a central aspect of the frame in which an analytic relationship may develop. Shortly after qualifying at the end of the 1980s, a colleague and I wrote a paper titled "The analyst in the counting-house: money as symbol and reality in analysis" (Haynes & Wiener, 1996). The paper explored the neglect of any serious study of the role and meaning of money, reflecting with some puzzlement on the absence of due attention to fees and the meaning of money during training. The situation now, almost twenty years later, has not altered significantly, suggesting that, for analysts, money continues to be "the last taboo" (Dimen, 1994), and more difficult to contemplate even than the emotional subjects of sex or death. There is a remarkable lack of interest in the subject of money, or, more likely, that thinking about money continues to represent an area full of conflicts and unresolved complexes for analysts who, it may be said, tend to suffer from "moneyblindness" (Lieberman & Lindner, 1987). Jacoby (1993), in a paper titled "Is the analytic situation shame-producing?", highlighted the shame-inducing nature of the analytic relationship because of its artificial inequality, but without any reference at all to the part that the fee could play.

In his book, *The World through Blunted Sight*, Trevor-Roper (1970, pp. 17–63), a consultant eye surgeon, writes of the "unfocused image" of people with poor sight and explores how optical anomalies, blunted sight as he calls them, can affect both perceptions of the world and the personality of those with visual impairments. He compares (1970, p. 31) how Keats, who was known to be short-sighted, focused on auditory subjects such as *Ode to a Nightingale* and *On the Grasshopper and the Cricket*, while the romantic imagery of Shelley, who had good vision, concentrated on the more distant evocations of the sky and the mountains. It is the unfocused image of money, its effects on the analyst, and, specifically, on the transference and countertransference landscape with which this chapter is concerned.

I recall a patient telling me how much easier it was for him to talk about his sexual fantasies and about the recent painful death of his father than it was for him to hand me a cheque for his sessions each month. The actual exchange of money for this patient evoked a strong negative transference, in which he felt he was being stolen from in order to nourish a needy and greedy mother. Another patient, angry about the length of the impending summer break, came into the consulting room and put her cheque directly into the wastepaper basket just next to my chair. The connection between money, love, and separation anxiety was palpable for her. A colleague related an incident where he inadvertently ended the session with a patient five minutes late. When the patient came to her next session, she had deducted from her bill the cost of the parking ticket she had incurred because of "his mistake", for which he had to pay. Clearly then, money is not only about the analytic frame, but is deeply embedded within the process of analysis itself. Money involves a real exchange, but it acquires symbolic and emotional value within the relationship for both patient and analyst. It resides in a unique and often uncomfortable psychological space at the intersection of the literal and the symbolic, involving both the external and internal world for both patient and analyst alike. It may be because of this that it is easier to turn a blind eye to money as a significant aspect of the relationship, avoiding the discomforts of greater consciousness that a clearer focus could bring.

The power of money

Money has been one of the greatest inventions in the world. It is essentially neutral, a means of exchange and a store of value, but no one is indifferent to it. Money is a screen that invites a multitude of different projections, always strong and often resistant to rational thought. Money is a reality, a thing in itself, but it also has symbolic significance. It is one significant measure of value, how we feel about ourselves and how we imagine others feel about us.

LeClair and Schneider (1968, p. 468) consider that money is any material object that performs one or more of five functions: it is a medium of exchange; a standard of value; a unit of account; a store of value; and a standard of deferred payments. The first is clearly the guiding principle of these literal, rather commercial definitions, but they are not irrelevant for analysts, since, without an exchange of money, there is no analysis. Even if patients are seen in an environment where the exchange of money is indirect, such as in the National Health Service in the UK, it is still there in the background, as individuals pay taxes that earn them the right to use such services.

Krueger (1991, p. 210) understands money in three different contexts:

- money as a medium of exchange for good and services;
- attitudes and values about money itself with their individual developmental components;
- money as a transference object with the potential to reveal not only the meaning money has for the individual, but also the sources of conflict and complexes.

It is highly likely that these contexts will not sit comfortably each with the other, but it is the last of Krueger's three contexts that is of particular interest here, with an opportunity to explore in greater depth the nature of the intrapsychic anxieties that money can arouse and how these have the potential to lead to transference and counter-transference enactments in the consulting room. His contexts seem to me to underplay the role and meaning of money interpersonally within the analytic relationship and specifically in the transference. It should be remembered, too, that money is a transference object not only for the patient, but also for the analyst.

What writing there is by analysts on the subject of money evokes strongly its emotional power. As early as 1913, Freud (1913c, p. 131) commented that: "money matters are treated by civilised people in the same way as sexual matters – with the same inconsistency, prudish-ness and hypocrisy". He then urges the analyst,

> not to fall in with this attitude, but, in his dealings with his patients, to treat money matters with the same matter-of-course frankness to which he wishes to educate them in things relating to sexual life. He shows them that he himself has cast off false shame on these topics, by voluntarily telling them the price at which he values his time. (p. 131)

It is difficult to disagree with the principle Freud is advocating here, but, in my experience, the "frankness" he refers to is often strikingly absent. I suspect this is because of analysts' defences against painful experiences associated with real shame about their financial needs rather than what Freud calls "false shame". It is interesting to notice, too, his comment in the same paragraph, given in parentheses, that "it is a familiar fact that the value of the treatment is not enhanced in the patient's eyes if a very low fee is asked".

Hillman (1982) has no doubt about the secrecy surrounding money matters, "patients more readily reveal what's concealed by their pants than what's hidden in their pants pocket" (p. 31). Guggenbühl-Craig (1982, p. 85) remarks along similar lines that, "money is a main projec-tion carrier for the soul. As with sexuality, so are secrecy, obsession and energy qualities of money".

Culturally, discussions about money are somehow un-English and generally seen as rather vulgar, so these quotations, illustrating clearly the inherent emotionality and complexity of money, are felt not only at a personal level, but also carry within them cultural and collective values. Our analytic concepts are severely stretched when considering this subject, and we cannot ignore the cultural climate in which attitudes to money reside. Of particular significance here is, first of all, that we are a female-dominated profession and, second, that the financial world crisis in recent years cannot but affect the culture in which we practise.

Women and money

The 23rd of October 2009 marked the eighty-year anniversary of the publication of Virginia Woolf's book, *A Room of One's Own*, one of the most important feminist texts of the twentieth century. Her book is a fictionalised narrative originally intended as two lectures to be given at the Cambridge colleges of Newnham and Girton to what must have been the early generation of women to go to university. It has been influential for women's literature for four main reasons:

- it dealt with the effect of poverty and silencing on women's writing;
- it discussed how women write under adverse conditions;
- it considered the subjects women should be able to write about;
- it looked at what use women make of inheritance when writing, pointing out that we think back through our mothers.

Woolf's main thesis was that, in order to write, women need both a room of their own and money. At that time, she considered £500 a year would be sufficient, though she did, in fact, inherit money from her aunt and later went on to make a good deal of money from her writing, £5000 in 1926. In terms of her talent and the money she earned, she was a successful writer.

Psychoanalysis is a female-dominated profession, and analysts need both a room of their own and also money in order to sustain an analytic practice. However, it is my observation that analysts tend to pay far more attention to the real and metaphorical room in which they work than the money they earn. Most analysts go to a great deal of trouble to make their consulting rooms good containing spaces in which to see their patients. This involves decisions about taste, about size, about temperature, about light, and about noise levels. A great deal of money can be spent to create this desirable room of our own! In her book, Virginia Woolf was, of course, talking not only about actual space, but also about symbolic space. This, too, is comfortable territory for analysts, as it is through a co-constructed symbolic space that the analytic relationship in all its aspects can develop and access to the unconscious is facilitated.

Neglected for the most part is attention to money, about which there is often silence. Some would consider that we do work under adverse conditions and, of course, we each draw on our own personal and cultural histories when it comes to attitudes to money. Had earning a great deal of money been our first objective, then we would have trained as bankers, surgeons, or lawyers rather than analysts. The work is appealing because we have some talent and competence for it (Wiener, 2007), and because we believe that we can make a difference to the lives of others who come to see us when in distress. We use our skill and our talent every day to help patients suffer their pain so they can develop in both their internal and external lives.

For women, in particular, it is the experience of a desire for money that arouses anxiety and conflict between fear of greed for asking too large a fee and experiences of shame about not earning enough. Recently, I facilitated a workshop on money at a psychotherapy organisation, attended mainly by women. A female colleague remarked during the discussion that she thought the participants seemed to be in competition for who could charge the lowest fee! Everyone laughed, of course, in recognition of the situation where the prevailing tendency can be to put fees down rather than up. The patient must come first.

For each of us, money has the power to constellate different states of mind. There is, first, the collective or archetypal reckless position, in which we can all become taken over irrationally by today's cultural consumerist pressures for retail therapy, manic activity, and the excitement and short-term gratifications around what money will buy. A well-known quotation puts its collective power with humour and a ring of truth: "In rich countries today, consumption consists of people spending money they do not have to buy goods they don't need to impress people they don't like" (Anon).

At other times, there is a much more sanguine and rational position where we need to feel secure and provide for our futures. Third, and somehow more difficult to admit, is the potential to experience greed, envy, and shame around money and the defences against these unpleasant emotions.

The impact of the present global crisis

Whether we like it or not, the present global crisis and subsequent recession has probably pushed money matters into our consciousness, offering an opportunity to do what we do best, to search for meaning in ourselves and our patients. It is impossible to avoid its impact on our external circumstances. It is not the first, and probably not the last, of such crises, but it has affected us all collectively and individually and its effects endure today. Many analysts would, I imagine, agree with the financial journalist Tett (2009), when she talks of her own initial perceptions that "Finance was presented as an abstract mathematical game that took place in cyberspace, and which could only be grasped by a tiny elite . . . without any reference to tangible human beings" (Tett, p. xii).

Turning a blind eye is more difficult if we are faced with loss of income and a need to negotiate reduced fees for patients affected too by the failures in the banking system, but money itself is really only the symptom. There has been a significant and shameful dent in our collective moral values and integrity.

The global economic crisis began in 2007 and has been the deepest and most dangerous financial crisis since 1929. Gone is the long-held belief that the market is inherently self-stabilising. During this crisis, we have seen the tightening of credit, declines in the stock exchange, liquidity problems in equity and hedge funds, huge devaluation of assets underpinning pension funds and insurance contracts, massively increasing public debt, and spreading currency volatility. There were warning signs, in the USA and in the UK, that we have been corporately living beyond our means. Most significantly, there were vast amounts of over-lending, what Tett has called "candyfloss money", akin to the way a small amount of sugar can be spun into a huge cone of candyfloss. There was a growing atmosphere of misplaced complacency in our financial system.

House prices began to fall and the banks, not surprisingly, curtailed lending. Banks were suspicious of one another and then they began to fail. In the UK, Northern Rock collapsed early in 2008 and our government decided to bail them out; then, on 14 September 2008, Lehman Brothers in the USA filed for bankruptcy when there was no longer any elasticity in the system and the American government would not bail them out. Businesses began to fail because individuals and companies no longer had access to their money, and this weakened all aspects of the economy. Banks and bankers became the centre of our collective rage in the knowledge that the containment of our financial needs was failing; we would all suffer, and the economic and social distance between rich and poor was widening once more.

There have been plenty of market crashes in history, of booms and of busts, but our present crisis stands out because of its sheer size; losses of between $2000 billion and $4000 billion (Tett, 2009). Tett considers that it has been a self-inflicted disaster, not triggered by the expenses of war, as is so often the case, or by a widespread recession, or an external economic shock, but because "bankers, governments and regulators have collaborated to build a system that was doomed to self-destruct" (p. xii).

Recent authors writing about the present crisis have largely similar views when it comes to a diagnosis of the crisis and possible treatment options. Stephen Green (2009, p. xi), considers that we are in the midst of a serious moral crisis that is essentially a crisis of trust,

> We are at one of those moments in history when it seems as if the tectonic plates are shifting. We are living through years in which a crisis has overtaken our increasingly globalized world, such as most of us have not seen in our lifetimes. There has been a massive breakdown of trust.

There have always been moral constraints on borrowing, what came to be called "the crime of usury", especially among Christians, and money-lenders have always been seen as cultural outsiders. It is not without a certain irony to realise that the word credit comes from the Latin word *credere*, meaning to trust. Green considers that we have lost faith in the institutions we had expected to contain us and our money, leaving a rather uncertain future and lack of confidence and hope.

Tett (2009, p. 116), talks of *a shadow banking system*, involving a lack of transparency, where risk could no longer be calculated. Credit, she thinks, is increasingly available through means other than the banks themselves and everyone is trying to find creative ways of seducing the public into excessive borrowing.

There is talk, too, of *a systemic and structural failure*, where governments, boards, and organisations have been neglectful and selfish in the ways in which they have overseen their markets. There has been a lack of communication and transparency both within organisations and between them.

Tuckett (2011, p. 187) interviewed fund managers about their attitudes and behaviour in relation to financial trading and highlighted the inadequacy of contemporary financial theory that *underestimates the complexity of decision-making*. He reminds us that "respondents . . . had to tolerate the experience of making decisions in uncertain and emotionally arousing environments, and were strongly influenced by what they imagined were the thoughts and reactions of those around them". Tett, too (2009, pp. 298–299), considers that the finance world's denial of wider social matters and bankers' tendency to treat their mathematical models as though they were an infallible guide to the future cuts to the heart of what has gone wrong. There has been a loss of holistic thought. Tett calls this a "silo" mentality, implying a small underground place where something is compressed. I imagine she is referring here to a process of compartmentalisation and fragmented practices in the financial system.

The term *affluenza* was first coined by an Australian, Hamilton (Hamilton & Denniss, 2005), to describe wasteful consumption leading to excessive debt, overwork, and a narcissistic, self-centred approach to the world.

James (2007) later developed these ideas, defining *affluenza* as a virus likely to increase our vulnerability to emotional distress because it places such a high value on making money, the acquisition of possessions, and how we are seen through the eyes of others. I suppose we might say that, to a greater or lesser extent, we are all suffering from *affluenza*, at some cost to other aspects of our lives.

Finally, the financial crisis has been influenced by *developments in technology*. Information and communications technology made possible much of the financial engineering that has led the system to crash. Moreover, its complexity and cost has made it non-transparent, not just for ordinary people and to government regulators, but for the financial community itself.

Authors have different views about the future, about how to learn from this crisis. Some are more cynical, inclined to think that we will return to more of the same but with possibly more controls in place over bonuses and expenses. Others urge us to remain connected with the dangers at all times: "Never in the field of financial endeavour has so much money been owed by so few to so many. And, one might add, with so little real reform" (Mervyn King, Governor of the Bank of England, speech to Edinburgh business leaders, October 2009).

Underlying globalisation are healthy archetypal urges to explore and to connect to others with curiosity, but, at the same time, the heightening and excitement of excessive risk-taking in our economy and its potential destructiveness has brought capitalism to its knees.

The significance of Jung's concept of the shadow is obvious here. Jung (1917, par.103) defined the shadow as "the negative side of the personality, the sum of all those unpleasant qualities we like to hide". Stein (1998, p. 106) puts it more elegantly: "the shadow is the image of ourselves that slides along behind us as we walk towards the light". The shadow usually has an immoral or disreputable quality, an aspect of our nature that we would prefer not to show to others and that is often highly resistant to consciousness and experienced in projection. Wharton (1990) distinguishes helpfully between two aspects of the shadow: what is not known and what is not liked, acknowledging that these may overlap. She also describes "the detached shadow" (1990, p. 279), using Peter Pan as an example of someone detached from his shadow and where "individuals suppress the awareness of 'two-ness' in themselves, the duality, the sometimes agonising conflict between what they would like to be and what they are, which is the essence of being human". We might speculate that this is exactly what bankers have enacted with little consciousness or sense of shame. Campbell's (1994, p. 315) idea of a "shame shield" to describe a defensive shield, a wish to disappear when under threat, is a helpful term to describe one of the defences in operation.

The effects of the banking crisis remains strong today, showing how greed, selfishness, and the imaginative power of money to bring ever greater wealth breed omnipotence and destructiveness. In Ovid's story, King Midas was granted the ability to turn everything he touched into gold, but when his food solidified and his drink turned to golden ice, his love for his gift turned to hatred. He renounced the gift and retired to the mountains, where he became a worshipper of the nature god Pan. The recent banking crisis then shows in high definition the shadow of money in action and terms such as "loss of trust", "collaborating", "seducing", "excitement", and "destructiveness" provide evidence of the extent to which the role of unconscious fantasy in decision-making is underestimated.

Midas, madonna, whore

My adaptation of the title of Welldon's (1988) ground-breaking book, *Mother, Madonna, Whore: The Idealization of Motherhood*, is intended to bring money under closer scrutiny in the consulting room, including our own wishes for "the Midas touch" and its effects on the transference–countertransference dynamics.

Tuckett's belief that we underestimate the emotional complexity of money and Tett's "silo mentality" are not the province of bankers alone, and it seems to me that analysts, too, unconsciously compartmentalise and underestimate the role of unconscious fantasy when it comes to decisions about money. The question here is why, and how best to understand the states of mind that underlie these tendencies.

Money may be a universal means of exchange, but, in analysis, it is a particular exchange. We must live simultaneously in the world of commerce alongside the world of sentiment. Warren Buffett, one of the wealthiest entrepreneurs in the USA, gives nearly all the money he earns to charity, stating that "we enjoy the process far more than the proceeds". However, most analysts are not rich, and while we certainly privilege the process and the analytic journey, we have financial needs and the proceeds have significance. What is more, we are dependent on our patients for our livelihoods. It seems to me that money within the analytic relationship constellates anxiety and tension for both patient and analyst because of the ever-present opposition between love and money. These can be experienced simultaneously in the form of pulls towards acquisitiveness or self-sacrifice, between need and fears of greed. Consider the following quotations as illustrations of these widespread tension-producing oppositions:

> The love of money is the root of all evil. (Bible: 1.Timothy)

> It is easier for a camel to pass through the eye of a needle than for someone rich to enter the kingdom of God. (Bible: Matthew 19:24)

But then:

> I'm tired of Love. I'm still more tired of Rhyme. But money gives me pleasure all the time. (Hilaire Belloc)

> For money has a power above the stars and fate, to manage love. (Samuel Butler)

Annual income twenty pounds, annual expenditure nineteen pounds, twenty six pence, result happiness. Annual income twenty pounds, annual expenditure twenty pounds nought and six, result misery. (Mr Micawber, *David Copperfield*, Dickens)

A focus on commerce alone can turn us into prospective whores to ourselves and our patients, but to hold in mind sentiment alone leaves us as one-sided madonnas. This is a central paradox for analysts, who also have to find a way to live with parallel paradox within their patients.

Shakespeare's *Timon of Athens* provides us with a chilling and challenging example of how difficult it can be to bridge these opposites. Timon was a wealthy Athenian who gave away money wastefully, and everyone wanted to please him to get more. His generosity gave him the illusion that he was wealthy in friendship. When his money ran out and his friends abandoned him, he discovered the hollowness behind his friends' interest in him; his love turned to hate and he left Athens to live in the wasteland outside the city. Greater consciousness released feelings of hatred and a determination to seek revenge. His belief, "I am wealthy in my friends", confused two forms of wealth in a society that valued only the monetary.

Marx (1844, pp. 147–148) uses the story of Timon to highlight two properties of money. First, how easily it can become deified, including its power to transform all human and natural qualities into their opposites, and, second, its base nature, the universal whore, the pimp of men and peoples. This is illustrated marvellously in Timon's speech in which money and rampant sexuality become almost indistinguishable:

> Gold? Yellow, glittering, precious gold? . . .
> This yellow slave
> Will knit and break religions, bless th'accurs'd
> Make the hoar leprosy ador'd, place thieves,
> And give them title, knee, and approbation
> With senators on the bench . . .
> Come damn'd earth,
> Thou common whore of mankind, that puts odds
> Among the rout of nations, I will make thee
> Do thy right nature.
>
> (Shakespeare, Timon, IV(iii), p. 1337)

For Timon, at the flick of a switch, his generosity metamorphoses seamlessly into hatred. Everything becomes its opposite, and Timon, who cannot live with ambivalence, dies.

For Jung, the alchemists' aim to make gold from base elements was a metaphor for the realisation of the self and the process of individuation. It was only quicksilver (Mercurius) that had the power to corrode the gold of the alchemists (Ann Shearer, personal communication). Are we surprised then, that money in the consulting room generates considerable anxiety, as there is always a trickster about, flicking a switch to change something into its opposite? For the most part, this concerns who comes first: the patient's need to pay less, or the analyst's need to feel effective by earning a decent living? In Jung's words (Jung, 1946, par. 384):

> the elusive, deceptive, ever changing content that possesses the patient like a demon now flits about from patient to doctor and, as the third party in the alliance, continues its game, sometimes impish and teasing, sometimes really diabolical.

For Jung (1948, par. 284), Mercurius has multiple aspects, but of relevance to money in the transference are his characteristics of duality with "innumerably inner contradictions [that] . . . can fly apart into an equal number of disparate and apparently independent figures". In Jung's words, he is also "the devil . . . an evasive trickster and God's reflection in physical nature".

Analysts hope to acquire through experience the ability to manage anxiety, to locate its source in themselves and then to come to some understanding of how it relates to the patient. This is the process we know well as countertransference. It is to be hoped that analysts are more able than Timon to bear ambivalence, but it remains the case that affects around money generate conflicting anxieties and residual complexes. Jung's (1946, pars 364–365) much-quoted comment implies that anxiety is an unavoidable aspect of psychic infection:

> the doctor by voluntarily and consciously taking over the psychic sufferings of the patient, exposes himself to the overpowering contents of the unconscious and hence also to their inductive action . . . the unconscious infection brings with it a therapeutic possibility – which should not be underestimated – of the illness being transferred to the doctor.

Bion (2005, pp. 104–105), too, makes the case that in any analysis, both parties will be anxious:

> in every psychoanalysis, when approaching the unconscious – that is, what we do not know – we, patient and analyst alike, are certain to be disturbed. In every consulting room, there ought to be two rather frightened people: the patient and the psychoanalyst. If they are not both frightened, one wonders why they are bothering to find out what everyone knows . . . I sometimes think that an analyst's feelings . . . are one of the few bits of what scientists might call evidence, because he can know what he is feeling . . . in real life you have an orchestra: continuous movement and a constant slither of one feeling into another. You have to have a method to capture all that richness.

Whether we are talking of Bion's "orchestra" or Jung's "unconscious infection", there is little doubt that money, with its capacity to trick and turn feelings into their opposite has the potential for transference and countertransference enactments in the consulting room for both patient and analyst.

Davies (2012), in a recent paper titled "Anxiety: the importunate companion", draws on George Eliot's description of anxiety as the "importunate companion, refusing to be utterly quieted even by much drinking". She reminds us that Freud's ideas about castration anxiety remain clinically relevant, but that they are in danger of being relegated to the history books with today's emphasis from Kleinian and the post-Kleinian practice on the twosome of the mother–infant relationship. Theoretically and clinically, this twosome privileges *separation anxiety* and the terrors that can be aroused due to early absence, dependency, and loss. This contrasts with the later, Oedipal, threats to effectiveness that are the main concern of castration anxiety. Davies points out (2012, p. 1104),

> in contemporary practice, the interplay of this duality has become somewhat unbalanced: we are more schooled technically in the interpretation of separation anxiety . . .[she argues] for a reinstatement of the place of castration anxiety and the concomitant centrality of sexuality and the law of the father in psychoanalytic theory.

She quotes Green (2005, p. 187) "father was to fade increasingly . . . castration anxiety saw its domain shrink in the face of anxieties linked to an exclusive mother–child relationship".

Today's emphasis, theoretically and clinically, on the significance for development of the early mother–infant relationship, involving attachment patterns and possible failures in attunement, is, of course, of supreme importance, but there is cause to question whether this permits space for money as a third, the firm father, regulating both the frame and the process. One of the dual functions of money is that, as part of the frame, it brings together patient and analyst and permits the relationship to continue. This is its positive function as a third; without an exchange of money, there is no analysis. Holmes (2001, p. 127) puts it well: "denial of the significance of money may represent a regressive wish to return to the pre-pecuniary state of mother–infant mutual absorption". The analytic work then is done for sentiment alone, for love and not for money.

More complicated is its role in the transference, as money serves also to keep analyst and patient separate, mainly because the exchange of money generates strong (albeit different) feelings within the relationship. It is here that the trickster inhabits the site of therapeutic action, sometimes turning human qualities into their opposite.

Analysis is a labour of love, of course, but we have to inhabit two worlds at the same time. Money is the third that reminds patient and analyst of the nature and the limits of their relationship, but the money metaphor generates anxiety for both patient and analyst. For the patient, money as an unwelcome third can turn the analyst in the transference into a hated Midas or whore when what desired is love—the madonna. My patient who deposited her cheque in my wastepaper basket presents a good example of this.

For the analyst, to remain solely in the domain of maternal preoccupation, attentive, of course, to the effects of breaks and separations, keeps both patient and analyst safe from the intrusion of money as a premature or unwanted third. It is only when analysts can learn to distinguish their own less conscious attitudes to money, including their shadow aspects such as shame, acquisitiveness, etc., from those of their patients, that they will be able to bear patients' negative projections and hatred. It is only then that money can remain firmly in the frame with the potential to foster development and a greater sense of effectiveness for both.

Money matters in the countertransference

Countertransference may be defined as the analyst's response to the patient's transference. It is an unconscious process and seen today as a central tool in understanding the dynamics of the analytic relationship, especially patients' transference. I have written elsewhere about countertransference as a form of active imagination, involving both the capacity to create a mental space and to use a mental function (Wiener, 2009, pp. 69–71). The analyst needs to create an internal imaginative space that is receptive to unconscious transference projections from the patient, as well as a reflective space to attribute meaning to the unconscious processes going on between them. When it comes to money, this emotional and reflective space can become infected by the projections on to money of both patient and analyst. The trickster is at work, and momentary internal shifts between experiences of separation anxiety and castration anxiety can lead to countertransference enactments.

Fordham's (1985, p. 142) comment about countertransference illusion is apt here:

> a countertransference illusion may have one useful characteristic: it demonstrates the fallibility of the analyst. Though optimally the illusion does not last for long, it does seem to place the analyst on the same level as the patient. In addition it reminds the analyst of his tendencies to become undesirably involved.

A natural focus for the emotional impact of money in the consulting room is the fee, and we do well to question ourselves as to whether we become "undesirably involved" when setting or reviewing a fee. I think that when we present our patients with a bill, this usually generates a regressive response, often resentment about paying with both personal and symbolic meaning for our patients and for us. Analysts, too, may experience regression in the form of a frisson of excitement when a cheque is put into their hands. They can feel angry when a patient "forgets" to pay the bill, and it is difficult to maintain an analytic attitude if money is short that month.

Some clinical vignettes

Vignette 1

At a meeting of training analysts in my own Society, there was a heated discussion about whether or not to set a maximum fee for supervising trainees. Some analysts were comfortable with agreeing to this in the knowledge that this fee was less than they might charge a non-trainee or a qualified analyst. They agreed to put the supervisee, struggling to meet the costs of training, first. Others preferred to charge supervisees the fee that represented for them what they felt they were worth. This led to a clash of moral values and a heated discussion, with some firmly of the view that this rate should be held to and others upholding their wish for personal freedom to charge what they wanted. The heat in the meeting could be seen to be a function of conflict between Midas-like negative projections of greed and inflation on those charging "high" fees on the one hand, and equally negative projections of needing to remain at all times a good object by keeping fees down on the other.

Vignette 2

A supervisee, qualified for several years, arrived at a session looking rather tense. He had been gradually building up his practice and wished for more intensive analytic work, to see patients several times a week. He told me that he was thinking of increasing his fees for new patients to between £50 and £75. He had recently begun a second analysis, and he had told me previously that this was the way his new analyst managed fees. There might have been other reasons for his tension when we met, but relevant between us were my complicated feelings. I felt on the one hand that my supervisee's tension concerned his fear that I might be angry and offended with him as I did not set my fees in this way, and also, because his top rate was considerably higher than the fee I was charging him at that time. I also had what could be described as a momentary feeling of castration anxiety, as if my effectiveness had been dented by his announcement. Why was I not charging higher fees? I sensed a possible split transference between me and his new analyst, but this did not feel appropriate or relevant to address directly in the session. I needed to help him understand and emerge from his personal money conflicts to a position where he could feel comfortable about setting his fees with his patients in his own way. The session highlighted a money complex of my own and led me to feel envious of my supervisee, who, at that moment, had discovered a capacity to manage love and money in relation to his patients in a more balanced way than I thought I could myself.

Vignette 3

A young male patient I have seen for over six years pays a low fee, negotiated with care by both of us to reflect what he could afford without any conscious resentment from me. He offered increases when he could afford to. Recently, he has changed career, taking financial and emotional risks to pursue his love of music. During this period, there were times when he had barely enough money to buy food or take the bus. However, it has always been important for him to pay me something as part of his appreciation of his analysis and to feel effective. He trusts that I am not resentful towards him for paying what he knows is a considerably reduced fee, and I trust that he will honour his debts. Once or twice, his cheques bounced, leaving him feeling ashamed and humiliated. Seeing holes in his shoes, I contemplated suggesting he pay me less, but considered this would increase his already vulnerable sense of his own potency. To prevent further problems with the bank, he began to pay in cash. He arrived at a session and presented me with an envelope containing cash, saying that he could not find the exact money and could I give him £10 change. At this point, my anxiety rose sharply and I experienced a strong resistance to handling cash in the room and rather quickly said I would take £10 off his next bill. I reflected later that my experience of intense discomfort at the thought of opening my purse and giving him the money enacted in me an unconscious identification with the whore or prostitute where cash in exchange for services became, for a moment, dirty money, the Devil's gold mentioned by Freud (1908b, p. 174). What was precious between my patient and myself, the fee, subject to loving negotiations from both of us over time, switched suddenly into its opposite, dirty faeces.

Vignette 4

A new female patient received the first monthly bill I presented to her saying, "Will you text me your bank details please?" I commented that it was not my practice to take direct bank-to-bank payments, leaving to one side at that moment the issue of texting as a mode of communication with patients. She looked at me as if I was really old-fashioned, telling me that she did not use chequebooks any more. Instinctively, I held to my position, aware that for her, getting a chequebook and remembering to bring cheques made me into the demanding other who was asking still more of her, rather than giving to her. This later turned out to mirror her own internal persecutor, driving her towards ever more professional and personal achievements. I reflected to myself later that as we move ever closer towards online banking, there will be a loss to the analytic relationship of the presence of a real, live exchange of money in the consulting room. How and when patients choose to pay us contains significant unconscious communications within the relationship about the analytic process. The loss of this process will be considerable should bank transfers become in time the only means of payment.

Vignette 5

A patient in a high status job, with whom I have been working for about three years, confessed shamefacedly one morning that she had just received an extremely large bill from the Inland Revenue for failure to fill in her tax returns. Although she sent money regularly to the Inland Revenue, she was eight years behind with her tax returns. I was very surprised to hear of her difficulties, as money was seldom talked about in sessions, and she paid me reliably without conscious complaint. A friend loaned her money to pay the bill, and much to her relief, most of the money was returned with the help of a new accountant, but this led in analysis to the emergence into consciousness of a powerful projection on to money. It was, in part, an anti-authority complex, a disguised attack on the controlling father Inland Revenue. More recently, she arrived at a session saying she had broken a front tooth that morning. She was less worried about vanity than the cost of dental treatment, which would take her finances, as she put it, "not to the bottom, but a good way down the lift shaft". We could revisit together her projections on to money and her feeling that she is always left to manage too much on her own. She recalled her parents' spending money on her younger sister but not on her. I reminded her of a time at the beginning of her therapy when she almost left because she did not think I liked her. She has always felt the less-loved daughter in the eyes of her mother. The incident connected once more, but in a different way, her relationship with money and her sense of deprivation and the absence of maternal love.

Conclusion

In this chapter, I have tried to understand in greater depth the continuing silence in the literature and in our training curricula about the subject of money. In the context of a profession dominated largely by women, and where we are all affected by a global banking crisis, the effects of which will be felt for many years to come, I have put forward two central reasons for this silence. First of all, that contemporary theory and practice, privileging the earliest relationship between mother and baby and the primacy of separation anxiety, make sustaining money as a potent third in the relationship more difficult. Second, that money is a trickster with the capacity to turn feelings into their opposites at the flick of a switch, creating a labyrinth of complexity in the relationship between love and money in the transference.

Our own attachment to money is likely to mirror other attachment patterns, and the shadow of money is being lived out as a cultural complex before our eyes. One of Warren Buffett's most famous quotes is that "in the business world, the rear view mirror is always clearer than the windshield". Keeping a sharp eye on the rear view mirror demands consciousness of the potential for a "detached shadow" in which our money complexes reside.

A line from Carol Ann Duffy's poem, "Mrs Midas", is the epigraph to this chapter: "and who, when it comes to the crunch, can live with a heart of gold?" The phrase, "heart of gold", with its poignant double meaning of coldness and kindness, does indeed get to the heart of the matter. In the poem, Duffy looks starkly through the eyes of Mrs Midas, reflecting with sadness on the coldness, the absence of warmth and touch, in a marriage to a man with money lust, who values the power of gold over relationship. For analysts, I would speculate that to "have a heart of gold" is to have discovered a balance between matters of the heart and money matters with our patients and within ourselves.

References

Bion, W. R. (2005). *The Tavistock Seminars*. London: Karnac.

Campbell, D. (1994). Breaching the shame shield: thoughts on the assessment of adolescent child sexual abusers. *Journal of Child Psychotherapy*, 20: 30–326.

Davies, R. (2012). Anxiety: the importunate companion. *International Journal of Psychoanalysis*, 93(5): 1101–1114.

Dimen, M. (1994). Money, love and hate: contradiction and paradox in psychoanalysis. *Psychoanalytic Dialogues*, 4: 69–100.

Duffy, C. A. (1999). *The World's Wife*. London: Picador.

Freud, S. (1908b). Character and anal eroticism. *S.E.*, 9. London: Hogarth Press.

Freud, S. (1913c). On beginning the treatment. *S.E.*, 9: London: Hogarth.

Green, A. (2005). *Key Ideas for a Contemporary Psychoanalysis*. London: Routledge.

Green, S. (2009). *Good Value: Reflections on Money, Morality and an Uncertain World*. London: Allen Lane.

Guggenbühl-Craig, A. (1982). Projections: soul and money. In: *Soul and Money*. Dallas, TX: Spring.

Hamilton, C., & Denniss, R. (2005). *Affluenza: When Too Much Is Never Enough*. Crows Nest, NSW, Australia: Allen and Unwin.

Haynes, J., & Wiener, J. (1996). The analyst in the counting-house: money as symbol and reality in analysis. *British Journal of Psychotherapy*, 13: 14–25.

Hillman, J. (1982). A contribution to soul and money. In: *Soul and Money*. Dallas, TX: Spring.

Holmes, J. (2001). Money and psychotherapy. In: *The Search for a Secure Base: Attachment Theory and Psychoanalysis* (pp. 123–133). Hove: Brunner-Routledge.

Jacoby, M. (1993). Is the analytic situation shame-producing? *Journal of Analytical Psychology*, 38: 419–436.

James, O. (2007). *Affluenza*. London: Vermilion.

Jung, C. G. (1917). The personal and the collective unconscious. *C.W.*, 17. London: Routledge.

Jung, C. G. (1946). The psychology of the transference. *C.W.*, 16. London: Routledge.

Jung, C. G. (1948). Alchemical studies. *C. W.*, 13. London: Routledge.

Krueger, D. W. (1991). Money, meanings and madness: a psychoanalytic perspective. *Psychoanalytic Review*, 78: 209–224.

LeClair, E. E., & Schneider, H. K. (1968). Some further theoretical issues. In: E. E. LeClair Jr. & H. K. Schneider (Eds.), *Economic Anthropology* (pp. 453–474). New York: Holt, Reinhart & Winston.

Lieberman, A., & Lindner, V. (1987). Unbalanced accounts: why women are still afraid of money. *New York: Atlantic Monthly Press.*

Marx, K. (1844). Economic–philosophical manuscripts I/3. In: T. B. Bottomore & M. Rubel (Eds.), *Karl Marx, Selected Writings in Sociology and Social Philosophy* (pp. 147–148). London: Penguin, 1956.

Shakespeare, W. (1952). *Shakespeare: The Complete Works*, G. B. Harrison (Ed.). New York: Harcourt Brace & World Inc.

Stein, M. (1998). *Jung's Map of the Soul*. Chicago, IL: Open Court.

Tett, G. (2009). *Fool's Gold:* London: Little, Brown.

Trevor-Roper, P. (1970). *The World through Blunted Sight*. London: Penguin.

Tuckett, D. (2011). *Minding the Markets: An Emotional Finance View of Financial Instability*. Basingstoke: Palgrave MacMillan.

Welldon, E. V. (1988). *Mother, Madonna, Whore: The Idealization and Denigration of Motherhood*. London: Karnac.

Wharton, B. (1990). The hidden face of shame: the shadow, shame and separation. *Journal of Analytical Psychology, 35*: 279–299.

Wiener, J. (2007). Evaluating progress in training: character or competence? *Journal of Analytical Psychology, 52*(2): 51–70.

Wiener, J. (2009). *The Therapeutic Relationship: Transference, Counter-transference and the Making of Meaning*. College Station, TX: Texas A & M University Press.

Woolf, V. (1929). *A Room of One's Own*. London: Penguin.

PART IV

TECHNIQUE: BORDERLINE AND PSYCHOSIS

CHAPTER SIX

Defences of the core self: borderline functioning, trauma, and complex

Marcus West

"The *via regia* to the unconscious, however, is not the dream, as [Freud] thought, but the complex, which is the architect of dreams and symptoms. Nor is this *via* so very 'royal', either, since the way pointed out by the complex is more like a rough and uncommonly devious footpath that often loses itself in the undergrowth and generally leads not into the heart of the unconscious but past it"

(Jung, 1934, par. 210)

T his chapter outlines a contemporary Jungian approach to working with patients with a borderline psychology, acknowledging that early developmental trauma underlies borderline modes of functioning but describing how Jung's underused concept of the complex still brilliantly accounts for many of the associated phenomena. Such traumas disrupt ego functioning, so that the vulnerable core is exposed and imperative "defences of the core self" are called up. The chapter extends and elaborates the concept of the complex, looking in detail at the "dual aspect" of its functioning. It also acknowledges the difficulty in reconciling and integrating early trauma-related internal working models (in both direct and reversed modes);

these are consequently constellated and reconstructed in the analytic relationship. This is a co-construction, involving both patient and analyst, and a particular analytic attitude and perspective is called for in order to work safely and effectively in this area. This work in the transference–countertransference allows the traumatic complex to be detoxified and integrated, freeing the individual to develop further and to function effectively and in a more fulfilling way.

Working with individuals with a borderline psychology presents certain challenges in therapy and analysis. To generalise for a moment: the experience of borderline individuals is very real, immediate, powerful, and raw. They are often disinterested in the "niceties" of analysis, as they want and need relief from their exposed, agonising, and unbearable-feeling situation, whether that is an immediate crisis or an intolerable long-term state of affairs. Characteristically, they react against the analyst's separateness, thinking, analysing, and self-containment: as a patient of Britton's put it, "stop that fucking thinking!" (Britton, 1989, p. 88). They frequently experience interpretations as unbearable criticisms, as they want the analyst to identify with them and reassure them that they are acceptable (exactly) as they are, and that the analyst likes and approves of them (the emotional tone of interactions is key); this is partly because their negative sense of themselves is intense.

As Fordham describes in his paper "Defences of the self" (the most-quoted paper in post-Jungian literature), patients react against the parts of the analyst that they see as technical and mechanistic, and they attempt to "unmask and obtain" a "good, hidden part" for themselves. Thus, they may treat the analyst's comments and interpretations as cold, unfeeling, and theoretical, or even as attempts by the analyst to defend himself against their own "infantile parts", which the patient maintains he is projecting into the patient; they may react "with denigration ending up in loud groans, screams or tears whenever the analyst speaks" (Fordham, 1974, p. 193).

He describes how the patient becomes extremely distressed and can come to feel that his pain, terror, dread, and confusion is directly caused by what he sees as the analyst's "sadism, cruelty and destructiveness". The analysis can run into considerable difficulty or impasse under these circumstances, with the patient becoming desperate and flooded with affect, such that the analyst might be led into relaxing boundaries, making disclosures, giving tokens, and so on. Fordham counsels that the analyst should not "try 'being himself' any more than he is already so doing by making confessions or giving information about himself etc."; he recommends that "the analytic attitude needs to be maintained" and that it is not desirable for the analyst to become "excessively passive or guilty at the amount of pain, terror and dread that the patient asserts the analyst causes" (1974, p. 196). Fordham describes these phenomena as part of a transference psychosis, where the patient is defending against what he experiences as "not-self" parts of the analyst, that is, parts of the analyst that are different from the patient.

While I agree with Fordham and his counsel about the analytic attitude, I have found his paper tantalising, as it does not adequately explain how and why these phenomena come about and, more particularly, how the situation might be resolved. Is the analyst to comply with the patient's wish for him to act as a mirroring self-object, as Kohut (1971) recommends? Or should they avoid "patient-centred interpretations" such as, "You are feeling envious that . . ." and emphasise "analyst-centred interpretations", such as, "You became anxious a moment ago when I . . .", which refer to the patient's concern with what is going on in the analyst, as Steiner (1993, Chapter Eleven) suggests? Furthermore, why is it not helpful for the analyst to let the patient know what they are feeling? What is being achieved when the analyst does not do so?

These are particularly apposite questions for Jungian analysts who, following Jung, will probably have come to trust in and respect the patient's "self" (the unconscious centre and totality of the personality) and to recognise that analysis is a process that deeply and intimately involves both patient and analyst, as Jung described so well (Jung, 1946). They are, thus, very likely to be open to acknowledging and exploring their own contribution to the two-person process of analysis. It is exactly these kinds of issues that led Jung into difficulties with his analysis of Sabina Spielrein and put him off working with patients with a borderline psychology, referring them on to colleagues, and saying that he preferred only a "mild transference" (Wiener, 2010).

Trauma and the disruption of ego functioning

My understanding of these phenomena is based on the recognition of the effect that early developmental trauma has in disrupting ego functioning: the emotional and autobiographical sense of self, thinking and self-reflection, self-containment, self-agency, and orientation towards reality. Infant development researchers such as Stern (1985) and Tronick (2007) have studied the nature of the interaction between the infant and his/her care-givers, which is essentially a turn-taking process where interactions call for a response from the other. Tronick and Gianino (1986) suggest that when there is a mismatch between the desired and actual response of the care-giver, the infant experiences distress and will act so as to try to repair the mismatch through signalling behaviours—cooing, gesturing, crying out, and so on. These patterns of disruption and repair are entirely normal in any interaction.

If the infant is successful in repairing the mismatches, the infant can "experience positive emotions and establish a positive affective core"; it increases their sense of agency (see Knox, 2011), and allows them to internalise a pattern of interaction that they bring to interactions with others (their internal working models (Bowlby, 1969)). However, if the infant is repeatedly unsuccessful in repairing mismatches, she comes to feel helpless, focuses her behaviour on self-regulation, limits her engagement with her social environment, and goes on to "establish a negative affective core" (Tronick & Gianino 1986, p. 156); this negative affective core is characteristic of borderline individuals (Kernberg, 1975; West, 2007). On a larger scale, these disruptions and failures to repair constitute early developmental trauma that may be brought about through, for example, the care-givers' depression, absence, inconstancy, emotional dysregulation, neglect, violence, and abuse.

Van der Kolk and others describe how such traumatic experience disrupts the individual's thinking and ego functioning. He writes,

> intense arousal ("vehement emotion" [Janet's term]) seems to interfere with proper information processing and the storage of information in narrative (explicit) memory so that memories of trauma may have no verbal (explicit) component whatsoever. Instead, the memories may have been organised on an implicit or perceptual level, without any accompanying narrative about what happened. (van der Kolk, 1996, pp. 286–287)

These experiential components—visual, olfactory, affective, auditory, and kinaesthetic—and trauma-related "ways of being with others" (Stern) are readily triggered in the analysis and represent intrusive experiences related to the original traumatic situation.

In addition, the individual has primitive, aggressive counter-responses to the violation of the core self (Neborsky, 2003), as well as so-called mammalian defence responses (fight, flight, freeze, and collapse), which may have become locked in the body awaiting release (Levine, 1997, 2005; Ogden, Minton, & Pain, 2006).

These sets of intense affective experiences, which cannot be processed by the individual's current ego functioning, thus form what Jung (1934) called feeling-toned complexes. In a neurotic personality, such complexes co-exist with the ego complex. However, if the experiences are of a critical intensity and difficulty and the traumatic complex is, as a result, sufficiently powerful, it disrupts the individual's normal ego functioning and ego complex, in so far as it has been established, and/or triggers the characteristic regression of borderline functioning. Herman, Perry, and van der Kolk (1989) argue that borderline personality disorder is, in fact, a form of post traumatic stress disorder. The disruption to the ego complex is the characteristic that distinguishes borderline from neurotic functioning.

I give below an extended clinical example and then describe the nature and functioning of complexes in the borderline situation, what is constellated in the analytic relationship, and how that can be most usefully worked with.

Clinical example

"Sue" came to analysis depressed and suicidal, having been dismissed from her job. In childhood, her mother had been severely depressed, and her father, who had been ambitious and materialistic, had been openly critical, dismissive, and disappointed in her and her younger brother.

In the early part of the analysis, Sue went into a steep decline, spending large portions of the day in bed. We made links between the past and her current situation: how she felt rejected and unappreciated in her old job as she had felt with her father, and that the world was an implacable place that did not respond to her or give her what she wanted and needed, as she had felt with her mother. During this period, it seemed significant to her that I could bear with her through her most desperate time and not be fazed by her despair or suicidal feelings.

After some time, Sue slowly got going again and applied for and, to her surprise, got a new job. However, she quickly felt unappreciated and criticised by her new manager and took little pleasure or comfort in the job as life still felt meaningless to her and, without a partner, she was convinced that it always would be. She was adamant that I appreciate how she had been treated unfairly—at home, at work, and in life in general—and she was insistent that I agree that certain figures in her life were really and authentically bad. If I seemed to suggest that her actions might have played a part, or if I said something sympathetic about her parents, she was furious with me and would accuse me of not understanding her (which she found particularly unbearable).

The analytic challenge was to accept fully her heartfelt experience and to make sense of it in such a way that it was not simply a collusion that might dangerously amplify the split: for example, "Yes, your new manager is terrible (you ought to make a complaint against her)", or did not leave me trying to supply the kind of (idealised version of the) experiences she had never had by forming a warm, special, exclusive, preoccupied relationship, or ensuring that I never did anything that resembled or triggered the original trauma, for example, by making interpretations that she might experience as critical.

In listening to Sue's experience (and others like her), I have come to realise (as have many others before me) that what she was experiencing in her life and in her relationship with me not only resembled, but was a detailed reconstruction of, her early experiences and patterns of relationship with her parents. The past is vitally alive in the present. I will describe how this began to manifest more fully and directly in the transference–countertransference.

A health scare meant that Sue had to ask to change some session times to attend medical appointments, and she was particularly exercised by whether I would find her alternative times and whether I would charge her if she missed a session under these "extreme" circumstances. I was very much aware of her rage and hatred towards people she felt were "heartless" and "uncaring", and I recognised that I was finding it difficult to think clearly about the issue and was tempted to bend my usual stated practice and not to charge her for one session for which I could not offer an alternative; however not to do so felt wrong to me.

With some difficulty, anticipating her reaction, I charged her for the missed session. She was furious and said she was disgusted with me, that she had not thought I would stoop that low, and that I was obviously only interested in money. I did wonder if she would leave the analysis, but she continued to attend, glowering and furious. I interpreted, with conviction, sensing the links clearly, that she was experiencing me as a mother who did not respond in a caring way to her needs and distress and who was too busy with others (viz. her younger brother), and as a father who was only interested in material things.

While she acknowledged this understanding, her rage and disappointment in me continued. Over the following weeks, as her rage remained unabated, I slowly came to recognise that, far from being the powerless victim that she saw herself as, she was treating me with powerful contempt, hatred, and disdain that was, to her, justified by my "wrongdoing". (This kind of moral outrage was familiar to me and I was, therefore, more able to think about it, whereas when I first met such outrage, I was convinced I had done something truly terrible and wrong (West, 2007, pp. 207–209).) I noted that her contempt seemed very similar to her father's contempt, which she had described so clearly.

Realising that this was a very delicate area, I began by interpreting her strength of feeling, hatred, and "power", and I suggested that she was very much in the active, angry, powerful (aggressor) role rather than in the passive, "done-to" (victim) role in which she usually saw herself. Recognising and owning this, with some difficulty, she seemed to become a bit less fragile and more robust as she connected with her power and agency.

Over the weeks, I expanded my interpretations to point out how she was adopting a role (internal working model) very similar to her father in her criticism of, and disgust with, me, and that perhaps she was unconsciously exploring what that was like "from the other side" (an identification with the aggressor); a little later, I pointed out that her withdrawal from me and her treatment of me as if I meant nothing to her reminded me of how I thought she might have felt with her mother's depressed withdrawal and rejection (for example, how I had felt she might leave the analysis when I had charged her for the missed session). These were particularly difficult things for her to acknowledge, as it was anathema to her to feel she might be "like them". It felt that the whole complicated, early set of relational dynamics, and the powerful feelings associated with them, were becoming increasingly constellated in the analytic relationship.

Despite a slight easing of the tension between us, in one session she told me with absolute, shocking certainty that I "didn't give a toss about her" and that I "hated her" (I did note that I had been less tuned-in to her emotional state that session, being slightly preoccupied with something myself). While her certainty that I hated her was shocking, I was able not to have a knee-jerk reaction of denial as I had come to recognise my own primitive (talion) counter-reaction to her treatment of me (Lambert, 1981): I had sometimes felt moments of anger and hatred towards her—some fleeting, some longer lasting. This was not my predominant attitude towards her, but, rather, a primitive reaction I was able to observe (Racker, 1958).

There is a strong tendency in therapy to try to reassure the patient in some way that their worst fears of how others may see them are not the case and that "I" (the therapist) "am not like that". In my experience, this attitude reinforces the splitting, as the therapist tries to remain the good figure in a way that is ultimately unhelpful to the patient since, while they might feel initial relief, they do not feel properly met or seen, and their core self-image and internal working models are not being addressed.

I began to explore Sue's reactions with her as if they were fact, referring interchangeably to the present and the past. I suggested that the most traumatic aspect of her early experience had become constellated between us—her feeling that her mother had hated her. (We could not know whether her mother had, in fact, felt this at times, although it seemed very possible/likely that she had, but it seemed certain that Sue had felt that she did and had felt mortified by her mother's irritation, abruptness, and withdrawal.) We began, very tentatively and sensitively, to explore this experience over the following weeks and months.

Co-construction and reconstruction of the original trauma

It has been my experience with patients with a borderline psychology that the original traumatic relational pattern becomes manifest in the transference–countertransference on a deep feeling level, and that only when this has happened, and only through it happening, is the traumatic complex worked through. This is partly due to the fact that the trauma disturbed the individual's ego functioning so that he or she has no effective, containing verbal narrative and the associated affects are so powerful and are, thus, enacted. As Freud said, "the patient does not say that he remembers that he used to be defiant and critical towards his parents' authority; instead, he behaves in that way to the doctor" (1914g, p. 150).

Beebe and Lachmann (2002) write illuminatingly of the way that the analytic relationship represents a co-construction by both partners in the analytic dialogue, and Davies describes what she calls a "therapeutic enactment" where there is,

> a collapsing of past and present; a co-constructed organization of the transference-countertransference matrix that bears such striking similarity to an important moment of the past that patient and analyst together have the unique opportunity to exist in both places at the same time. (Davies, 1997, p. 246)

In practice, this co-construction occurs through sometimes subtle and sometimes not-so-subtle cues, actions, and behaviours. Thus, it is likely that Sue's conviction that I hated her was cued by my slight distraction on that particular day and that this constellated her traumatic experience of feeling hated. Previously, my charging for the missed session had clearly triggered her experiences related to her father and money, and my general analytic stance, being not overtly warm and expressive, would have been unconsciously associated by her with her mother's withdrawn, depressed behaviour. (I should add that I naturally respond to what patients say, seeing the analytic process as essentially a dialogue. Patients are usually able to come to recognise my contained depth of feeling through the sometimes heartfelt interpretations I make, born out of the real experiences between us, but that will be after they have worked through contrary experiences, such as those related, in Sue's case, to her depressed mother.)

Similarly, Sue induced feelings of frustration, impotence, and hatred in me over time by, for example, repeatedly frustrating my interpretations, attempts to link, relate, have a dialogue, or to move towards a more positive or optimistic outlook (setting up an experience very much like that which she had experienced with her depressed mother—a projective identification). Thus, her conviction that I hated her would also be due to the implicit knowledge that she had behaved this way towards me and that, on the most primitive, talion level, such responses would have been constellated in me— whether I was conscious of them or not (see below). I do not, there-fore, see her experience as "simply" a projection of her own hatred of those who were unresponsive towards her, although that was certainly part of it.

It is these "relatively minor" cues and associations with the origi-nal trauma that can trigger powerful reactions in the patient that seem out of all proportion to the situation—the trigger itself may not even be recognised. (The Boston Change Process Study Group (2010) describes how apparently surface interactions such as these are, in fact, foundational, in the sense of being the key elements of an indi-vidual's experience rather than "deep" drives or defences.) Sue was aware of the apparently disproportionate nature of her reactions and they caused her much confusion, shame, and self-recrimination. Understanding them in relation to the trauma helped her accept and understand them in a way that she did not find punitive and could readily appreciate.

In regard to the co-constructions, Davies and Frawley write,

> included in our conceptualization of the transformational aspects of the treatment are the patient's experience of the analyst's availability and constancy, the analyst's willingness to participate in the shift-ing transference-countertransference reenactments, and, finally, his or her capacity to maintain appropriate boundaries and set necessary limits. (1992, pp. 30–31)

The analyst, therefore, needs to recognise when certain roles, feelings, and dynamics are being constellated inside themselves and the patient: among them, passive, powerless, masochistic (victim) roles; omnipotent, sadistic, powerful (aggressor) roles; heroic, idealised, "good" (saviour) roles; distant, uncaring, neglectful (uninvolved parent) roles; naïve, ever-hopeful, wanting to please (innocent) roles, and so on (Davies & Frawley, 1992; Gabbard, 1992; Karpman, 1968).

If the analyst tries to remain seen simply as "good" and helpful, resisting the more negatively toned roles, they can be led into trying to prove themselves in the kinds of ways that Fordham describes: being especially warm and kindly, making personal disclosures, offer-ing frequent extra sessions or phone calls, and generally relaxing boundaries (see also Davies and Frawley, 1992, pp. 25–34; Britton, 2003, Chapter Three). The opposite of this is also possible, with the analyst becoming punitive and hyper-critical, or hopeless and despondent. While such enactments are inevitable, they are problematic if they become persistent and are not recognised, considered, and worked with.

It can take some time and experience for the analyst to recognise and to feel comfortable in working with these primitive counter-reactions in themselves. Thus, with Sue, it took some effort on my part to resist the kindly "saviour" roles that she was encouraging me to adopt and to face her hurt, disappointment, and outrage; connecting to my primitive counter-responses of anger, frustration, and hatred helped to ground me more fully in the wider picture of what was going on.

While the analyst's thinking and ego functioning can allow vital space to consider and understand what is being constellated in the transference–countertransference (rather than act), their tolerance and forbearance can also amount to them being heroic or masochistic; indeed, there may be times when the analyst needs to stop the patient from verbally or even physically attacking them or infringing or eroding boundaries stating, perhaps, that the analysis will be terminated if the behaviour continues (see West, 2007, p. 22 for an example). If the analyst resists these more problematic roles, insisting implicitly or explicitly that "they are not like that", the patient will need to work all the harder before the analyst finally "gets the point" and registers the reactions that the patient needs them to feel, thus properly constellating and making real the otherwise inaccessible experience.

Disclosure

Sue was quick (in a paranoid way) to want to know whether I did hate her, implicitly seeking reassurance that this could not be true. The pressure on me was intense to offer reassurance that this was not the case, which, in various subtle or not so subtle ways in the past, I am sure I had given. It was an important evolution in my position that I could stay with this and not simply offer reassurance: the process of analysis is as much about the analyst's readiness to face certain feelings as the patient's[1] (although the analyst's readiness to make a certain interpretation might reflect the patient's readiness to be able to bear and receive such an interpretation; in other words, it is some-thing that evolves as part of the process of analysis).

I have found it unhelpful to confirm what I am actually feeling, as this immediately closes down the analytic work-space and the person tends to conclude that I feel "only that"; therefore, I have come to say, often from quite early on in an analysis, that I do not answer questions about what I am feeling (although I will acknowledge if I have been defensive or have said something that I later realise is unhelpful, and I may well apologise for that). I realise there is a tension between the "reality" of the experience between patient and analyst and the analyst not disclosing what he is feeling; however, this is necessary if the patient's feelings are going to be understood as symbolic commu-nications rather than simply "who they are". This is particularly intense with patients such as Sue, whose experience is very powerful, real, and raw.

If the analyst does start making disclosures, then the analytic working space is lost and something is being concretely enacted. The patient will register this and may have varying reactions, from initial relief and satisfaction to anxiety, fear, and a sense of unsafeness. I have found that these issues related to the analyst's containment, analytic stance, and the maintaining of their thinking and ego func-tioning are often reconstructions of early interactions. Sue, for exam-ple, would frequently have to reassure her mother that she loved her, or tell her what she was feeling, or fend off vehement questioning from her father about what she was doing and why.

There is an intense sense of threat and envy when the analyst does not respond to interactions/questions as the patient implicitly expects (thus protecting their core self in a way that the patient was, tragically, unable to do).[2] It is exactly these kinds of internal working models, stored in implicit/procedural memory (Knox, 2003), that are so compelling for patient and analyst. It is important that these issues do not become simply battles of will and that the analyst can continue to think about and explore these interactions, particularly looking for earlier blueprints.

Sue stating that I hated her led us to explore her growing aware-ness of the range of her feelings towards me—sometimes angry, hate-ful, envious, and murderous, sometimes warm, grateful, appreciative, and loving. She was able to see that the relationship could bear this range (thus lessening the need for splitting, where good and bad must be kept unrealistically apart). One element of her concern that I might hate her was related to her wish that I might be the hoped-for, idealised, loving mother-father-analyst, which emerged at this point; I will discuss this further below.

The dual aspect of the complex

One difficulty for the analyst (and the patient) in recognising the different roles that are being constellated in the analytic relationship is the primacy of the original trauma with which the patient naturally identifies—the wound comes to dominate the patient's sense of themselves.[3] Related to this, Fonagy, Gergely, Jurist, and Target (2002, pp. 11–14) describe how the child internalises an "alien self"—the abusive part—and, in order to feel coherent, needs to find someone on to and into whom to eject it, and then to relate to it through projective identification. Thus, they remain trapped by, and in thrall to, their bad objects. As Liotti (2004, p. 478) writes, it is precisely because these patterns—victim and aggressor—are so powerful and conflicting that the child is not able to construct a unitary, coherent, and cohesive identity. This is another way of saying that the traumatic complex disrupts the ego complex and compromises the individual's ego functioning.

With Sue, I frequently found myself experiencing her as, at the same time, the wounded, rejected child and the wounding, rejecting parent. Often this was at exactly the moment that she was experiencing me as wounding and rejecting and was, perhaps, unconsciously excited by rejecting and wounding me. It seems to me that such moments demonstrate most clearly the Janus-like, dual aspect of the complex, where the trauma-related internal working model is being expressed in direct mode (corresponding with Sue's original traumatic experience) and in reversed mode (in identification with the aggressor). This corresponds with Jung's theory of opposites (1955) and what Perry (1970) called the bi-polar nature of the complex.

I have come to see how the internal working model becomes installed in the individual's procedural memory and operates on different levels, similarly to what Jung described in relation to symbols (Jung, 1917, pars 121–150). Thus, an important part of the working through of the complex with Sue was in recognising, over time, how she felt rejected, criticised, and killed off by her parents and others (on the objective level), by herself, passively, in the form of a critical super-ego (on the subjective level), by me (on the transference level), and by the world, feeling herself everywhere scapegoated, criticised, unwelcome, and unwanted (on the archetypal level).

In addition, however, we slowly recognised how she rejected and criticised others (on the objective level), how she actively rejected and criticised herself, having no sympathy for her rejected child-self and wanting to get rid of it (the subjective level), how she rejected and criticised me (the transference level), and how she wanted to obliterate and reject others and the world (the archetypal level).

This reversed, identification-with-the-aggressor mode also represented Sue's own primitive, talion response to her father's criticism and her mother's withdrawal, where she fought "like with like" (Lambert, 1981). As Levine (1997, 2005) describes, these primitive fight, flight, freeze, and collapse responses can become locked in the body, having been unable to be released at the time—he calls them uncompleted action tendencies—either because it was not possible or not safe to do so: for example, it is not safe for the child to fight back against the bullying father. For the patient to recognise and accept the way they may be acting in identification with the aggressor thus represents a significant development in working the complex through, not only because there is no longer a need for the role/dynamic to be denied and projected (and a vital part of themselves is being accepted), but also because there is invariably something useful and necessary in that mode of being.

To give one example of this, in becoming more able to bear experiences of not being responded to, and in recognising that sometimes she did not want to respond to others, Sue became more able to allow both herself and me not to react to every feeling she had. Thus, she was sometimes able to put to one side what she was feeling in the service of "getting on with life", a vital element of ego functioning.

As part of owning her identification with the aggressor we also recognised how Sue unconsciously induced others to reject and hate her (I have described, above, how this occurred in the transference). This is what Winnicott (1960) would call taking the trauma into her sphere of omnipotence; Freud (1914g) would see it as an aspect of repetition compulsion and I would suggest it was an aspect of working on the complex so that it might be mastered and worked through.

Sue needed to be able to bear, take control of, and think about these hateful interactions, coming to bear and understand what might be going on in the other person's mind through experiencing her own feelings of hatefulness; this is an element of what Fonagy (1991) calls mentalisation.

It is important that the analyst also comes to recognise, in his own life and in his conduct of analysis, the way that his own early traumas operate in both direct and reversed modes, and, thus, that he might subtly and unconsciously re-enact what was done to him. It is also important that analysts recognise their own "borderline" part that wishes to avoid conflict, opposition, and separateness and to be experienced as "good". Britton (2003, p. 56) gives one example of this in terms of the analyst responding to the patient's unconscious invitation to regard himself as the transcendent love-object of the patient's Oedipus complex.

The internal working model operating on the archetypal level reflects the frequently recurring emergence (Knox, 2003) of these patterns of relationship with which we are all the time engaged (Jung describes how he uses the term archetype to "coincide with the biological concept of the 'pattern of behaviour'" (Jung, 1958, par. 566)). We all know individuals who might be seen as "cold", "cruel", "heartless", "rejecting", "critical", "unresponsive", and "murderous", or "warm", "kind", "generous", "friendly", "approachable", "loving", and so on; it is through these emotive figures and ways of being that the patient engages the analyst on a primitive level, and unconsciously primes and encourages him to behave in certain ways and not others. When the pressure is intense, this can sometimes amount to what Knox (2011, Chapter Five) calls "indexical communication".

Trauma and the violation and exposure of the core self

This priming and cueing is made so much more powerful and compelling due to the disruption of the borderline individual's ego functioning, so that their core self is viscerally exposed, and, as a result, the individual will need to engage in what Bion (1959) called "excessive projective identification". Defences of the core self are, thus, called into action; these are "imperative", and the analyst will naturally identify and resonate with them. As we know implicitly that the core self must be protected at all costs, the analyst is strongly influenced to take an active role in the regulation of the patient's affective experience (Stern, 1985), regulation that is a natural element in human relationships, particularly with infants.

I am using the term "core self" here to refer to the largely nonverbal, early-developing, sensitive, affective core. While the core self is vitally attuned to the environment and performs unconsciously many sophisticated functions of appraisal and self-regulation,[4] it requires the individual's effective ego functioning to achieve a manageable level of experience and, in particular, a balance of regulation by self and other (see Beebe & Lachmann, 2002). The term "core self" overlaps with, but is different from, Jung's concept of the self (see West, 2007, Chapter Six) in that what emerges from the core self reflects the individual's internal working models, which, although held with utmost conviction, cannot be trusted as a guide in analysis. The core self does, however, represent a vital manifestation of early experiences and patterns of behaviour, and what emerges is invaluable if seen in those terms.

The nature of the core self is such that it requires the analyst's identification, synchrony (Schore, 2003) and regulation; this is another perspective on what Freud (1900a) called primary process functioning, or what Matte Blanco (1975, 1988) described as the symmetry. This was reflected in Sue's insistence that I see things her way, identify with her and her position, and that I act so as to make her feel all right (regulate her affective state). It is only the development of the individual's own ego-functioning and self-agency, largely through bearing and understanding their own experiences through the process of analysis, that the core self can come to feel safe and contained.

Ogden, Minton, and Pain (2006, p. 3) describe how early trauma triggers body-based responses which form the core of the individual's identity. Thus, Sue's early experiences of lack of response from her mother, and her inability to repair such mismatches, led her to form a negative affective core (Tronick & Gianino, 1986) that generated beliefs such as "I am unlovable" and "no one would want me". She had become incapacitated, hopeless and "frozen", feeling despairing and unable to affect others, and, thus, she "required" me to come to the rescue and "pick up the pieces" of her life (an aspect of a borderline personality organisation (West, 2007, Chapter Eight)). She had, thus, incorporated the primitive "freeze" response and, from that, built her "way of being with others" (Stern 1985). Another thread for Sue was her "fight" response to her father's threat, attempting to control the other person, angrily blaming them for causing hurt or anxiety (aspects of a narcissistic personality organisation (West, 2007, Chapter Seven)).

Other patients have a "collapse" response to threat and trauma, thus feeling unviable in the world, and they build on this response by suspending their own idiom (Bollas, 2000). They dedicate themselves in a loving and/or desperate manner to an other they hope will take over their care and regulation, but they feel suicidal (a form of collapse and self-annihilation) when this does not occur (a hysterical personality organisation (West, 2007, Chapter Nine)). Others react to threat by withdrawing to a place of self-soothing and self-regulation, demanding/hoping that the other will make an ideal world in which it will be safe to be fully themselves (a schizoid personality organisation (West, 2007, Chapter Ten)).

As Bollas (2000, p. 4) says, these are natural forms of defence that we all adopt at times; it is only when one form comes to predominate in a particularly powerful way that the individual becomes fixed in a rigid personality organisation. In this chapter, I have described "borderline functioning" in a broad manner, focusing on the core negative sense of self, the disruption of containing ego functioning, and the exposure of the core self that is common to all these personality organisations. I could identify all these forms of relating in Sue at different moments, although the frozen, bleak, hopeless, negative sense of herself and the angry, blaming, attacking modes were primary, relating to experiences with her mother and father, respectively.

I found that identifying and discussing these primitive, body-based responses with Sue and helping her understand that they were natural counter-responses to the trauma helped her to feel less shame in relation to them and to begin to recognise and accept them more in herself (see Ogden, Minton, & Pain, 2006).

"Only what is really oneself has the power to heal"

Naturally, I supported the constructive, agentive elements of Sue's functioning, for example, by encouraging her to recognise that she was well placed for a dreaded annual work assessment. However, this had only limited success, as the dynamics of the traumatic complex itself needed to be explored, lived, and worked through.

A major dynamic for her was not accepting herself as she was, feeling that she was flawed and wrong, and wanting to be different. She felt, in relating, that experiences of unresponsiveness and criticism were intolerable and "wrong", so that she found it impossible to accept herself and exist in the world as it was. In contrast to this was her deeply held wish for a partner who would accept and love her, make her feel good about herself, and be constantly available. Thus, she wanted to avoid anything that triggered the original trauma and sought to enlist me in protecting her from it. We were, thus, almost always (characteristically) working on the edge of what felt impossible for Sue to bear.

Sue's wish to avoid the traumatic experience was understandable, but ultimately futile, and the analyst's task is to help the patient bear the dreaded and previously unbearable experiences by understanding and working through them in the transference–countertransference. There were significant moments in the analysis when, implicitly and explicitly, I was able to challenge her view that non-responsiveness, criticism, or someone else's hatred was unbearable, most specifically when she accused me of hating her. Furthermore, in discussing her fear that I hated her, we were also able to explore her wish for me to be the all-loving mother-father-analyst. This was particularly difficult for her to acknowledge, as she did not believe it was possible for her, a cause of much despair.

Grasping these nettles brings relief to both patient and analyst, as, finally, painful reality can be accepted rather than avoided. This represents what Symington (1983) calls the analyst's "act of freedom" or, in Kleinian terms, the analyst not succumbing to projective identification but moving into the depressive position. This is one of the hallmarks of analysis, in contrast to therapy, as analysis aims to stay with what *is*, to recognise that the patient's experiences can and "must" be borne, and that, ultimately, "only what is really oneself has the power to heal" (Jung, 1928, par. 258).

For Sue, this meant, among other things, discovering that not every pressure or goal was bad, not every judgement was punitive and cruel, not every boundary or lack of response was a rejection, and not every person in authority was hostile or oppressive. She became able to relinquish her hope for an idealised solution (Stark, 2006) and own the elements that were "really herself". Contrary to what she might have expected, I found this moving and enlivening, which deepened our relationship considerably. I think she registered this and felt deeply responded to and accepted.

Reconstruction and the analytic attitude

The patient's demand for the analyst's identification puts great pressure on the analyst from the start. Understanding these pressures and dynamics as co-constructions and reconstructions allows the patient's experiences and impulses to be accepted and respected (a partial identification) and their origins understood, minimising punitive interpretations and ascriptions of destructive intent: for example, "you are sabotaging yourself". Recognising the "symbolic", that is, reconstructive/communicative/purposive nature of the patient's demands, creates much-needed analytic space, which, in turn, allows the understanding and containment of needs and drives that feel very real, immediate, powerful, and compelling. Such co-constructions and reconstructions can deeply affect both analyst and patient, drawing on their core selves. It is for this reason that working with individuals with a borderline psychology is such a personal as well as a professional challenge.

Interpretations must not become "tired" reconstructions of past events, but rather be born out of the analyst's immediate experience. Ideally, they are rooted in the transference–countertransference dynamics that capture the compelling manner in which trauma-related internal working models structure the present. This is not about what happened in the past, it is about how the past affects the present.

These are some of the many ways I worked with Sue during the years of the analysis, circumambulating (as Jung would say) the traumatic complex and working through it, thus allowing Sue to function in a more effective and fulfilling way.

Conclusion

The framework outlined here both overlaps with and differs from the Kleinian framework of paranoid–schizoid and depressive positions and the functioning of projective identification, as well as with Sandler's (1976) view of role responsiveness. While Freud abandoned his seduction theory and Klein emphasised the patient's instinctual aggression, this framework embraces both the trauma and the individual's counter-responses to it and recognises the way that the conflict between these two is central to the difficulty in forming a coherent and inclusive identity and effective ego functioning. The perspectives of early relational trauma, reconstruction, the complex, and, in particular, its dual aspect, represent powerful tools in identifying and working with this conflict and the associated pressures and dynamics. The framework offers an accessible, comprehensible, non-punitive, and effective way in which to work with individuals with a borderline psychology.

Notes

1. In the book *We Need To Talk about Kevin* (Shriver, 2010), it is clear that it was Kevin's mother's (understandable) difficulty to own and constructively use her hatred for her son (which he clearly knows about) that meant that his intense negativity (a counter-response to her hatred) could not be resolved, with tragic consequences. It is only when his own hatred has been manifested in his killing his schoolmates, and the victims' families' counter-hatred of him has been constellated "out there", that mother and son are finally reconciled and their primary attachment needs are met (see Winnicott's (1949) paper "Hate in the counter-transference").

2. Cordelia's refusal to answer the questions of her father, King Lear, in the manner he wanted was central to the tragedy that followed—he disowned and banished her—although he soon fell foul of his less true daughters, sinking into a "madness" associated with the disillusionment of his omnipotent phantasies and only belatedly recognising Cordelia's integrity and fidelity.

3. Individuals who identify primarily with the aggressor present more rarely for therapy, although they might come seeking help, for example, with anger management or with a crisis for which they recognise they are responsible.

4. As Winson writes, "Rather than being a cauldron of untamed passions and destructive wishes, I propose that the unconscious is a cohesive, continually active mental structure that takes account of life's experiences and reacts according to its scheme of interpretation" (1990, p. 96).

References

Beebe, B., & Lachmann, F. (2002). *Infant Research and Adult Treatment: Co-constructing Interactions*. Hillsdale, NJ: Analytic Press.

Bion, W. R. (1959). Attacks on linking. *International Journal of Psychoanalysis*, *40*: 308–315.

Bollas, C. (2000). *Hysteria*. London: Routledge.

Boston Change Process Study Group (2010). *Change in Psychotherapy: A Unifying Paradigm*. New York: Norton.

Bowlby, J. (1969). *Attachment and Loss, Vol. 1. Attachment*. London: Hogarth.

Britton, R. (1989). The missing link: parental sexuality in the Oedipus complex. In: R. Britton, M. Feldman, E. O'Shaughnessy (Eds.), *The Oedipus Complex Today* (pp. 83–102). London: Karnac.

Britton, R. (2003). *Sex, Death and the Superego: Experiences in Psychoanalysis*. London: Karnac.

Davies, J. M. (1997). Dissociation, therapeutic enactment, and transference–countertransference processes: a discussion of papers on childhood sexual abuse by S. Grand and J. Sarnat. *Gender and Psychoanalysis*, *2*: 241–257.

Davies, J. M., & Frawley, M. G. (1992). Dissociative processes and transference–countertransference paradigms in the psychoanalytically oriented treatment of adult survivors of childhood sexual abuse. *Psychoanalytic Dialogues*, *2*: 5–36.

Fonagy, P. (1991). Thinking about thinking: some clinical and theoretical considerations in the treatment of a borderline patient. *International Journal of Psychoanalysis*, *72*: 639–56.

Fonagy, P., Gergely, G., Jurist, E., & Target, M. (2002). *Affect Regulation, Mentalization and the Development of the Self*. London: Karnac.

Fordham, M. (1974). Defences of the self. *Journal of Analytical Psychology*, *19*(2): 192–199.

Freud, S. (1900a). *The Interpretation of Dreams*. *S.E.*, *4*. London: Hogarth.

Freud, S. (1914g). Remembering, repeating and working-through. *S.E.*, *12*: 145–156. London: Hogarth.

Gabbard, G. O. (1992). Commentary on 'Dissociative processes and transference–countertransference paradigms' by Jody Messler Davies and Mary Gale Frawley. *Psychoanalytic Dialogues*, *2*: 37–47.

Herman, J. L., Perry, J. C., & van der Kolk, B. A. (1989). Childhood trauma in borderline personality disorder. *American Journal of Psychiatry*, *146*: 490–495.

Jung, C. G. (1917). On the psychology of the unconscious. *C.W.*, *7*, R. F. C. Hull (Trans.). London: Routledge & Kegan Paul.

Jung, C. G. (1928). The relations between the ego and the unconscious. *C.W.*, *7*, R. F. C. Hull (Trans.). London: Routledge & Kegan Paul.

Jung, C. G. (1934). A review of complex theory. *C.W.*, *8*, R. F. C. Hull (Trans.). London: Routledge & Kegan Paul.

Jung, C. G. (1946). The psychology of the transference. *C.W.*, *16*, R. F. C. Hull (Trans.). London: Routledge & Kegan Paul.

Jung, C. G. (1955). *Mysterium Coniunctionis, C.W., 14*, R. F. C. Hull (Trans.). London: Routledge & Kegan Paul.

Jung, C. G. (1958). Schizophrenia, *C.W.*, *3*. *The Psychogenesis of Mental Disease*, R. F. C. Hull (Trans.). London: Routledge & Kegan Paul.

Karpman, S. (1968). Fairytales and script drama analysis. *Transactional Analysis Bulletin*, 7: 39–43.

Kernberg, O. (1975). *Borderline Conditions and Pathological Narcissism*. New York: Jason Aronson.

Knox, J. M. (2003). *Archetype, Attachment, Analysis: Jungian Psychology and the Emergent Mind*. New York: Brunner-Routledge.

Knox, J. M. (2011). *Self-Agency in Psychotherapy: Attachment, Autonomy and Intimacy*. New York: Norton.

Kohut, H. (1971). *The Analysis of the Self*. New York: International Universities Press.

Lambert, K. (1981). *Analysis, Repair, and Individuation*. London: Karnac.

Levine, P. (1997). *Waking the Tiger: Healing Trauma—the Innate Capacity to Transform Overwhelming Experiences*. Berkeley, CA: North Atlantic Books.

Levine, P. (2005). *Healing Trauma: A Pioneering Program for Restoring the Wisdom of your Body*. Boulder, CO: Sounds True.

Liotti, G. (2004). Trauma, dissociation, and disorganized attachment: three strands of a single braid. *Psychotherapy: Theory, Research, Practice, Training, 41*: 472–486.

Matte Blanco, I. (1975). *The Unconscious as Infinite Sets*. London: Karnac (Maresfield Library).

Matte Blanco, I. (1988). *Thinking, Feeling and Being*. London: Routledge.

Neborsky, R. J. (2003). A clinical model for the comprehensive treatment of trauma using an affect experiencing–attachment theory approach; In: M. Solomon & D. Siegel (Eds.), *Healing Trauma: Attachment, Mind, Body and Brain* (pp. 282–321). New York: Norton.

Ogden, P., Minton, K., & Pain, C. (2006). *Trauma and the Body: A Sensorimotor Approach to Psychotherapy*. New York: Norton.

Perry, J. W. (1970). Emotions and object relations. *Journal of Analytical Psychology, 15:* 1–12.

Racker, H. (1958). Psychoanalytic technique and the analyst's unconscious masochism. *Psychoanalytic Quarterly, 27:* 555–562.

Sandler, J. (1976). Counter-transference and role responsiveness. *International Journal of Psychoanalysis, 57:* 43–47.

Schore, A. N. (2003). *Affect Regulation and the Repair of the Self.* London: Norton.

Shriver, L. (2010). *We Need To Talk about Kevin.* London: Serpent's Tail.

Stark, M. (2006). Transformation of relentless hope: a relational approach to sadomasochism. Accessed July 2012 at: www.lifespanlearn.org/documents/STARKtranform.pdf .

Steiner, J. (1993). *Psychic Retreats: Pathological Organisations in Psychotic, Neurotic and Borderline Patients.* London: Routledge.

Stern, D. N. (1985). *The Interpersonal World of the Infant.* London: Karnac, 1998.

Symington, N. (1983). The analyst's act of freedom as agent of therapeutic change. *International Review of Psychoanalysis, 32:* 218–220.

Tronick, E. (2007). *The Neurobehavioural and Social-Emotional Development of Infants and Children.* New York: Norton.

Tronick, E. Z., & Gianino, A. (1986). Interactive mismatch and repair: challenges to the coping infant. *Zero to Three, 6*(3): 1–6. Also in: Tronick, E. (2007), *The Neurobehavioural and Social–Emotional Development of Infants and Children* (pp. 155–163). New York: Norton.

Van der Kolk, B. (1996). Trauma and memory. In: B. van der Kolk, A. McFarlane, & L. Weisaeth (Eds.), *Traumatic Stress: The Effects of Overwhelming Experience on Mind, Body and Society* (pp. 279–302). New York: Guildford Press.

West, M. A. S. (2007). *Feeling, Being and the Sense of Self: A New Perspective on Identity, Affect and Narcissistic Disorders.* New York: Karnac.

Wiener, J. (2010). Working in and with the transference. In: M. Stein (Ed.), *Jungian Psychoanalysis* (pp. 188–200). Chicago, IL: Open Court.

Winnicott, D. W. (1949). Hate in the counter-transference. *International Journal of Psychoanalysis, 30:* 69–74.

Winnicott, D. W. (1960). Theory of the parent–infant relationship. In: *Maturational Processes and the Facilitating Environment* (pp. 37–55). New York: International Universities Press, 1965.

Winson, J. (1990). The meaning of dreams. *Scientific American, November*: 86–96.

CHAPTER SEVEN

Beneath the skin: archetypal activity in psychosis

Maggie McAlister

"And what rough beast, its hour come round at last
Slouches towards Bethlehem to be born?"

(Yeats, 1919)

My interest in writing this chapter has emerged from my long-standing involvement in working with patients with severe and enduring mental health problems, particularly psychosis. I have been employed in an inpatient secure psychiatric hospital within the National Health Service for the past sixteen years, where the Forensic Psychotherapy Department offers group and individual treatment to mentally disordered offenders, as well as running Reflective Practice groups for staff members on the wards. We are working with patients who have a diagnosis of severe and enduring mental illness, largely paranoid schizophrenia, and who have committed grave offences. They come into contact with our service via the Criminal Justice System and their offences are often violent, and carried out largely as a result of their psychotic beliefs. They are, therefore, deemed to need treatment within a medium-security hospital setting in order to modify and risk assess their dangerousness. One can say of this client group that their symbolic mental functioning has broken down, leading to very concrete states of mind, as seen in their psychosis as well as in the enactment of their offences (Cordess & Cox, 1996). The offending behaviour also can be thought of as a wish to evacuate, through action, overwhelmingly intolerable states of mind (Morgan & Ruszczynski, 2007).

For the purposes of this chapter, I intend to explore Jung's legacy in working with psychosis, in particular the emergence of his theories of archetypes and the collective unconscious, and how these ideas might link creatively with contemporary clinical work and psychoanalytic theories. I am especially interested in drawing some parallels between the work of Jung and Wilfred Bion, specifically how psychotic archetypal activity might relate to Bion's later theories about mental functioning and areas of mental life that he describes as pre-natal functioning. This area of mental functioning Bion sees as thoughts that have not yet had a psychic birth, thoughts that are proto-mental, somatic–psychotic, and in the realm of "nameless dread". Bion described these as "thoughts without a thinker", which indicate the presence of a more profound aspect of the mind, housing "unthought thoughts" from which thinking emerges. On the whole, the ideas that Jung developed early in his career in relation to psychosis remained largely unchanged throughout his life. On the other hand, Bion's ideas did undergo a transformation and were largely ignored by his psychoanalytic colleagues as too "mystical". My intention in this chapter is to explore how Jung's concept of archetypal activity, as seen in psychosis, might resonate with Bion's later theories, in particular, the teleological aspects of the Jungian Self, and Bion's concept of O.

In order to explore these ideas further, it is important to first contextualise the main theories of Jung and Bion as emerging initially from their work as psychiatrists and their profound study of psychosis, from which both extrapolated a deeper understanding of the mind in illness and in health. One could also say at this point that both men had a personal experience of something akin to a psychotic breakdown: Jung, when he split from Freud, and Bion (Bion, 1982) who writes that he "died" on the Amiens–Roye road in 1917, an event that he felt was never sufficiently understood by Melanie Klein in his later analysis. An element in both of these experiences is a personal relationship to the areas of mind that one thinks of as psychotic, and a lifelong development of clinical enquiry as a result of these experiences.

When faced with a patient with deeply held psychotic beliefs (i.e., beliefs that are delusional and have no relationship to reality), the task for the analyst is to attempt to understand the potential meaning of the content of the psychosis while at the same time recognising that the psychosis is, in itself, an attack on meaning and a replacement of, or defence against, reality, that is, an attack on the subject's own mind, the object that can perceive reality. Although many of the patients with whom I work have a diagnosis of formal thought disorder, one often discovers that there is one particularly persistent delusion or psychotic narrative that holds a compelling reality for the patient—a reality in the internal world, if not an external reality. Delusional beliefs are extremely persistent and enduring, despite all attempts at reality testing, and in my forensic setting they can create extreme danger, as it is often these beliefs that have led to violent offending in the past. In the fragmentation of the mind, the psyche appears to produce a container, as it were, into which the parts of the self can be re-gathered and meaning restored, even though what is communicated is mad and, to a large extent, meaningless. It is also often after the fragmentation of the mind that the psychotic beliefs begin, as a way to shape meaning out of, or defend against, an experience of nameless dread. This idea was explored by Schmidt in his paper "Psychic skin" (2012), where, following on from Bick (1968) and Symington (1985), he describes the achievement of a psychic skin as providing a containing and protective function of the psyche. In psychotic states, this containing function is breached and the individual is left in constant fear of spilling out into "disintegrated states". What the individual disintegrates into is, in some ways, the focus of this chapter, as, in the absence of a containing ego function, the psyche falls or disintegrates into a deeper layer of archetypal material, or beta-elements, an idea that has been explored by Dehing (1994) in his paper "Containment—an archetype? Meaning of madness in Jung and Bion". The loss of the psychic skin, or alpha function, creates the search for a different kind of container: beta elements/archetypal activity seeking a "realisation" to produce a "conception". This different kind of container is what seems to be produced in the positive symptoms of schizophrenia: delusions and hallucinations that seek to evacuate/expel (and, in some ways, communicate) not only the catastrophe of the psychosis, but also, by synthesis, the *meaning* of it. For example, a male patient was approached by police when he had been standing against a school wall for several hours with his arms and legs splayed. He called to them to stay back as he was caught in a spider's web and was afraid they would likewise become ensnared. The imagery of the spider's web created psychic meaning for an experience that was very real, terrifying, and utterly "unknowable" for the patient.

Jung's early work in psychosis and main theories

Jung was one of the earliest pioneers in the field of analysis to work with severely ill patients, and, towards the end of his life, he commented that in 1900 he was the very first to work psychotherapeutically with schizophrenia, which did not begin in psychoanalysis until the 1950s with the work of Bion and Segal. Jung's deep interest in psychosis remained active and strong until the end of his life. In 1956, five years before his death, he wrote "Recent thoughts on schizophrenia", and, in 1957, the paper "Schizophrenia". His later papers remain consistent with his clinical findings in his earlier work, and from these papers one can identify four main points about Jung's ideas about psychosis:

● the disintegration of thoughts to the points of meaninglessness. There is a destruction of all former connections;
● the very foundations of the personality are impaired. The unity of the personality is almost irreversibly damaged;
● the ego loses all power to resist the power of the unconscious;
● there is an emergence of a collective component to psychotic imagery.

As a young psychiatrist, Jung worked at the Burghölzli, the main psychiatric hospital in Zurich, and, under Eugen Bleuler, began using association tests to probe the minds of psychotic patients, which led him to formulate the theory of complexes. He wrote his doctoral dissertation on the disintegration of ideas in dementia praecox, the condition Bleuler renamed schizophrenia, meaning "divided mind". In this early work, Jung discovered that the contents of delusional beliefs in schizophrenia could be recognised as having a compensatory function, but he found that they were disintegrated to the point of meaninglessness. However, unlike the psychiatric colleagues of his day, for whom the content of delusional beliefs was largely irrelevant and unimportant, Jung was interested in discovering the meaning of these psychotic experiences for the individual. He stated,

> In many cases in psychiatry, the patient who comes to us has a story that is not told, and which as a rule no one knows of. To my mind, therapy only really begins after the investigation of that wholly personal story. It is the patient's secret, the rock against which he is shattered. In therapy the problem is always the whole person, never the symptom alone. (1963, p. 138)

This intuitive understanding led Jung to spend many hours working psychotherapeutically with patients, listening closely to them and attempting to reach them. He describes this rather beautifully as "a kind of attentive entering into the personality of the patient" (1963, p. 150). He stated,

> Through my work with the patients, I realised that paranoid ideas and hallucinations contain a germ of meaning. A personality, a life history, a pattern of hopes and desires lies behind the psychosis. The fault is ours if we do not understand them. (1963, p. 149)

This early, ten-year period at the Burghölzli sowed the seeds for many of Jung's later theories, and, from his description of his work at this time, we also get an insight into the beginning of his method, his way of being with his patients, based very much on individuality. "I treat every patient as individually as possible, because the solution to the problem is always an individual one" (1963, p. 152). This kind of attentive entering into each individual case led Jung to put a strong emphasis on the doctor as person. The nature of psychotic upheaval forced him to realise that in the therapeutic situation, the therapist as well as the patient may be called upon to undergo profound development. He used the idea of chemical interaction to describe how thoroughly patient and therapist interact with one another. For this reason, he advised that a prospective analyst have a training analysis, to learn to know his own psyche and take it seriously before attending to the psyche of another. Jung was the first to insist on a training analysis, and it is was one of his important contributions to psychoanalysis. These ideas are later found in the work of Searles (1965) and Bion's ideas of projective identification as a communication, where the therapist must largely bear the impacts from the patient.

Jung's basic attitude to the psyche was that affect was the central organising principle of psychic life (1907). "The illness often breaks out at a moment of some great emotion" (Jung 1908, par. 333). This led him to consider the impact of trauma, or unbearable affect, on the ego, and he saw this as something that cannot be processed by the ego; it must be split off. The psyche's normal reaction to a traumatic event is to withdraw from the scene of the trauma. However, if withdrawal is not possible, then a part of the self must be withdrawn, and for this to happen the otherwise integrated ego must split into fragments or dissociate. Jung saw dissociation as a normal part of the psyche's defences against trauma's potentially damaging impact, which he demonstrated with his word association test. Furthermore, Jung placed equal emphasis on the traumatic impact of unconscious phantasies as well as the actual traumatic event. He saw traumatic unconscious phantasies as having the same impact as real traumatic events. The parts of the psyche that are split off and dissociated allow external life to go on, but at a great cost. The trauma ends and its effects might be largely lost to consciousness, but the dissociated affects continue to haunt the individual in the form of certain images which cluster around a strong affect—what Jung called the "feeling toned complexes". Jung discovered that these disturbing aspects of the psyche, which are completely split off from the rest of the personality, exert an autonomous influence on the ego, operating almost like sub-personalities at times of severe stress. In his essay on trauma, he wrote,

> . . . a traumatic complex brings about dissociation of the psyche. The complex is not under the control of the will and for this reason it possesses the quality of psychic autonomy. Its autonomy consists in its power to manifest itself independently of the will and even in direct opposition to conscious tendencies: it forces itself tyrannically upon the conscious mind. The explosion of affect is a complete invasion of the individual, it pounces upon him like an enemy or a wild animal. I have frequently observed that the typical traumatic affect is represented in dreams as a wild and dangerous animal – a striking illustration of its autonomous nature when split off from consciousness. (1928, pars 266–267)

In this way, Jung was interested in dissociative splits in the psyche, or vertical splits, which separate off entire aspects of the personality into discrete entities. An important point to make here is that Jung intuited that the agent doing the splitting was something other than the ego, because of the strength of the dissociation and the autonomous way the split-off contents could act on the ego. He saw the ego as being but one of many "complexes", and this is a new perspective, fundamentally different from Freud's formulation in which the psyche is seen as part of a topographical structure, with the ego as the repressing agent. From this, one sees the emergence of Jung's concept of the self, which he conceived of as a central organising archetype within the psyche, underpinning all psychic activity within the individual, and constantly evolving to create psychic growth and new potential. It is beyond the ego, as it contains and transcends ego functioning, encompassing a psychic totality, conscious and unconscious. The self cannot be fully known as it is unconscious and always evolving, ineffable and infinite, the central archetype, within which all other archetypal activity is produced and contained.

Jung's conceptualisation of vertical splits in the psyche and feeling-toned complexes came from work with patients suffering with acute forms of psychosis, most notably schizophrenia. Jung was aware of the numinous power of these split-off contents and the way in which they appear to possess the individual and overwhelm the ego completely. This numinous power of the unconscious contents was evident in the power, terror, and awe his patients felt for their hallucinatory and delusional experiences. The experiences did not feel as if they were originating from within, but had the quality of a compelling external force or agency. "It is as if the very foundations of the psyche were giving way, as if an explosion or an earthquake were tearing asunder the structure of a normally built house" (1939, par. 522).

Jung viewed the inner world of his psychotic patients as filled with gods and demons that exerted irresistible power over the mind and defied all attempts at reality testing. Furthermore, these inner figures had a quality of timelessness; they were infinitely enduring and changeless. When Jung then experienced his own "psychotic crisis" after his break with Freud (1912–1916), he began an intense period of work on his own personal "confrontation with the unconscious", and it was here that he approached the meaning of his experiences with a "synthetic–constructive" method, feeling that Freud's "analytic–deductive" method was too limited. This personal experience was pivotal to the development of two profound and far-reaching approaches to the psyche. The first was his emphasis on a synthetic–constructive treatment method (linked to the activity of the self). The second, his awareness that the psyche is embroiled in eternalities, led him to the idea of archetypes and the collective unconscious, which enabled him to explore the meaning of psychosis in its religious or mythic aspects. He states, "As early as 1909 I realised that I could not treat latent psychoses if I did not understand their symbolism. It was then that I began to study mythology" (1963, p. 153).

His study of mythology gave birth to a method called amplification, in which mythological content is used to amplify the psychotic material in order to discover the purpose or goal of the psyche. Jung's approach in working with such cases was that there had to be a search for meaning, leading him to ask such questions as "what does this symptom mean for the development of the whole person?" or "what is the purpose of this symptom?" This search for a purpose or constructive meaning applies to all aspects of work, including dreams as well as symptoms. In this way, Jung saw value in some of the most disturbing symptoms of severe illness, regarding them not as purely pathological, but also as an attempt by the psyche to heal itself. In the case of severe illness, Jung saw the teleological aspects of hallucinations and delusions as being purposive for the psyche, as holding meaning in relation to the development and goal of the individual.

Jung's personal psychotic crisis concluded with his publication of *Symbols of Transformation* (1912), a major work in which his departure from Freud's psychoanalysis is made clear. The main focus of this work is the analysis of a psychotic case, Schreber, and their correspondence about the case, towards the end of their collaboration, illustrates the fundamental conceptual differences that ultimately led to their split. One of their disagreements was regarding the existence of an archetypal layer of material, the other the teleological purpose of the psychosis. In *Symbols of Transformation*, Jung firmly introduces his synthetic–constructive method in its purposive aspect. He writes,

> When we apply these insights to that class of mental patient to which Schreber belongs, we must, from the objective–scientific standpoint, reduce the fantasy-structure to its simple fundamental elements. This is what Freud has done. But that is only one half of the work. The other half is the constructive understanding of Schreber's system. The question is: What is the goal the patient tried to reach through the creation of his system?" (1912, par. 408)

Behind Schreber's psychosis, Jung saw the constant unconscious activity of the self as attempting to heal pathological splits, particularly between the maternal and paternal self-objects. Schreber felt that God was trying to transform him not only into a woman, but also a man and a woman in one person, "having an intercourse with myself". This kind of sexual imagery is very resonant to Jung, and he often used sexual metaphor to describe cogently psychic processes: the union of opposites, the syzygy of male and female, as in the Rosarium wood carvings, and his alchemical writings in the *Mysterium Coniunctionis*. In this search for separation and new union, Jung felt that the first and main task for the psyche was separation from the mother. This was a very important and far-reaching formulation of the essential problem facing the psyche, and it was years before the mother–infant relationship became a primary focus in psychoanalysis, notably in the work of Winnicott, Bion, and Segal. Jung anticipated this development through his own interpretation of the Schreber case, although his emphasis was always more on the archetypal mother than the personal mother. However, in post-Jungian thought, there would be more of the interplay, or indivisibility, of the personal and archetypal, how the archetypal needs to be humanised through contact with, and attachment to, the personal mother. In the developmental post-Jungian school, we recognise the interdependency of the personal and archetypal levels of the psyche: what is personal has an archetypal dimension and what is archetypal has a personal dimension. If there is a difficulty in the personal realm, however, one "disintegrates" into the archetypal realm, with all the benefits and perils that this entails.

Bion's early work on psychosis

Whereas Jung's interest in the psychotic imagery of his Burghölzli patients feels lively and excited, Bion seems to start from a very different place. Reading Bion's early work on psychosis, we are met with a very bleak landscape indeed, a language of abstractions and mathematics, a grid and alpha–beta elements. He was concerned with the process of how we know what we know, the evolution from inborn psychic structure to psychic existence, how a rudimentary proto-thought becomes a thought available for thinking, that is, becomes a psychic event.

Bion's careful scrutiny of the process of thinking was born from his early work in groups (1961), where, through the discovery of basic assumption activity (fight/flight, dependency, and pairing) in the "basic assumption group", he recognised the existence of universal unconscious behaviour, born from emotional experience, which affects the conscious activity of the "work group". This led him to conceive of a kind of "proto-mental life" in the individual and the group, from which thinking emerges. When he came to work more specifically with psychosis, he developed far-reaching theories of the mind. The writings collected in *Second Thoughts* outline his major theories at the time (1967). Bion conceived of what he called "beta elements", sensorial impressions that are not yet represented on the psychic level, but which are found in the body, the psychosomatic realm, and in "positive" psychotic symptoms such as hallucinations and delusions. These beta elements needed the action of "alpha function" (found in the mind of the mother—her reverie) in order to be transformed into "alpha elements"—thoughts that become available for thinking.

> Normal development follows if the relationship between infant and breast permits the infant to project a feeling, say, that it is dying into the mother and to reintroject it after its sojourn in the breast has made it tolerable to the infant psyche. If the projection is not accepted by the mother the infant feels that its feeling that it is dying is stripped of such meaning as it has. It therefore reintrojects, not a fear of dying made tolerable, but a nameless dread. (Bion, 1962, p. 116)

Like Jung, Bion also saw the psyche as being based on affectivity, and he replaced Freud's drive theory with the idea of emotional links between objects—love, hate, and knowledge (L, H, K). The experience of nameless dread is psychotic in nature, and, when reality is too dreadful to bear, a defence against the experience is produced.

In this way, Bion sees hallucinations as an evacuation of beta elements through the sensory perceptive organs, creating "bizarre objects". Delusions are, likewise, an attack on reality, and a total replacement of knowledge (K) with omnipotence ($-K$).

Although Bion was concerned with the psychotic mechanisms that produce symptoms such as we see in formal thought disorder, he was less concerned with the content of delusional beliefs except that they served a function in evacuating intolerable experience, expressing hatred of reality. However, Bion did conceive of psychosis as containing the personal "myth" of the patient, conveying a psychotic narrative (alongside "sense"—the sensorial experience of the psychosis, and "passion", the feeling-tone of the psychosis) that, similarly to Jung's conception, contains a germ of meaning. It is his later work that begins to move more into areas that we might think of as particularly "Jungian", as follows.

Jung's archetypal activity and Bion's pre-natal functioning

Jung's concept of archetypal material may find some resonance in what Bion later came to conceive of as "pre-natal" aspects of psychic functioning. This is an area of psychic life that I understand as relating to thoughts that have not yet crossed the contact barrier between unconscious and conscious. In his later work, Bion became interested in the idea of rudimentary sensory development in foetal life as he traced back developments in his earlier work on psychosis about proto-mental phenomena and proto-mental systems (1961), which he later recast as beta elements (1962). His thinking about beta elements developed into the conjecture that they might link up with corresponding mental counterparts (inherent preconceptions) to form primitive proto-conceptions awaiting psychic birth and post-natal development for further processing (Grotstein, 2007). His interest in this area was about the quality of the caesura (act of "birth") in which these proto-conceptions can link up, or connect with, a realisation leading to the development of thought and alpha function. ". . . can we catch the germ of an idea and plant it where it can begin to be developed until it acquires the necessary maturity to be born?" (Bion, 1980, p. 84).

The pre-natal aspects of mental functioning, therefore, require a caesura/container in order to gestate and become incarnate, or finite, as opposed to remaining in an infinitised (unconscious) state. Thus, the troubling beta elements of pre-natal life need to meet a caesura, a contact barrier or membrane which can function as a boundary between pre-natal and post-natal existence, or conscious and unconscious systems, and which unite, disunite, and define separate parts of the mind (Grotstein, 2007, p. 257). Without a contact barrier or membrane, this thinking apparatus is seen to have enormous damage and deficits, as observed in patients with formal thought disorder and psychotic processes. This leads to an overwhelmingly concrete state of mind where there is an enormously damaged capacity to separate inner and outer reality. Patients who develop enduring psychotic illness can be thought of as having had a catastrophic breach to this contact barrier or thinking apparatus, a catastrophe that Bion states is signalled by their psychosis. When this breach becomes overwhelmed by crisis, it is then that psychotic delusional beliefs often develop, almost as a way for the damaged psyche to create meaning and develop a new container, serving to protect the individual from further crises. This is what Bion refers to as the "myth" of the psychotic patient. The psychosis, in this sense, becomes a matter of an attempt to create a container for meaning, although this meaning is a transformation in $-K$ as opposed to O, an omnipotent "knowing" of reality, rather than an "unknowing" in the service of individuation.

Jung's teleological self and Bion's transformations in O

We can compare Jung's concept of the self to Bion's conception of O, which Grotstein has defined in the following way. "O designates an ineffable, inscrutable, and constantly evolving domain that intimates an aesthetic completeness and coherence". He refers to it by different terms, "Absolute Truth", "Ultimate reality", or "reverence and awe". "Thoughts without a thinker" derive from O. They are the 'unborns,' the 'intimations of immortality' that we seemingly experience as located within our inner cosmos, but they are placeless, unlocatable" (Grotstein, 2012, p. 1).

If we think of archetypal activity as being the "unborns", the "intimations of immortality", we can see a strong resonance between Jung and Bion's interest in this area of mental functioning, which is similar to psychotic thinking. I am thinking particularly of the content of delusional systems, which often revolve around powerful archetypal images and figures such as gods and demons. Grotstein states, "O overreaches heaven and hell ('nameless dread') in its paradoxical sweep" (Grotstein, 2012, p. 3).

The "paradoxical sweep" is central to the idea of the self as an archetype, a bi-polar totality encompassing light and dark. For individuation, one needs to consider the dark side of the self, the "hell" of

O as part of what O encompasses. Jung is clear that the primal self is an integrate of extremely powerful energies (love and hate, creation and destruction). There is no moral judgement on what is dark and light, rather that creativity, like God, is morally neutral. It has two sides, construction and destruction. Both are in the service of the whole. In the same way, he saw the archetype of the self as having this bi-polar, morally neutral quality. Therefore, the activity of the self may not be in the service of the ego but will be in the service of the whole, the totality of the psyche.

The mythic language: clinical vignette

When we encounter something akin to a breach in the psychic boundary that separates the collective from the personal unconscious, we are faced with a substream of psychic material that Jung thought of as archetypal and Bion conceived as "O", a universal mythic language that transcends and completely overwhelms the psychic boundaries of the individual. In this way, psychotic material is binocular in that it both communicates this breach through the content of the psychosis and signals what Eigen calls a "state of disaster" (Eigen, 2010, p. 47) for the individual, a collapse of meaning and an attack on reality and one's perceiving mind. Darren Aronofsky's film *Black Swan* is an interesting example of a psychotic state in this binocular vision. The central character, a prima ballerina who is under extreme pressure rehearsing the lead role in *Swan Lake*, begins to develop delusions about her skin. The delusions take the form of the appearance of an outbreak of something beneath her skin, which we discover to be feathers. This becomes clearer as she struggles to integrate the Black Swan and White Swan in her performance, and also in her personality. The background story is her attempt to separate from her controlling, intrusive relationship with her mother, who keeps her infantilised and de-potentiated throughout the film. In terms of the specific symptom of her delusional system, there is the signalling of a breach of psychic reality through her delusions about her skin, her psychic skin as it were, but also the communication of the quality of that catastrophe through the content of her delusional system, the emergence of the Black Swan character. Experienced first as a sensory impression/ "outbreak" through her skin, the delusion overwhelms her body and physical self entirely, and, correspondingly, her ego functioning and persona utterly, to an ultimately devastating conclusion. The idea of delusions, with their dual functions, acting as a psychic skin has been discussed by Schmidt (2012).

To protect confidentiality, I have disguised the following clinical vignette and drawn on a number of cases that share common factors without losing any of the main features and central dynamics of the work.

Mr Z is a man in his forties who has been in our secure unit for a number of years following an index offence of grievous bodily harm with intent as a result of paranoid delusions about his skin. This took the particular form of believing that there was a military weapon being designed by the government that specifically attacks the skin of the victim, leaving permanent disfigurement. However, the weapon itself leaves no trace and is only known about through the effects that it causes, which is to gradually change the appearance of the skin so that it becomes permanently scarred and disfigured. The nature of the attack is largely a psychological one, in that the victim is not disabled or impaired, but can continue to function and live life. Therefore, the damage stays at the level of appearance, and, in this sense, is largely a "psychological attack". These beliefs led Mr Z to believe that he was the victim of such an attack, targeted by government agents who had used this weapon through an open window in his room while he was sleeping. When he woke, he felt that a catastrophic breach had taken place, and, frightened for his life, he became paranoid and then committed a violent act, which he perceived as self-preservative. This involved burning and attacking the skin of a passer-by whom he was convinced was attempting to harm him in some way. Mr Z managed to escape, and a few nights after the attack, while looking in the mirror, he pieced together his (delusional) understanding of what had happened: that the passer-by was an agent with a secret weapon that had damaged his skin and that there was a governmental conspiracy to disfigure people in this way.

The creation of his delusional system, in front of a mirror, was an attempt by his psyche to piece together a meaningful explanation for an overwhelmingly fragmented or disintegrated state that was experienced as intensely threatening, persecuting, and a breach of his body boundaries, or psychic skin. In this way, there was a descent into a mythic narrative that held together an omnipotent "knowing" of what had taken place, for what otherwise would remain meaningless, unknowable, and utterly terrifying. The archetypal stratum of material in this case is that of losing one's skin, being penetrated and damaged by a toxic substance that permanently destroys one's body boundary, burning and disfiguring one's identity and sense of personal integrity. The beta elements in this case have a sensory quality of burning and acute impingement, an attack on one's essence, which Mr Z describes as "implanting a psychological attack" beneath the skin.

When I first started seeing Mr Z for psychotherapy, this narrative had been modified somewhat by his cognitive recognition that these ideas were delusional. However, at times of strong emotion, he was inclined to resort to seeing his beliefs as factual and real, and they continued to exert a strong compulsion for him during the course of our work. In our first meeting, he sat with arms crossed, engaging in a dialogue with me that mainly took the form of questions and answers, as if I were a legal representative, or an agent myself, and he was attempting to ward off any contact that might be experienced as too penetrating and damaging. Despite my attempts to offer transference interpretations based on the quality of our interaction and ways in which he might be quite anxious about me and what I was attempting to discover or implant within him, this remained a central feature of our interaction.

The first "breakthrough" came several months later, when I felt Mr Z had relaxed sufficiently to begin speaking more freely and spontaneously during our sessions, often about difficulties in his past and in his relationships with his family, but also ruminating in considerable detail about aspects of his legal case. It was during one such rumination that he spoke about the belief that he had been "stitched up" by his solicitors and the legal doctors involved in the decision about whether he had been fit to plead and stand trial for his index offence. I became aware that I, likewise, could be perceived to be stitching him up in that, by opening up with me, he was demonstrating that he was still a risk to the public due to his persistent beliefs about the military weapon and the delusional idea that I and others knew about it and hid this knowledge from him for our own ends. It was likely that he was experiencing the whole treatment as a potential stitch-up. I reflected on these thoughts, presenting them to him as a possible dilemma, in that he was unclear about my intentions, whether or not

I would do him further harm. This startled him, but it seemed to hit a nerve, as he was at pains to impress upon me that this was not the case. However, after this, over time, we were able to begin to find a language together which acknowledged the conviction of his beliefs, while keeping them suspended as something neither true nor false, thereby not becoming too invested in whether or not they were objectively. This allowed us some "triangular space" (Britton, 1989) in which to consider the emotional reality of the beliefs (Bion's "sense, passion and myth"), the experience of acute attack, and impingement affecting his identity and sense of self, which he must keep at bay, at all costs. In thinking about the constructive–synthetic meaning of his illness, I attempted to treat it as a subjectively real emotional experience, leaving the other objective reality of the beliefs outside the remit of our work. I began to focus on the personal myth of the delusions, as containing something very real for the patient at an emotional and psychological level. This followed from his own insistence that the attack was mainly a "psychological one". In this way, we were able to begin examining his beliefs as something that contained a compelling psychological reality for him and become more focused on understanding the meaning of this.

My approach in working with Mr Z was an attempt to understand the teleological purpose of these dangerous beliefs, in so far as they were, in themselves, a communication of meaning of the inner state of Mr Z and, like Schreber's, served a goal that Mr Z is trying to reach. So, immediately one is faced with a question about how to think of such material from a synthetic–constructive position, from a position of something "not yet known".

Countering this is Bion's understanding of psychosis; the underlying problem that whatever psychotic imagery can mean is overshadowed by the fact that a catastrophe is signalled, as Eigen put it, "Psychotic language is like an SOS in progress" (2010, p. 48). The burning skin solution had the quality of a beta element in that it was raw sensorial data, with a pronounced alien character, and the strength and autonomy of the delusion that erupted at a time of violent affect had completely overwhelmed Mr Z's capacity for ego function/reality testing. However, in thinking about the idea that archetypal activity contains some alpha elements within it, there is an aspect of the delusional beliefs that serves to communicate and seek a "realisation" in which to produce a new conception through the action of container–contained. My model in working with a patient such as Mr Z is an attempt to use my countertransference as a way in which to provide reverie and alpha function for the patient. Sometimes, Mr Z has experienced me as also being aligned to the conspiracy, feeling that if he discussed these matters with me in too much detail, I would "stitch him up" to the Ministry of Justice and prevent his eventual discharge. In this way, I become personified as the "breach" within the room, within the relationship. Mr Z has been the "victim" of many such breaches in his early life, and his psychotic system can be seen as an attempt to ward off any further breaches to his psychic skin. The work we have been engaged in is an attempt to discover a language that has the potential to express this sensorial experience (of being invaded, attacked, conspired against) and define its psychological meaning, giving psychic birth to an archetypal experience that otherwise remains in an "unborn" state. In working with psychosis, the therapist must bear witness to the emerging meaning of the psychotic language and imagery and supply a context. With Jung and Bion, the particular emphasis is an attentive entering into the personality of the patient in order to recognise these states of disaster and bear them for the patient, whom they both understood could not bear witness, but could only become embroiled in an infinite cosmos, becoming orphans of O.

To turn to literature for a moment, I think this predicament is beautifully expressed by Yann Martel in his novel *Life of Pi*. In a section where the orphaned, shipwrecked Pi is adrift on his life-raft during the night, he is overwhelmed with terror by the canopy of stars and the attendant experience of vast emptiness and no-thingness around him.

> The volume of things was confounding – the volume of air above me, the volume of water around and beneath me. I was half moved, half-terrified. I felt like the sage Markandeya, who fell out of Vishnu's mouth while Vishnu was sleeping and so beheld the entire universe, everything that there is. Before the sage could die of fright, Vishnu awoke and took him back into his mouth. (Martel, p. 177)

Direct experience of archetypal experience, without the mediation/containment of the ego, is to become an orphan of the Real—an orphan in the way Bion felt he was orphaned on the Amiens–Roye road. The central challenge in working with psychosis is how to contain and mediate an experience and plant the germ of meaning where it can begin to be developed until it is ready to be born. This is the synthetic–constructive approach at its best, describing an evolution from inborn psychic structure to psychic existence; allowing the birth of a thought that is not a rough beast, neither a god nor a demon, but fully "realised" suffering made incarnate, human, and finite. Bion believed that the true purpose of analysis was to learn how to "suffer", to acknowledge and bear the reality of experience (Bion, 1970, p. 7). This is the fundamental difficulty of work in the area of psychotic illness.

Acknowledgement

I would like to thank John Gordon for invaluable help and comments on an early draft of this chapter.

References

Bick, E. (1968). The experience of the skin in early object relations. *International Journal of Psychoanalysis, 49*: 484–486.
Bion, W. R. (1961). *Experiences in Groups.* London: Tavistock.
Bion, W. R. (1962). A theory of thinking. *International Journal of Psycho-analysis, 43*: 4–5.
Bion, W. R. (1967). *Second Thoughts.* London: Karnac.
Bion, W. R. (1970). *Attention and Interpretation: A Scientific Approach to Insight in Psychoanalysis and Groups,* London: Karnac.
Bion, W. R. (1980). *Bion in New York and Sao Paulo.* Strathtay, Perthshire: Clunie Press.
Bion, W. R. (1982). *The Long Week-End 1897–1919: Part of a Life.* F. Bion (Ed.). Abingdon: Fleetwood Press.
Britton, R. (1989). The missing link: parental sexuality in the Oedipus complex. In: R. Britton, M Feldman, & E. O'Shaughnessy, *The Oedipus Complex Today* (pp. 83–101). London: Karnac.
Cordess, C., & Cox, M. (Eds.) (1996). *Forensic Psychotherapy: Crime, Psychodynamics and the Offender Patient.* London: Jessica Kingsley.
Dehing, J. (1994). Containment—an archetype? Meaning of madness in Jung and Bion. *Journal of Analytical Psychology, 39*: 419–461
Eigen, M. (2010). *Madness and Murder.* London: Karnac.

Grotstein, J. (2007). *A Beam of Intense Darkness: Wilfrid Bion's Legacy to Psychoanalysis*. London: Karnac.

Grotstein, J. (2012). Bion's "transformation in 'O'" and the concept of the "transcendent position". Accessed at: www.sicap.it—merciai/bion/papers/grots.htm.

Jung, C. G. (1907). *The Psychology of Dementia Praecox, C.W., 3*, R. F. C. Hull (Trans.). London: Routledge.

Jung, C. G. (1908). *The Content of the Psychoses, C.W., 3*, R. F. C. Hull (Trans.). London: Routledge.

Jung, C. G. (1912). *Symbols of Transformation, C.W., 5*, R. F. C. Hull (Trans.). London: Routledge.

Jung, C. G. (1928). *The Psychological Foundations of the Belief in Spirits, C.W., 8*, R. F. C. Hull (Trans.). London: Routledge.

Jung, C. G. (1939). On the psychogenesis of schizophrenia, *C.W., 3*, R. F. C. Hull (Trans.). London: Routledge.

Jung, C. G. (1956). Recent thoughts on schizophrenia, *C.W., 3*, R. F. C. Hull (Trans.). London: Routledge.

Jung, C. G. (1958). Schizophrenia, *C.W., 3*, R. F. C. Hull (Trans.). London: Routledge.

Jung, C. G. (1963). *Memories, Dreams, Reflections*, A. Jaffé (Ed.). New York: Random House.

Martel, Y. (2002). *Life of Pi*. Edinburgh: Canongate Books.

Morgan D., & Ruszczynski, S. (Eds.) (2007). *Lectures on Violence, Perversion and Delinquency: The Portman Papers*. London: Karnac.

Schmidt, M. (2012). Psychic skin: psychotic defences, borderline process and delusions. *Journal of Analytical Psychology, 57*: 21–39.

Searles, H. F. (1965). *Collected Papers on Schizophrenia and Related Subjects*. London: Hogarth Press and the Institute of Psychoanalysis.

Symington, J. (1985). The survival function of primitive omnipotence. *International Journal of Psychoanalysis, 66*: 481–487.

Yeats, W. B. (1919). The second coming. In: *W. B. Yeats Selected Poems* (p. 124), 1991–2000 Penguin Modern Classics. London: Penguin.

PART V
TECHNIQUE: INTEGRATION

CHAPTER EIGHT

Creating a skin for imagination, reflection, and desire

Brian Feldman

Introduction

The creation of a secure internal space for the experience of thought, imagination and reflection occurs within the intersubjective matrix of the relationship between baby and (m)other (Ainsworth, 1978; Stern et al., 1998; Tronick, 2007). The development of this secure internal space depends both upon the innate capacities of the infant, the quality of the infant–(m)other attachment, and the ability of the infant–(m)other couple to co-create meaningful experiences that can be generated, integrated, and assimilated and that, over time and through the repeated experience of meaningful interaction, form the scaffolding and structure of the infantile psyche. Interactions between baby and (m)other that involve the surface of the body, the skin, are critical in the evolution of the infant's sense of a bounded internal space that is separated from the external world through a boundary experienced as the skin (Bick, 1968). When the experience of the skin as a boundary between the internal and external realms has evolved, the individual is able to experience living within their own individual skin, separate but interconnected with significant others. Secure attachment (Ainsworth, 1978) is facilitated through the evolution of a primary skin function (Feldman, 2004) that can serve as a container of psychological and emotional experience, and this primary skin function evolves through the sensitive interactions, both bodily and emotional, between the baby and the mothering figure. Bick emphasises the importance of the capacity of the (m)other to physically *hold* the baby in whatever physical or emotional state the infant is in. The mother's capacity to both tolerate, mediate, soothe, and transform the often terrifying mental states of the baby into more manageable and digestible experiences (Bion, 1962) is another significant factor in the evolution of a secure attachment relationship and in the development of a primary skin function. Infant observation using the Bick (1964) method has been helpful in being able to understand the importance of the skin in infancy, and has helped to provide evidence that the evolution of a healthy primary skin function promotes containment, reflection, and thought. The emergence of a secondary skin function involves bodily defences such as repetitive movement, freezing (Fraiberg, 1987), and addictive and auto-sensuous behaviours to help contain unbearable affects often stimulated by separation and abandonment (Tustin, 1990). In this chapter, I shall try to show how both primary and secondary skin functions develop within the context of two observations of infants from different cultural backgrounds, one from North America and the other from Latin America. I will also explore the importance of the primary and secondary skin functions for contemporary analytical work.

The significance of the infant observation method and its relevance for the development of theory

Through the careful observation of infants, we have been able to see that as development unfolds the skin becomes an increasingly important container of psychological, emotional, and erotic/sensuous experience for the infant (Anzieu, 1989; Bick, 1968; McDougall, 1989). The transformation of the somatic skin into an internalised psychic skin is facilitated through complex interactional sequences between baby and (m)other: the infant's ongoing bathing in words (Anzieu, 1989), the emotional interchanges that provide the baby with the psychological nourishment related to affective attunement (Stern, 1985), and physical touch, which, when sensitively experienced, provides a foundation for the evolution of the primary skin function (Feldman, 2004). Early interpersonal experiences within the infant–(m)other couple that impede the development of a coherent psychic skin or primary skin function are often a major focus in the analysis of children, adolescents, and adults who suffer from identity disorders, eating disorders, disorders of the skin, sleep disorders, and auto-sensuous addictions that can impede both psychological growth and the development of individuation processes. These disorders can be related to the emergence of a secondary skin function (which Bick calls second skin), that impedes psychological and emotional development through the excessive use of bodily defences. When bodily defences are dominant in the personality, emotional development can be severely impacted.

Within the field of analytical psychology, Fordham (1985) suggested that the individuation processes as well as the capacity for symbolisation begin in infancy and that when symbolisation difficulties emerge in the analysis of the child, adolescent, or adult, then the infantile components of the psyche need to be explored in depth. In this regard, Fordham expanded upon Jung's original speculations on the meaning of the symbol, symbolisation, and the transcendent function in analysis, and he explored the developmental origins of the capacity to use symbolisation processes for the purposes of growth, development and individuation.

In analysis, when symbolisation processes mediated by the transcendent function are optimally operational, individuation and integration are able to proceed. However, when these processes are not able to function properly, the analysand can become mired in developmental impasses that are often dominated by what Fordham calls defences of the self (Fordham, 1985), and what Tustin (1990) terms autistic defences and autistic states of mind. Fordham (1985) made a major contribution to analytical psychology by emphasising that the self can become dominated by defensive patterns or defences of the self that profoundly curtail the possibility of developing functional symbolisation capacities. These defences of the self often have their origins in infancy, when bodily processes are unable to be transformed into a capacity for thought and symbolisation. The infant can remain stuck in auto-sensuous activities that preclude the growth of mental capacities such as reflective and imaginative functioning as well as symbolisation processes. Tustin (1990) and Bick (1968) have emphasised that the defences of the self are often experienced in a

sensory and bodily way, and that a secondary or defensive skin function can develop that impedes psychological, mental, and emotional
growth. Data from infant observation, infant research, and attachment
theory all point to the hypothesis that a secure attachment relationship
between a neurologically healthy baby and a stably present, mindful,
and sensitive attachment figure(s): male and/or female, father and/or
mother, or parents of either gender in a homosexual relationship
forms the foundation of healthy symbolisation, reflective and imaginative processes upon which the scaffolding (Vygotsky, 1997) of all
later psychological developments take place.

The infant observation method and its significance for analytical practice

The data from infant research and infant observation have an important relevance for the practice of analysis. Using the (m)other–infant
metaphor, we can speculate that, in analysis, the development of
symbolisation processes in the analysand are dependent upon the
analyst's capacity to maintain a symbolic attitude that provides a
secure internal space in which the meanings of images, reveries,
memories, and sensory experiences can unfold and take shape in the
potential space of the analytic encounter. Jung's concept of the analyst's symbolic attitude can be linked to Bion's conception of maternal
reverie. According to Bion (1962), maternal reverie fosters the transformation of sensory experiences of the infant into more mentalised
symbolic schemes that, in turn, create and facilitate the possibility of
the generation of meaning for the infant. The same can be applied to
the analytic couple. Using the mother–infant metaphor, Bion (1962)
postulates that the (m)other, in a state of reverie, is able to receive,
via projective identification, the infant's unmetabolised, unmentalised
sensory experiences, and transform them through a striving for
understanding into an emotional–bodily experience that is bearable
and manageable for the baby. Through this interactional sequence, the
baby feels more adequately held by the (m)other, and more contained
within her/his mind. We can see this type of interchange in infant
observations when a sensitive care-giver is able to communicate to the
baby both verbally and sensorially (through touch and holding) that
the baby is distressed, and that the care-giver is receptive to reflecting

on the baby's distress without immediately trying to change the baby's emotional or mental state. This requires of the care-giver a capacity to tolerate not knowing initially what the baby's distress may be about, while maintaining an emotional presence with the baby until the distress can be better understood and some meaning made out of the co-created experience. The care-giver in this interactional and intersubjective sequence provides what Vygotsky (1978) would term mediation, the provision of support and understanding that fosters the infant's growth and development. Given a healthy baby (neurologically and developmentally), this usually leads to the baby's becoming calmer and more secure (from an attachment standpoint) and fosters the experience of the (m)other as a secure base who provides safety, security, and comfort (Ainsworth, 1978).

The primary and secondary skin functions
as viewed through the lens of infant observation

Observation of babies with Bick's methodology indicates that there is a desire for a containing experience that involves the nipple securely held in the mouth, the sucking motions that lead to a good feed, the tactile feel of (m)other's skin, and the experience of being securely and firmly held in (m)other's arms. When this deeper connection is made between infant and care-giver, it can lead to a shared experience of satisfaction, mystery, and pleasure that helps to reinforce the baby's experience of security and primary (sensory and psychological) containment. This type of satisfying experience for both (m)other and baby leads the baby to develop a primary skin function and provides a scaffolding (Vygotsky, 1997) for the evolution of a psychological container. With the development of a primary skin function, the baby feels secure within his own skin and is able to tolerate periods of separateness from (m)other without undue anxiety. These experiences lay the foundations for a secure sense of self in relationship to an other and foster the development of reciprocity, containment, and intersubjectivity. The primary function of the psychic skin (Feldman, 2004) provides a vessel or container that retains positive affects of goodness, fullness, warmth, and love and is supported by the bathing in words and affects that the care-giver engages in for the benefit of the infant's growth and development.

The French analysts Anzieu (1989) and McDougall (1989) present the helpful metaphor of the skin as a containing psychic envelope. The skin envelope as a mental representation emerges from the interplay between the mother's body and the child's body. When the containing function is adequately introjected, the baby is able to acquire the concept of a space within the self and can begin to conceptualise that both she and her (m)other are contained within their respective skins. When a faulty skin function develops, a defensive process can emerge that Bick terms a "second skin" function. When a secondary, or faulty, skin function develops, the infant can evolve a precocious independence from the primary attachment figure and can appear to be functioning in an autonomous manner. This premature autonomy can mask feelings of excessive anxiety, extreme forms of avoidant attachment, and the use of auto-sensuous behaviours for self-soothing and comfort. A second-skin defensive pattern can also lead to the excessive use of thinking, language, or muscularity to help create a feeling of pseudo-containment.

This type of second skin phenomenon was apparent in my observation of infant Maria. In the following sequence, muscularity is used as an attempt to contain unbearable, painful emotions, and this points to the possibility of defensive elements emerging within the infant, as psychic development is impeded.

Infant observation vignette: Maria at four months and two weeks

When I arrive for the observation, I let myself into the house, as requested, without knocking or ringing. Maria is alone in the family room, strapped into a mobile chair with wheels. The family have always waited expectantly for the observation, have never cancelled a meeting, and have expressed very positive feelings about having me observe Maria in the context of family life. It is 8.30 a.m. Maria cannot move the mobile chair as it is on the carpet. As I sit down to assume my place of observer, I begin to hear stirring in the background. Anna, Maria's thirty-eight-year-old mother, comes into the room, smartly dressed for work in a neat business suit and conveying an air of self-importance. She is a manager in a technology company in Silicon Valley and is about to go to a business meeting. Anna enters the room with a flourish and appears to demand all of our attention. Her presence catches Maria (and me) by surprise. I sense mother's height-ened emotionality, the feeling of her being in a hurry to get to work and taking little note of us in the room. She seems preoccupied and excited. Anna has a big smile on her face. After a few moments of scur-rying around the room she asks me how I am doing, but there is not much space to say more than a few words as she is in perpetual motion. I am wondering if she really wants to hear anything, but is being polite in asking. We exchange pleasantries. Anna says nothing to Maria, or to the au pair, Jane, who has just come into the family room. She does not come over to Maria, who has been looking at her intently throughout this episode. After a few more moments, Anna leaves with a dramatic flourish, saying nothing. She does not say goodbye to Maria or kiss her goodbye. There has been no transitioning. I am feeling star-tled by Anna's lack of recognition of Maria's need for physical and emotional contact and transitioning. The lack of ritual around separa-tion (and attachment) is bewildering to me and I am left wondering and reflecting about it in the observation. I allow myself to be in reverie, while at the same time I am observing Maria and her response to the separation. I notice that Maria has been watching her mother closely as she moved around the room in a flurry of activity. She continued to look for her mother as she left the room, and continued to stare at the door through which she exited. I sensed that she was wait-ing for mother to reappear. After a few more moments, and without Anna reappearing, Maria became fussy and started to cry, a cry that I had not heard before. Its intensity and pain startled me, and I began to have anxious and depressive feelings related to the abrupt separation. Maria started to cry in a low melodic way, not very vigorous or distressing at first, but increasing rapidly in intensity and level of distress. After a few minutes, her cry becomes strong, loud, uncontrol-lable. I observe her crying for several minutes, feeling an emotional pain and struggling to stay in my position as observer, as my desire is to comfort Maria. However, I continue to observe. Jane, the au pair, looks at me with an expression of confusion and distress, as if saying "what should I do now?" Jane is also anxious, feeling as if she cannot think and take action. She goes hurriedly into the kitchen without comforting Maria. After several minutes, Jane comes back into the family room, comes over to Maria, takes her out of the chair, and holds her. Maria remains distressed, continues to cry, and is inconsolable. Then Jane puts Maria back into her chair, quickly goes back to the kitchen and comes back with a warmed bottle filled with expressed milk. Jane gives the bottle to Maria, who remains in the chair. Jane holds the bottle while Maria sucks from it. Maria sucks vigorously on the bottle in a somewhat frantic way, gasping for air. She moves her body back and forth in a rhythmic manner in an attempt to self-soothe. After about a quarter of the bottle is gulped down, she suddenly stops sucking. Jane then removes the rubber nipple from Maria's mouth. Maria begins to cry again. Jane quickly puts the rubber nipple back in Maria's mouth without saying anything, and Maria again sucks vigorously and intensely. My reverie at this moment is of a baby frantically searching for mother's breast and, unable to find it, becoming distraught and desolate. I then begin to have another, more distressing fantasy, an image of mother being ripped away from Maria's stomach and in the process pulling away some of Maria's flesh, leaving a dark void. I wonder, is this what Maria is trying to fill up with her frantic activity? I then have a reverie of some of my analysands who suffer from eating disorders. Is what I am observing related to their frantic search for an unobtainable nourishing breast that cannot be found? Is it this kind of experience that can trigger their bingeing episodes? I am beginning to feel a chill, a chill I have not felt before. I feel empty and cold. I am wondering if this is related to the dread and terror of separation/abandonment from a nourishing, containing, holding, and available (m)other in infancy. As I continue to keep my attention focused on Maria, I observe that she is calmer; she has been able to feed and soothe herself. Jane takes her out of the chair, and again Maria appears upset and begins to cry. She puts her head against Jane's shoulder and appears to respond to the softness of Jane's skin. After a few moments, she falls asleep and the observation ends.

Maria's response to mother's abrupt separation, which included a lack of transitioning, led her to use bodily defences related to the secondary skin function. Her body became rigid and frozen as a way of coping with the unbearably painful feeling surrounding the abrupt separation by mother. When the au pair came to her, she was inconsolable, and then Maria focused on the rubber nipple and fed voraciously as a way of coping with what at the time were unbearable anxieties and emotions. My experience in the moment of the observation was that she felt uncontained by mother and dropped from mother's mental and emotional preoccupation. For Maria, being separated from mother in this way meant being torn away from her and her containing presence. She tried to gain control over these dreadful feelings by making her musculature stiff and frozen. In this way, she could attempt to control and stop feeling flooded by unbearable primitive affects. When she latched on to the rubber nipple and gulped voraciously, she appeared to be in frantic search of an object that she could hold on to and control. She could fill her stomach with a warm substance that could give the illusion of a nourishing mother and, at the same time, fill the internal void and take away momentarily the cold, rageful feelings. The frantic aspect of this sequence appeared to be triggered by feelings of disconnection and a dark feeling of dread that is difficult to name and give shape to.

The significance of the secondary skin function in clinical work in contrast to normal development of primary skin function

In my analytic practice with children who have identity disorders, eating disorders, or addictive behaviours, I have found that auto-sensous activities such as rocking, masturbating, or bingeing are ways of providing a feeling of pseudo-containment in the face of often unmanageable emotional experiences. The experience of containment offered by these behaviours is short-lived and needs to be repetitively re-enacted in order to experience a feeling of calmness and control over these painful emotional states. The primary self of the infant has its own defensive system that is activated when there is environmental failure (Fordham, 1985). These defence systems arise spontaneously out of the bodily and psychic self and are designed to preserve a sense of individual cohesion and intactness. These defences of the self create an impermeable barrier, a second skin, between the infant's self and the environment, and the processes of deintegration–reintegration and assimilation–accommodation are prevented from evolving. In extreme cases, the infant can evolve rigid, autistic-like symptoms of a second-skin nature that thwart psychological development. In the infant observation with Maria, I think we can see the emergence of these secondary skin defences, which often have an auto-sensuous nature. Although related to Fordham's concept of defences of the self and Tustin's autistic defences, this defensive pattern involves the body to a great extent, and describing it as a secondary skin defence seems closer to the actual experience.

In contrast to the secondary skin function, the primary skin function provides a sense of a secure envelope in which emotional experience can emerge and unfold without the infant or child being overwhelmed or overly anxious. The primary skin function leads to the feeling of being comfortable within one's own skin; that one has a separate and unique identity, and can interact with others without excessive fear of merging or loss of identity. To feel comfortable within one's own skin is the outcome of optimal ordinary development. Through analysis, a child with faulty development can be helped to experience their own agency and their impact upon others, and to discover that primary attachment figures can be a secure base from which to explore themselves and the world around them.

Infant observation vignette: Esperanza at five months and one week

The evolution of a primary skin function could be observed in Esperanza, a Mayan/Hispanic baby whose parents had immigrated to California from Central America.

When I arrive for the observation, mother asks me to go into the bedroom, where Esperanza is lying in a bassinet on her parents' bed. Mother is giving her a bath. Esperanza appears calm, yet alert. Mother is speaking to Esperanza in Spanish with an intonation that echoes the rhythms of Esperanza's vocalisations. Mother gently covers Esperanza's body with warm water, rubs her skin, and bathes her with soap. Esperanza has a small rubber ball in her hand that she holds with a certain determination and focus. All the while she maintains a gaze on mother's face and eyes and does not look around the room or at me. As mother shampoos her head with vigorous strokes Esperanza remains relaxed and calm, allowing her head to bob up and down a bit, responding to the strokes of mother's hands without uttering any sounds of protest. Mother then tells me that Esperanza remains calm when she has something in her hand, and then she does not cry. As mother is talking to me, she gently bathes Esperanza's genitals in an unselfconscious manner. Mother goes through the ritual of rinsing Esperanza a number of times, each time passing her hands over Esperanza's head, chest, arms, and legs. Esperanza appears to calm as mother strokes her body, and she then closes her eyes and appears to drift into a reverie state. When mother stops touching her, Esperanza opens her eyes and looks towards mother, as if to orientate herself after her reverie. Mother continues the rinsing a number of times and lifts Esperanza on to her legs, turning her around so that her back faces me. She then turns her around again and says to Esperanza in Spanish, "How delicious is the water. Thank you, God, for the water. What would happen to us if we did not have water?" I sense Esperanza's pleasure in the moment and her close emotional connection with mother. Esperanza has a radiant smile, and she then looks away from mother with a strong and firm gaze. She conveys a sense of presence and embodiment in her fleshy baby's body. I feel touched and privileged to witness the intimacy between infant and mother. Esperanza's radiant smile evokes a smile in her mother, who then continues with the bath as she and Esperanza are immersed in the pleasure of their interchange.

The aesthetic and spiritual life of the baby and the emergence of the primary skin function

Virginia Woolf's (1976) concept of moments of being is helpful in understanding the aesthetic and spiritual dimensions of this experience, and they add to our understanding of the emergence of the primary skin function. Woolf writes about the ways in which ordinary experience can become filled with importance, and that these moments of being coalesce to become the "invisible and silent scaffolding" of our lives (Woolf, 1976, p. 73). According to Woolf, moments of being provide the foundation for our experience of self. They involve the integration of past experience into the present, providing us with the narrative of our lives. During the two years of my observation of Esperanza, I kept being drawn back to the moments of being that provided the secure foundation for her later development. These experiences provided a feeling of containment within her own skin. At first, the experience was primarily sensuous and took place on the surface of her skin. As Esperanza's development unfolded, the sensuality of her skin experience became more internalised and later symbolised in her play. Esperanza's experience of these skin episodes became encoded in her psyche, and provided the foundation for emerging capacity for containment and relationship.

She began to feel comfortable in her own skin, and later her capacity for empathy towards others could be observed. The past experience of the skin became integrated with the present experience of self and other. Woolf poetically describes this experience of integration of past into the present:

> The past only comes back when the present runs so smoothly that it is like the sliding surface of a deep river. Then one sees through the surface to the depths. In those moments I find one of my greatest satisfactions, not that I am thinking of the past; but that it is then that I am living most fully in the present. For the present when backed by the past is a thousand times deeper than the present when it presses so close that you can feel nothing else. (Woolf, 1976, p. 98)

Esperanza's experience of being bathed in the warmth of the water and the warmth of mother's words is a moment of being that structures and nourishes the felt experience of containment. This facilitates the formation of a primary skin function that enables Esperanza to feel safe and secure within her feminine body. The mother's touch, the warm water, being contained in the bath and feeling securely held within mother's mind all form the background for the emergence of this primary skin function. The experience in the bath becomes an unconscious narrative of the self where past and present can become integrated, "the present is experienced as sliding over the depths of the past, creating a fullness" (Woolf, 1976, p. 98). Woolf's insight into the impact of these moments of being is expressed poignantly, as follows:

> I reach what I might call a philosophy; that behind the cotton wool is hidden a pattern; that we – I mean all human beings – are connected with this; that the whole world is a work of art; that we are all parts of the work of art. (Woolf, 1976, p. 72)

We can understand more about the importance of these moments of being if we look closely at recent infant observation research done in a laboratory rather than in-home observation using the Bick method. Laboratory observations by infant researchers Ainsworth (1978), Beebe and Lachman (2002), Stern (1985), Schore (2003), and Tronick (2007) provide substantial evidence that the intersubjective field is a continuous, reciprocal system in which each partner is contextualised by the other. This gives scientific support to Woolf's poetic description of the primary skin function. Development proceeds as self and other are involved in interactions that are mutually regulating. Empirical infant research describes patterns of interaction that enable analysts to observe the non-verbal processes that lie behind the verbal exchange. Individual organisation is continually shaped by the dyadic context. In the realm of infant–care-giver relationships, there are three major interacting units that constitute the system: the parent as a self-organ- ising, self-regulating unit; the child as a self-organising, self-regulating unit; the parent–child dyad as an interactive field with a unique organ- isation of its own. This also applies to analytic work, as both analyst and analysand are continually influencing and being influenced by the other's words, feelings, and actions. Particularly at the non-verbal level, mother and infant, as well as analyst and analysand, participate in a moment-to-moment co-ordination of the rhythms of behaviour. Symbolisation and imaginative processes require a matrix of relation- ship in which to develop; they do not develop spontaneously. This relational and intersubjective matrix is at the very heart of contempo- rary analysis and is grounded in the child's earliest experience of inter- change and reciprocity. Tronick (2007) terms these dyadic states of consciousness, and he notes that when the collaboration of two brains is successful, each fulfils the system principle of increasing its coher- ence and complexity. At the moment the dyadic system is created, both partners experience an expansion of their own state of consciousness. The boundary or psychic skin surrounding their individual experi- ences expands to incorporate elements of consciousness of the other in a new and more coherent form.

Observation of newborn babies indicates that the baby has the potential for integrative experiences at birth and that these experi- ences are mediated through the interactive bodily–emotional dialogue with the (m)other. The baby's innate, archetypal potential for the experience of self is facilitated through the experience of touch, smell, taste, sound, and sight. The experience of self is mediated through his interactions within an interpersonal environment that is sensi- tive and resonant to his needs. It is within this relational context that body image and identity development begin to unfold. The infant's active engagement with his care-givers leads to processes of deintegration–reintegration (Fordham, 1985) and increased differenti- ation through what Piaget (1951) terms assimilation and accommoda- tion. In these processes, experiences (both personal and archetypal) are internalised and an inner world becomes structured through the introjection of relationships and affects with significant attachment figures in the infant's life.

Another way of looking at the concept of moments of being, both in relation to analytic work and the emergence of a primary skin function in infancy, is presented by Stern and colleagues (1998) in their paper "Non-interpretive mechanisms in psychoanalytic therapy: the 'something more' than interpretation". The "'something more' than interpretation" is a concept that applies to an analytic treatment that is grounded in contemporary laboratory studies of infant–(m)other interaction. Stern found that such moments of authentic interpersonal connection between infant and (m)other, or analyst and analysand, can have a therapeutic effect, transforming the analysand's relationship with the analyst as well as contributing to the analysand's sense of having an authentic, alive self.

These moments form the foundations of the primary skin function, as well as promoting the development of a secure attachment. Such moments of meeting can become significant turning points in analytic treatment as well as in an infant's development, as I have tried to show through the infant observation of Esperanza. In the observation of Maria, I have tried to demonstrate how moments of non-being or failures of meeting also have a fundamental role in an infant's development and can lead to the formation of a secondary skin function that impedes development. Both infant observation using the Bick method and infant research done in laboratories seem to be reaching similar conclusions about the importance of moments of being or non-being, or moments of meeting or failures of meeting, for the infant as well as the analysand. Following Fordham's lead, analytic work that is done with an understanding of the dynamics of the infant–(m)other relationship and grounded in infant observation research is critical in helping analysands to form a secure internal space where emotional, imaginal, and reflective processes can unfold and individuation and growth can be facilitated.

Conclusion

Using the infant observation method, we can see how the primary and secondary functions of the skin emerge through the complex interactional sequences that take place between the baby and the significant attachment figures in her life. Through the careful observation of babies at home, we have been able to formulate new theories based on a view of the earliest psychic development of the infant. Fordham emphasised that observation must always come before theory, and that if our observations point us in new directions, our theories might need to be modified and transformed (private communication). Theories of psychic skin, starting with Bick's seminal papers, have helped us to understand and work with patients who might have been inaccessible to us before. Greater empathy and understanding can be brought to those interrupted in their individuation processes, with symptoms such as eating disorders, self-mutilating behaviours, sensations of feeling "skinless", and other disorders that involve the body. By providing a secure frame and a containing analytic skin, we can enable analysands to explore the preverbal and infantile origins of their difficulties. The primary skin function develops as the analysand is able to work through infantile experiences, both internal and external, that have led to difficulties in experiencing emotional containment and secure attachment. The secondary skin functions have helped to protect the analysand from feeling overwhelmed with unbearable anxiety. As the primary skin function emerges, the analysand can experience his or her feelings, thoughts, and sensations without feeling overwhelmed, and a capacity for reflection, imagination, and desire evolves. The creation of this secure internal space leads to the capacity to be separate. It is an important developmental task of infancy and a significant focus of analytic work for patients without such a secure space.

References

Ainsworth, M. D. (1978). *Patterns of Attachment*. Englewood Cliffs: NJ: Lawrence Erlbaum.

Anzieu, D. (1989). *The Skin Ego*. New Haven, CT: Yale University Press.

Beebe, B., & Lachman, F. (2002). *Infant Research and Adult Treatment*. New York: Analytic Press.

Bick, E. (1964). Notes on infant observation in psychoanalytic training. *International Journal of Psychoanalysis, 45*: 558–566.

Bick, E. (1968). The experience of the skin in early object relations. *International Journal of Psychoanalysis, 49*: 484–486.

Bion, W. R. (1962). *Seven Servants*. New York: Jason Aronson.

Feldman, B. (2004). A skin for the imaginal. *Journal of Analytical Psychology*, 49(2): 285–311.

Fordham, M. (1985). *Explorations into the Self*. London: Academic Press.

Fraiberg, S. (1987). *Selected Writings of Selma Fraiberg*. Columbus, OH: Ohio State University Press.

McDougall, J. (1989). *The Theaters of the Body*. New York: Norton.

Piaget, J. (1951). *Play, Dreams, and Imitation in Childhood*. New York: Norton.

Schore, A. (2003). *Affect Dysregulation and the Disorders of the Self*. New York: Norton.

Stern, D. N. (1985). *The Interpersonal World of the Infant*. New York: Basic Books.

Stern, D. N., Sander, L. W., Nahum, J. P., Harrison, A. M., Lyons-Ruth, K., Morgan, A. C., Bruschweiler-Stern, N., & Tronick, E. Z. (1998). Non-interpretive mechanisms in psychoanalytic therapy: the 'something more' than interpretation. The Process of Change Study Group. *International Journal of Psychoanalysis*, 79: 903–921.

Tronick, E. (2007). *The Neurobehavioral and Social–Emotional Development of Infants and Children*. New York: Norton.

Tustin, F. (1990). *The Protective Shell in Children and Adults*. London: Karnac.

Vygotsky, L. (1978). *Mind in Society*. Cambridge, MA: Harvard University Press.

Vygotsky, L. (1997). *The Collected Works of L. S. Vygotsky*, Volume 4: *The History of the Development of Higher Mental Functions*. New York: Plenum.

Woolf, V. (1976). *Moments of Being*. London: Harcourt Brace.

CHAPTER NINE

From not knowing to knowing: on early infantile trauma involving separation

Alessandra Cavalli

O ne of the main reasons that brought Jung to separate from Freud was Freud's belief that infantile experience is paramount and profoundly influences the person that each of us becomes. Jung felt this approach was deterministic and, convinced that there must be more (Jung, 1961; Kerr, 1994; McGuire, 1974), he plunged into the scholarly study of our written heritage: philosophy, physics, and metaphysics, anthropology, astrology, and mythology. In his search for this unknown "more", Bion's O (1970), Jung sought guidance from the experience of those who had lived before. By finding other ways of understanding the psyche, he hoped to prove that Freud was wrong.

Ironically, separating from Freud was problematic for Jung precisely because it evoked his own unknown and unresolved infantile trauma of separation. Writers including Winnicott (1964), Jackson (1963), Satinover (1985), Fordham (1985), Feldman (1992) and Meredith-Owen (2010, 2011) have discussed the mental crisis Jung suffered as a result, elaborating on this early trauma and how it informed his personality, and how analytical psychology is founded on Jung's attempt to make sense of what he was experiencing and his internal working through.

Liber Novus, The Red Book (2009) is the testimony of how Jung was able to emerge from his mental crisis, out of the darkness of his unconscious to be reborn alone, without the help of a mother. Instead, he created a matrix for himself using the written heritage he studied. In the *Red Book*, he constructed a boundary around this unknown past experience and found a way to deal with the beta elements provoked by his traumatic separation from Freud. Yet, despite his capacity to heal himself and to create an entire psychology based on explorations into his self, it is possible that Jung did not understand the infantile origins of his trauma.

Vestiges of experiences that have not been contained and mediated by the maternal matrix are not available to explicit memory (Mancia, 2007). They are stored in implicit memory, so have emotional impact but no meaning. Unlike the repressed unconscious posited by Freud, these primitive memories have never been represented mentally and, therefore, cannot be expressed. They affect the personality because they inhabit a "non-existent" desert of the mind, which has no name. These memories emerge only as acting out, as symptoms that need a semantic significance. Emotional events in the present reconnect us with suppressed emotional events in the past in such a way that past and present become inseparable, conflated.

His break with Freud brought Jung into contact with an earlier traumatic experience of separation that had been suppressed (to use Green's 1998 formulation). By containing it, he was able to explore it, and this contributed to a growing sense of self (Jung, 1961). Some of Jung's legacy to us is represented by his clinical and theoretical research into these areas of the individual's primal proto-mental experience and its relationship with reality.

In this chapter, I use a clinical case to look at early infantile trauma involving separation. My aim is to think about technique, and how to work with patients who present an ego that has varying degrees of maturity and strength, but contains a split-off part, a fragment or pocket with associated non-ego contents. Particular attention is paid to the need to create a maternal matrix (what Botella and Botella (2005) call figurability) in which the patient's early trauma can be recovered and the split-off part can be integrated. Even with a considerable level of ego development, it is a constant threat to stability to have such an unintegrated primitive area in the personality. Relating to one specific case, I focus on the rigidity of those areas, and on the difficulty of spotting them in analysis. Progress in analytical theory and technique must be sought at the frontier of analysis, in the difficulties that might seem impossible to overcome. This frontier is a "no man's land", open to progress as well as to failures. This is the zone of the unrealised trauma (Bion's Caesura, 1977). A psychic trauma becomes known when it is recognised as such by the analyst and/or by the patient. It acquires full significance when both realise this (Baranger, Baranger, & Mom, 2009).

When dealing with pockets of preverbal areas, one finds an absence of representability; instead, there are subjective states of feelings and body sensations with phantasies attached, which have never been tested in reality, confusion between subject and object, and symbols expressed in a very concrete way. Although Jung had little to say about these problems, much of his work was concerned with them (Jackson, 1963). In his search for "more", Jung did find O, the truth, although he could not understand it in the way we can now think about it. Nevertheless, he lived it, and experienced the phenomena that represented it. Experience precedes knowing about it.

At the end of the chapter, I come back to Jung and this quest. I pay particular attention to the problem of knowing, Bion's K, with the aim of showing that in order to stay open to Jung's dictum "there must be more", to stay open to O, we must challenge our knowledge again and again and accept that what seemed known to us (K) can suddenly turn out to be a belief, a false certainty. This realisation is possible only if we allow ourselves to be touched by O, by the truth, and experience its phenomena. The challenge of O reframes our knowledge (K) anew, allowing us to grow and develop. In a sort of parallel process, both patient and analyst are faced with this difficult exercise. The challenge consists in being open to experience, in breaking and repairing theory in the struggle to evolve. Understanding can be only in transformations in O, which then must be understood. In this respect, Jung created a precedent.

A few thoughts on early infantile trauma involving separation

In his paper "Abandonment in infancy" (1985), Fordham made an important distinction between separation and infantile trauma involving early separation, which he called abandonment (1985, p. 21).

According to Fordham, abandonment is a traumatic experience and differs from other forms of separation in which sadness, pining, and grief are experienced. In abandonment, there is no internalised image of a mother who can physically hold and mentally contain her infant, because the actual mother has left her infant without her mediating and containing function. Experiences that have not been mediated by the mother, for which no maternal matrix has been provided, are split off, dissociated, and not integrated into the rest of the personality. They are known only implicitly, and so affect the rest of the personality in the form of symptoms, or through acting out. As somatic delusion–illusion, preverbal bodily events that have never become word, they trap the person and prevent development and growth. The problem in analysis is how to create a container in which the terrifying somatic event can emerge, so that a matrix can be provided, and, with it, meaning.

In the following case material, I present the problem of patients who have employed early defences against abandonment and the difficulties for both patient and analyst in their quest to transform "O" into "K".

Clinical presentation

The patient "lost" her mother when she was a few months old. While her mother was ill (present, but absent for her infant), she was brought up by another member of the family, who looked after her in a rigid and strict way. My patient was not conscious of this trauma as she became very attached to the maternal substitute, who loved her but created for her a container similar to a psychic straitjacket. This took the form of strict rules that the infant had to follow: no sucking, sleeping on command, potty on command, weaned at four months and fed with a spoon on command. This maternal substitute could be viewed as emotionally abusive, but she provided a strong container for the patient's infant self. Like an iron box, it held the infant together, preventing her from breakdown after the traumatic loss of her absent-but-present mother.

The patient is a well-adapted woman who has been successful professionally. She came to analysis because she felt she was approaching a mid-life crisis and had lost a sense of direction. She had always felt that life was a fight that had to be endured, and her description of this fight had the intense quality of something in her internal world that had to be understood. Only in retrospect did it become clear that this patient had created around herself a strong defence, and she was operating in life like a soldier who would attack any problem, external or internal. Her "credo" was that she had to be good, and everything that was in the way had to be annihilated, including emotions, feelings, and thoughts that could be considered by her as "bad". Her understanding of the world was black and white, and while she was operating for the world to become white, she was totally unconscious of this, and had no means of knowing herself or others in a more realistic way. In her mind, it was a matter of will power.

First dream of the patient:

> I was riding a bicycle. This seemed to be my task, just going on and on pedalling, every push on the pedal felt difficult and heavy, only at some point I realised that I was pulling a rickshaw, which was attached to the bicycle. I understood that it had always been there. I looked back, and in it was another me, in a comatose state. She woke up, had a look around and passed out. I realised I had to keep pedalling and pedalling. I became aware that I had always taken this other me with me.

Through the image of the dream, we began to think of a split-off part of her that was traumatised. This part was carried around by another part of her, and a lot of energy was employed in this difficult exercise. We began to think that our difficult task in analysis was to get to know the split-off and traumatised part in relation to her early history and in relation to herself.

First break: separation and hallucinations

Freud described the splitting of the ego as passive, an ego subjected to a traumatic event allows itself to be split. For Klein, trauma splits the ego and while one part remains in contact with reality, the other part, and the object attached to it, stops developing. According to Fordham, it is not the ego that splits, but two different experiences that remain separate because they are irreconcilable. These are linked with two experiences of the object to which the self was relating. Although the self has the capacity to link experiences (ego bits), some ego bits can remain unintegrated. Following Fordham's hypothesis, I began to think of my patient as having had two experiences of herself in relation to her object: these two experiences seemed to be linked in a way that had to be understood, and while one was positive and growth-promoting, the other seemed to be unthinkable and dreadful. The dream seemed to be showing in a powerful way that the patient had not been able to integrate these two experiences into herself. Something had made her feel totally helpless, and a helplessness that had no name emerged in this image of an ill, comatose part of the personality which could not sustain contact with reality and had no way of expressing itself. The challenge of the work was to create a boundary around this something that had no name. The dream represented the first attempt of her psyche to find meaning for something unknown that needed understanding.

The dream was an image of an experience of total loss and helplessness that had been introjected, but never understood. Confirmation of this became apparent in her relationship with me in the sessions. I began to have two experiences of my patient on the couch: a very alive woman, energetic and full of interest, and one who would suddenly become silent and lost. Although she was alert in these lost moments, she could not free associate; she was "blank". If asked what she was thinking, she would reply, "Nothing, I am only waiting for you to tell me what to do." Slowly, we began to understand that she would put herself on hold and wait for instructions. In the first part of the analysis, it was difficult to know what might have provoked these moments, which did not seem to be connected with anything. When she became blank she had two experiences of the analyst, first as the lost mother, and then as the maternal substitute who would rescue her.

I began to relate to the patient's blankness as to her early trauma. The lost mother was somewhere present in the analysis, but then the patient lost the analyst and related to her as to a substitute mother / analyst who would tell her what to do and think. I began to imagine that the blanks represented an experience so confusing that it would re-traumatise the patient again and again. The trauma had happened so early that it had no form, only confusion, confused and confusing nameless dread. There was no way of expressing it. I began to imagine that the part of the personality linked to that experience of early loss was still attached to the self, but had lost all hope of being found.

Perhaps the rigid rules of the maternal substitute, like the rigid rules of the analysis to which the patient had committed eagerly, provided a container for the patient's past experience. Because of anxieties and confusion, the part of her personality that lived alienated at the edge of the self had not developed the ability to create the symbolic structures by which we face absence and loss. Nevertheless, in analysis, the repetition of an early experience could be observed and some understanding could begin to take place.

I began to understand her silences—at the beginning of the week, in the middle of a session, or during the last session of the week—as a re-enactment of her early trauma: the straitjacket of the analysis was holding her together, but the loss of her mother was re-enacted again and again without the possibility of understanding it. In blank moments, the patient was motionless, at times she felt cold and would cover herself with a blanket. Sometimes, her stomach would produce noises. It took a long time for us to understand their meaning, and I will return to this. I began to postulate in myself that the blank moments were attached to the rest of the session by feelings that at that point we did not know about. As the rickshaw was attached to the bicycle by a link, these unknown feelings were the link between two experiences of my patients in relation to her objects. We did not yet know about them, as my patient did not seem to feel anything.

When the first summer break arrived, I was curious to see if the blanks could be accessed or if we had come close to them in some ways. With the break, the straitjacket of the analysis would be lost, and I wondered if the loss might reconnect my patient with the experience of the abandonment. The patient experienced this first break as a catastrophe. She hallucinated my presence, and these hallucinations, although very frightening and confusing, helped her to survive.

Some thoughts

It took some time for us to understand that the hallucinations were not serving the purpose of reconnecting the patient with me or her analysis, they were simply helping her to keep away from the split-off part of her personality. While the separation could have helped her to contact something of that early experience, by hallucinating my presence she was defending again and in a more manic way against the terror of the early experience. By keeping me with her all the time, the patient had not separated from me, as if the summer break had not taken place. It was possible to make a first hypothesis according to which the lost object (the primitive mother) had not been represented internally. By fusing with an experience of the lost object, my patient was telling me that it was possible to think of her early experience with the lost mother having been very ambivalent. She seemed not to have been able to create a good and a bad image of the lost mother, but only to identify with an idealised aspect, the love-giving mother. During the break, she was desperately trying to identify with this aspect of her mother in relation to me in order to protect herself from her mother as the aggressor, the lost mother. This powerful and terrifying aspect of her mother was still unknown to us and had no representation in her mind.

We began to think of the mini-breakdown she experienced during the summer as a way to keep away from a catastrophic childhood experience in which she had not been held or contained, mentally or physically. Idealising was a defence against a terrifying experience that had to be avoided at all costs. The straitjacket of the mother substitute and the analysis could now be thought about as the rickshaw containing an unknown experience which had to become known.

After the first summer break

After the break, the patient began to complain about feeling confused. This confusion had the quality of a primitive confusion, a product of her earliest relationship in which the search for clear and differentiating answers was not adequately met. It is possible to postulate that, when the primary self of my patient was hit by reality with the loss of the mother, a "patch" (the phantasy of fusion) was produced, which protected the self from the impact of unbearable reality. Her initial dream gained a new meaning: it was as if the whole self of my patient was moved by the phantasy of reunion, the capable part of the patient, with the traumatised helpless part attached, was moving through life with the unconscious hope of refinding the lost mother of infancy. Perhaps my patient had spent all her life hoping to be reunited with the lost idealised object, and this hope gave her the motivation to move on in life. The patient had transferred this hope to me, and, indeed, she had been able to reunite with an aspect of me during the break, but it was the idealised me, while the me who had left her was blanked out.

During the break, the "comatose" part was abandoned again. I had become the mother substitute who had taken the mother from the infant. In order to survive the loss, the patient hallucinated the lost mother-me and survived the break in the same way she must have survived the maternal abandonment. We can see that the summer break was a lost opportunity for mourning. The repetition of a past experience was the only way the patient was able to cope with a situation in the present that was linked with a past experience. The repetition was also a defence against an experience that could not be recovered. In identification with the abandoning mother-me, the patient was re-abandoning herself, as she preferred to be fused with an idealised me, leaving in the rickshaw a dead–alive part of herself.

The question remained as to which experience of the object the comatose part was relating to. Also, what were the feelings that were linking the two experiences of the object? There seemed to be no representation of them. "In parallel to the symbiotic relationship with the idealised object, there is always a symbiotic relationship with the dead alive object" (Baranger, 2009, p. 215). In the unknown content of the split-off part was a terrible experience of the object and of herself, and knowing it created a terrible confusion in my patient. This confusion was one way of understanding the link between the two experiences of my patient and her mother. Secondary splitting and idealisation were employed in the struggle against a primitive and unbearable confusion. This confusion had to be tolerated in our work for the two experiences to become closer and known.

Encouraging my patient to think about the break, to tell me how she felt, to clarify the content of her hallucinations, was a way of getting her to look at it as a real event, in which I had not been with her. By showing her that I did not know what had happened to her, I encouraged her to think about it, to test her desire to deny something real that troubled her, which she did not want to know about. By attempting to ignore the hallucinations, she was keeping the comatose part of herself in a dead–alive state. As if repeating the abandonment of her mother, and in identification with her, she was leaving the other part of herself to deal with a lost object that was constantly re-traumatising her. It was extremely difficult to keep in my mind the part of her that needed to be attended to, but which my patient disregarded with considerable nonchalance.

After the second summer break

When we resumed work after the second summer break, my patient said "No" to me. She did not want to come back to her analysis. For a long time she kept saying "No" to me. It was difficult to understand which experience she was refusing. Was it a "No" to possible depressive feelings due to the break and the experienced cruelty of the mother-me? Or was it a "No" to the substitute mother-me who was asking her to enter again the straitjacket of the analysis? Although terribly painful and difficult to deal with, this "No" was the beginning of a breakdown of an unthinkable past experience that needed to be understood.

While the patient was silent and uncooperative on the couch, I began to hope that I could become someone else, not a better mother, not a better maternal substitute, but a thinking object that could provide a matrix for the terrible experience which until then had never been understood.

It was at this point that I began to think of the hallucination as a form of protection, an early form of relationship that was known but which, like the womb, needed to be mourned. Then she had had another early experience, one that had not been fully known, which was difficult to represent and understand. Looked at in this way, her "No" could have a new meaning. It could be understood as a "No" to any other experience of me but the idealised one, to her fear of having to come to terms with an unrepresentable reality, to her rage with me for forcing her to look at the status of things, and, possibly, as a "No" to mourning the womb-like relationship she wanted to have with me. Her "No" also meant having to accept a relationship to the blank experience.

While the patient was beginning to separate from the maternal substitute by saying "No" to me, she was also expressing the unresolved feelings that were connecting the two experiences of her mother. From the beginning of the analysis, these feelings were expressed in the form of sounds produced by her stomach. As she became more in touch with the feeling of confusion, these stomach sounds gradually diminished, and finally they disappeared.

The two experiences of the same object and herself, linked together, could now begin to be analysable. Slowly, it became possible to bring them closer in relation to her early experiences and to me.

The idealised object and the dead–alive object were now the same in their two manifestations, as well as the good-person aspect of the patient and her dead-like other aspect that needed to be understood. Bringing these two aspects closer was creating a great deal of confusion. This confusion was in some way a confirmation that the loss had happened at an early stage in which clear differentiation had not taken place.

Some thoughts and further developments

I began to understand the two images of my patient with their mirror objects as having their origin in early states of primitive identity between infant and mother.

In Fordham's language, the adoring baby adoring an adoring mother in parallel to a dead-like baby mirroring a dead-like mother could be understood as two archetypal experiences. Subject and object could not be differentiated because of lack of containment. The experience and its representation were identical, and symbolisation was not possible. Re-enactment was the only way to symbolise and transform what could not be digested and understood. In Kleinian language, the infant part of the patient had introjected but not assimilated both aspects of the mother and identified with them. With her "No", the patient was rebelling against the lost idealised mother, the maternal substitute, the old known way of relating.

According to Klein, if the ego bit rebels against the experience, the object attached to the experience also rebels. It was likely that the semi-dead-like aspect of the object would now become a persecutor, and that I would become that aspect of the object in the transference. For this part of the ego, the infant and her experience of that aspect of her mother were still undifferentiated. By describing to my patient what I thought was happening, I hoped to create a matrix for understanding, for representability and differentiation. This understanding might provide an antidote to her fear of a persecuting me, which, like the dead-like mother, would be a persecuting experience that my patient had to avoid at all cost. Perhaps she was afraid of falling to pieces if she were forced to reconnect with that early experience.

For Klein, the fear of disintegration is mitigated by the introjection of the ideal breast and identification with it. This protects the infant from the knowledge of a persecutory breast, which becomes a superego that persecutes the ego bit. The rickshaw, like the iron box of the maternal substitute that had saved her from disintegration during that early experience, was now trapping my patient in such a way that she could not move on.

The patient's infant part was maintained in a near-death situation to avoid feelings of needs, rejection, and helplessness. It was to avoid those feelings that my patient was rebelling against her analysis and me. By rebelling, her dead-like part was waking up, and, in an omnipotent way, she was denying our work, her dependence on me, possible depressive feelings, rage and hate: a survival defence against helplessness. Her insistence on wanting to leave me had a psychotic quality. For Bion, the psychotic is what has not become a thought, but has remained an allergy to the frustration of an absence. This was the blank that my patient and I were hoping to transform into a feeling and a thought.

The early relationship of my patient with the mother was broken by the trauma of her absence. In that absence, there was a no-thought, an emptiness that was held together by a second skin, an armour, the iron box of the maternal substitute. I was hoping to find in the archae-ology of her mind a "tooth, one mandible, and reconstruct a whole personality from this fragment" (Green, 1998, p. 659). This fragment, possibly her feeling of confusion and the sounds of her stomach, was the first link between the two experiences of the mother that my patient had been unable to know about.

Inside the rickshaw

The patient's stomach sounds needed particular attention. Instead of becoming alive, something would be evacuated through her intestine. It is possible that these sounds were a defence against devastating emotions. Her "No" was a last desperate attempt to control emotions that were attached to the experience of the lost mother. Now that she was becoming separate from the idealised object-me, and I was becoming a persecutor, the unresolved feelings attached to the expe-rience of the loss of the idealised mother were becoming free and could no longer be controlled.

The difficulty in the analysis was to help the patient to feel all these feelings in such a way that when the phantasy attached to the perse-cutor became known, or a partial representation of it, the feelings attached to that experience would feel less persecuting because they were known and the patient had learnt to feel them. Encouraging the patient to stay in touch with these feelings was difficult because they were frightening her. She had no experience of being physically held when she had powerful bodily feelings that felt as if they were fragmenting her. She had been abandoned to them.

Second part of analysis

In the second part of her analysis, my patient began to feel something she did not know about, which evoked panic in her. By now, although reluctant, she seemed determined to understand herself, and a different relationship between us could emerge. It seemed that my curiosity and attention to her had stimulated a similar interest in herself. Her "No" to me slowly unfolded into a "Yes" to herself, and then into "I want to know more about myself". The panic was evoked by a long known and suppressed sensation that we identified as a feeling of utter helplessness.

This coincided with our understanding of a recurrent dream in which she was in bed, paralysed. Understanding the dream was perhaps the second element in the difficult construction of a representation of the experience of the lost mother. Although my patient's conscious self was very ambivalent about the analysis, her unconscious seemed willing to cooperate by providing elements that were paramount in our work of constructing a matrix of figurability (Botella & Botella, 2005). It was deeply moving for my patient to identify the feelings of total helplessness that the dream described. A once unbearable bodily event now had a name and could begin to be known and thought about.

My patient had been contained by the womb and had adapted to her mother's care after birth, but, with the premature loss of her mother, she was trapped in the iron box of the strict rules of the maternal substitute. This new container had become a prison from which my patient could not escape. By putting a name to this old, unknown bodily sensation, we were able to transform it into a thought. Helplessness could be understood and felt.

The experience of rejection for my patient had been so profound that she maintained the near-death situation to avoid the feelings connected to it. Instead, the experience seemed to be encapsulated in a terrible sense of helplessness that she had converted it into a sort of religion. This was her destiny.

In order to know more about her lost capacity to form a representation of the lost object and its mirror image of the lost baby, we needed to find ways of exploring the delusional aspect of the absent mother mirrored by the abandoned baby. As we did with the hallucination related to the idealised object, we needed to connect with a delusional representation of the loss in the negative.

By allowing me to become a companion to explore with her the persecutory feelings that inhabited the void, helplessness, shame, and fear, the patient was moving away from experiencing me in the transference as identical to her experiences. I was becoming the provider of the maternal matrix that she needed. Once separate, I was available to investigate, question, and think about what had not seemed knowable to her. In this process, her suppressed feelings could become felt, known experiences.

Slowly, the terror of abandonment could be explored again and again with all the feelings attached to it. My patient could develop and connect with a third position from which she was able to observe, feel, and think. From this position, the patient could begin to separate from the lost object, and finally begin to dream something about the unknown experience. With this, symbolisation could begin.

Coming closer to the delusional aspect of the suppressed experience and its possible representation

Around this time, my patient dreamt that she was in a room with a terrifying presence. In the dream, she thought it was probably the devil. We were beginning to connect to the experience of the lost mother and the feelings that were connecting her with that experience of the mother. A few months later, a second dream brought us closer to that experience.

> I am at the hairdresser. He not only cuts my hair, he also asks to me to talk freely and express my thoughts. I do this but then admit to myself that I was communicating with the devil. The devil was a sort of friend who would help me, but also a terrifying agent.

This dream gave rise to many memories: my patient's childhood fear of the devil, her terror of the dark, and finally an association with the film *Rosemary's Baby*.

Slowly, she began to trust that the good hairdresser/me could create order in her head, transforming beta elements into thoughts. An image was becoming available to her, and words could be found to describe something that until then had remained unthinkable. Only by accepting the devil as a container could the content of a terrifying experience become known and thinkable. Was this unwanted baby a devil? Was this why she was abandoned? Or, worse, was this baby the daughter of the devil itself?

While this dilemma remained unthinkable, my patient had spent her life wanting to punish herself, or aspiring to saintliness to eliminate the devil part of herself, and/or feeling damned by birth as a daughter of the devil and without hope of salvation. There seemed no way for her to escape this destiny, trapped in the iron box of her infancy.

Now that we were slowly able to make meaning, and some possibility of understanding could emerge, the capacity to create a phantasy could be recovered. This meant that bodily events could be linked with images that had been lost, and the ego could find again the lost sense of fit between mind and body. Finally, we understood the two aspects of her symbolic experience of the devil:

- the hateful abandoned child is abandoned by a horrified mother;
- this child can only hide what it fears is its devilish nature, in terror of finding out that her nature cannot be transformed.

This unconscious dilemma had been trapping my patient: she could not escape her nature, but, if her nature were discovered, she would be punished and abandoned again and again.

Now we could understand her profound fear of relating to others, her fear of being rejected, and, with it, the fear of meeting the real self she could not escape. In parallel, we were able to understand her fear of meeting the devil in the other. The constant terror of this made her feel she had to be very good, but also to punish herself for desiring freedom, which would have damned her if she had attained it.

The phantasy of the devil was a very primitive way of representing the terrible experience of hate and loss, and it was necessary to transform this first delusional representation of her experience into one closer to the truth, to reality as it is. This primitive defence against early loss could be relinquished when something that had remained unknown could be recovered and reintegrated. Finally, the feelings connecting my patient with that early experience could be felt in relation to others without their delusional components. By integrating a suppressed experience, my patient was reaching a level of separateness that is the foundation for the capacity to experience wholeness and passions.

Conclusion

The potential for wholeness and a sense of self resides in primal emotional experiences: they are true. These primitive experiences need to be understood (K). This understanding brings us closer to "O", reality as it is, and our unique relationship with it. The attempt to experience reality, and our capacity to know about it, needs to meet with adequate conditions in order for us to develop an evolved sense of being. This includes a capacity for mental growth and a development towards integration of experiences. The fluctuation between states of disjunction and wholeness is a lifelong task, which includes the capacity to separate from primitive phantasies and identification with aspects of the parents, to bear affects, and to transform them into emotions, feelings, and thoughts. When an experience cannot be represented, it can only be enacted: indigestible facts (beta) cannot be understood and transformed. This represents an obstacle to the growing sense of self, to K, and to O.

In the difficult task of sustaining patients in their search for self, the analyst must find ways of becoming a sort of auxiliary conscious and unconscious ego, able to perform for the patient what has gone amiss, such as the capacity to create meaning between mind and body, and to (re)find the ego's sense of fit between mind and body (Garland, 1998). For my patient this has meant being able to name previously unnameable primitive experiences that belonged to the past but were active in the present, and to find a different way of knowing herself in relation to them as they are. In our work together, in our investigation of O, we have been able to come closer to beta and to O.

As I have broken down theories and put them together again, I have tried to make sense in myself and for my patient of her

unknown experience, which she has now understood in a different way. I have used the patient's past as a beta element that had
to find new meaning in the present. This transformation brought
integration of a split-off emotional experience of the past that was
always present and, although unknown, was connecting all her
emotional experiences in such a way that present and past were
confused.

I have tried to construct a matrix around an infantile experience.
Using free association, the theory of child development and observation of the patient's capacity to relate to me, I have formulated with
the patient a way of making sense of her past experience and transforming it into something new. Preverbal bodily events that had
remained somatic delusions could now become known. The grip of
bodily events and of their resulting delusional–illusional states could
be relinquished. In this chapter, I have shown how somatic delusions
could become feelings and thoughts. Two different primitive
emotional experiences of my patient in relation to others could be put
together, and the feelings attached to them could be felt and understood in relation to her experiences.

My clinical approach is similar to Jung's, keeping open to "O". I
have tried to link my reverie to the childhood experience of my
patient, relating to it from a personal, individual point of view. I
found archetypes of the collective unconscious and personal unconscious phantasies. Jung sought something "more", and I have tried to
show that this more—in Bion's language, beta and O, the ongoing
search for meaning (K)—requires elaborating on emotions and an
analyst who is very much in touch with feelings. It is primal emotional
truth that we need to reach: every emotional experience in the present
reconnects us with those in the past. The past obscures the present,
and past emotional experiences must be integrated in order to understand the present.

Like Jung after his break with Freud, my patient and I encountered
suppressed events that were hidden but present and which were trapping her. Understanding and transforming them freed my patient
from imprisonment. We approached the unknown past with courage
and curiosity and were able to transform beta and O into K. This
transformation has helped my patient, like Jung (1961), to achieve a
sense of wholeness and of self. Our work brought us closer to the real
thing, to O.

References

Baranger, M., Baranger, W., & Mom, J. M. (2009). The infantile psychic trauma, from us to Freud: pure trauma, retroactivity and reconstruction. In: M. Baranger & W. Baranger, *The Work of Confluence*. London: Karnac.

Baranger, W. (2009). The dead alive. In: M. Baranger & W. Baranger, *The Work of Confluence*. London: Karnac.

Bion, W. R. (1970). *Attention and Interpretation*, London: Tavistock.

Bion, W. R. (1977). *Two Papers: The Grid and Caesura*. London: Karnac, 1984.

Botella, C., & Botella, S. (2005). *The Work of Figurability*. London: Routledge.

Feldman, B. (1992). Jung's infancy and childhood. *Journal of Analytical Psychology*, 37: 255–274.

Fordham, M. (1985). Abandonment in infancy. *Chiron*, 3–21.

Garland, C. (1998). *Understanding Trauma*. London: Karnac.

Green, A. (1998). The primordial mind and the work of the negative. *International Journal of Psychoanalysis*, 79: 649–666.

Jackson, M. (1963). Symbol formation and the delusional transference. *Journal of Analytical Psychology*, 8: 145–159.

Jung, C. G. (1961). After the break with Freud. In: *Memories, Dreams, Reflections*, A. Jaffé (Ed.). New York: Random House.

Jung, C. G. (2009). *The Red Book*. New York: Norton.

Kerr, J. (1994). *A Most Dangerous Method*. London: Sinclair-Stevenson.

Mancia, M. (2007). *Feeling the Words*. London: Routledge.

McGuire, W. (Ed.) (1974). *The Freud/Jung Letters: The Correspondence between Sigmund Freud and C. G. Jung*, R. Manheim & R. F. C. Hull (Trans.). Princeton, NJ: Princeton University Press.

Meredith-Owen, W. (2010). Winnicott on Jung: destruction, creativity and the unrepressed unconscious. *Journal of Analytical Psychology*, 56: 56–75.

Meredith-Owen, W. (2011). Jung's Shadow: negation and narcissism of the self. *Journal of Analytical Psychology*, 56: 674–691.

Satinover, J. (1985). At the mercy of another: abandonment and restitution in psychotic character. *Chiron*: 47–86.

Winnicott, D. W. (1964). Memories, Dreams, Reflections by C. G. Jung. *International Journal of Psychoanalysis*, 45: 450–455.

PART VI
THE FUTURE

CHAPTER TEN

Friendship: beyond Oedipus*

Stefano Carta

I n this chapter, I will explore the theme of friendship as a transformation of that libidinal love that characterises the Oedipal
complex with its implicit themes of betrayal and narcissism. My
aim is twofold. First, to show how these issues describe a harmonic
dialectic formation which, starting from the original force of libidinal
love, may, or may not, evolve and mature during a person's life or a
patient's analysis. I believe that friendship, if defined in a certain way,
is truly the highest and most mature form of human relationship—one
of the deepest embodiments that the *elixir* of individuation may take.

In my view, the relationship between libidinal love—as a sort of
prima materia and the *lapis* of friendship—is deeply bound and rooted
within the very essence of the "analytical situation", so much so that
its history and vicissitudes may be traced back to the birth of psychoanalysis and analytical psychology as a direct product of the original
relationship between Freud and Jung. As I will try to show, the transformation of Oedipal love into friendship is neither easy nor obvious.

---

* An earlier version of this chapter, "Narcissism, solitude, friendship: notes on the therapeutic alliance in the context of the Freud–Jung relationship", was published in
September 2012 in the *Journal of Analytical Psychology*, 57(4): 483–499.

Neither has it been sufficiently analysed, or been given the role that I believe it should have.

My second aim is to show that such a relative lack of attention to friendship is due to the specific legacy and shadows of the personalities of the "founding fathers" and their relationship, which influenced, and perhaps still influences, our own analytic identities (here including our psychoanalytic colleagues).

For this reason, I begin by briefly recalling what I think is a fundamental tenet of the Freud–Jung relationship: its intrinsic Oedipal nature. My intention is not to analyse the relationship between Freud and Jung *per se*, but to *recall it* to shed some light on the nature of friendship and its meaning within both our own psychological life as subjects, and our "institutional identity" as analysts.

My starting point is Carl Meier's reaction to the reading of the whole correspondence between Jung and Freud, after Anna Freud had found the missing half of the letters in a trunk. While reading the letters written by Jung alone, Meier had felt only a moderate interest, yet, when he was able to read the whole exchange, he wrote a letter to Kurt Eissler dated 14 January 1955 that opened with these words: "My first impression is truly that of a 'devastating tragedy'" (McGuire, 1974, p. xxiv).

I think that we must begin from here and ask ourselves: what happened between Freud and Jung? What did Meier's sentence really mean? Why, in short, did he evoke a tragedy, and a *"devastating tragedy"* at that?

I believe that Meier's words were not chosen lightly. He really did mean tragedy, and for more than one reason. The first is that, if we consider the relationship between Freud and Jung from its human side, as I am trying to do here, one can have few doubts that it was deeply marked by the Oedipus complex in which Freud played the role of the father and Jung the son.

For Freud, Jung is the favourite son, "the man of the future" (Gay, 1988, p. 201). Like a modern Abraham, Freud sees in Jung the man who will ensure his progeny and the future of his own creation: psychoanalysis. It is commonly known that Freud fainted twice in Jung's presence and that he himself interpreted such fainting as a reaction to the death wish that he thought his favourite son held for him.

However, for the Oedipal tragedy to occur, it is not enough that just one of the two actors will participate: Laius and Oedipus call to each other and each in turn replies. If Freud alone had played a role in a huge enactment of the great castrating father, while Jung was immune to its complementary role, nothing would have happened: their relationship would have died as an emotionally inert matter. Freud faints because, like Laius, he recognises his own son who waits for him at the crossroads.

In March 1909, when there were yet no apparent signs of their future break-up, Jung wrote to Freud,

> You may rest assured, not only now but for the future, that nothing Fliess-like is going to happen. I have experienced so much of that sort of thing; it has taught me to do the contrary at all times. Except for moments of infatuation my affection is lasting and reliable. (McGuire, 1974, letter 135J, pp. 211–212)

Surely we do not need to wait for Freud's essay on negation to understand the real meaning of this hint about Fliess, in which Jung already foresees the destruction of the Oedipal father. The very same Jung who will write a flood of words on the characteristics of complexual affectivity shows here an incredible touchiness when he *believes* that Freud criticises him or does not appreciate him enough. Once again, I am not speaking of Jung, but of Oedipus, before his venerated castrating father.

The paranoid death anxiety in which Jung was destined to become a psychological assassin inhabited Freud both as a person and as a Jew. He saw Jung at first as the son who would save the psychoanalytic Thebes from the plague of scientific derision and from isolation, and, at the end, as the crazy and violent renegade. One could cite numerous examples to show Freud's identification with the role of Oedipal father, not least of which is that he used to write to Jung calling him "son".

Jung, in turn, treats Freud in an absolutely idealised manner. In 1908, he writes, this "undeserved gift of your friendship is one of the high points in my life which I cannot celebrate with big words" (McGuire, 1974, letter 72J, p. 72), and goes on to say he feels obliged to ask Freud ". . . to let me enjoy your friendship not as one between equals but as that of father and son".

Towards the end of their personal relationship, in a letter of December 1912, Jung, extremely irritated at an interpretation (moreover correct) that Freud made of a *lapsus calami* of his, will write to him these words: "...Your technique of treating your pupils like patients is a *blunder*. In that way you produce either slavish sons or impudent puppies ..." (McGuire, 1974, letter 338J, p. 534). Even if, in the light of history, Jung's criticism appears objectively well grounded, his tone is of someone clearly involved in the same emotional picture he is trying to criticise.

Examples of the Oedipal nature of the relationship between Jung and Freud are many, but here I must stop. It is indispensable, however, to add what might seem a relatively unimportant observation. In this entire correspondence, Jung never goes beyond addressing Freud as "Herr Professor" while Freud goes so far, in the central years of their mutual infatuation, to call Jung "lieber Freund", or dear friend. If this asymmetry gives rise to some suspicion, the question now is: were these two ever really friends?

I would have to answer "no". The relationship between Freud and Jung had nothing of friendship about it. It is permeated with that acquisitive eros, of that passion which, in a sense, is the very opposite of friendship. Here, the interesting point is that the same tie that bound them together also ensnared the two great masters, the same type of eros or, if you like, the same libidinal investment, one quite similar to that which, in the analysis of unconscious infantile derivatives, is called "transference neurosis". The question then becomes, if these two were not friends, for what reasons were they not?

In the first place, I would argue, because each was moved by a predatory love for the other: each expected the other to be what he wished him to be. Each of them wished to bind himself to the other, and this desire was expressed by the Oedipal script that an entity much greater and more powerful than the two masters had reserved for them, what the Greeks called *Ananke* (fate).

Freud felt betrayed by Jung, and, to all intents and purposes, Jung did betray him, although the same could be said reciprocally. In this intense Oedipal love, betrayal, the ambivalent counterpart to love, is part of the script, even if it appears too often in the guise of pure destructivity. The phrase used by Maier can now be commented upon: the tragedy was devastating, first of all, because, as is consubstantial with tragedy, the hero (and here we have two) voluntarily chooses the destiny that will destroy him; second, because this event is in itself a tragedy foretold, already written, rediscovered, and reinvented by Freud. Last, because its missed transformation, its failed transcendence, determined some important outcomes within the analytical situation—outcomes that we shall investigate shortly.

It is true that Freud distanced himself from Jung and strengthened his psychoanalytical creation. Jung moved away from Freud and became completely Jung.[1] Nevertheless, on a human level, their affair was tragic because, in the dialectic between salvation and annihilation, intrinsic to the notion of tragic, the salvation was directed toward the elaboration of their respective theories and clinical practices, while the human relationship was destroyed.

It is my view that the myths that govern psychic life are manifold, perhaps innumerable, and that, therefore, no single myth can be guaranteed a central role, as is the case of Oedipus. My view acquires a particular importance with respect to the question: if Freud and Jung acted out in full an Oedipal relationship, could another alternative be imaginable? Or, in other words: from the Oedipal *telos* that was secretly interwoven in the relationship, could a transformation or transcendence have followed? I believe that this question is central, fateful, and not only for Freud and Jung, but also for our patients and for ourselves. What is the alternative to Oedipus? Only its being "crushed", as Freud believed? A sacrifice either heroic or painful? In short, only a loss to the point of castration? Or is there really something else in psychic life, something *wholly other*?

I think that Oedipus, together with the constellations of the other tragedies of mythic stamp, first of all that of Laius, but also those of Clytemnestra, Agamemnon, Orestes, or Antigone, fill an important role for what one could call the process of weaning from infantilism. Surely the Oedipal complex, as it has been interpreted for more than a century, represents a fundamental aspect of the underlying archetypical weaving in the relationship of the child with its parents? Also, as infantilism is the cause of the vast majority of cases of neurotic unhappiness, it is clear that the Oedipus–Laius complex, with its variations, has a central role. This discovery alone—the unveiling of the mythical structure of the psyche and the psycho-mythical reinvention of the Oedipus story—would make Freud an absolutely enormous figure both as a scientist and as a human being.

However, if we speak of taking leave of the realm of the mothers, of the loss of dependence and of the infantile omnipotence/impotence, it is legitimate to ask ourselves if this taking leave will lead us into some *other* psychological place. Allow me to emphasise this passage. Here, the Oedipal relationship is approached not with regard to its causes or its particular vicissitudes, but to its latent aims. From this perspective, the question is not whether Freud and Jung were perfect actors in a tragedy already written and played out infinite times before, but *why* did this happen? It is this question we must pose ourselves, and that neither Freud nor Jung was able to ask himself: "What is the reason, the *aim* of this situation? Is this the only form of relationship possible or can it transcend itself into something else?"

I returned to these details of the very complex relationship between Freud and Jung because I think that neither asked himself this question, nor were they able to transcend the nature of their relationship. Most of all, because the vicissitudes of their relationship have had considerable effects on the analytical theories and practices of future generations, as well as on the history of the analytical movements. One need only think of the trans-generational dynamics of analysts, trained in their turn by their analysts almost as if to become faithful spiritual sons, or, sometimes, schismatic opponents.

It may well be, too, that the splitting of the analytical community is a direct result of the failed transformation of the relationship of the two great masters into a successful friendship. Now, on the other hand, we can respond to the question central to the *telos* of the Freudian Oedipal conflict. One may formulate the hypothesis that it was precisely due to what happened with Jung—as previously with Breuer, Fliess, Stekel, and Adler—that Freud could coalesce into an extremely powerful theory his own Oedipal psychic equation, that is, through establishing the highly peculiar psychoanalytic setting, which is wholly directed towards the infantile prehistoric past and its manifestation through transference neurosis. However, I believe that such a technical and theoretical setting might tend to prolong interminably many analyses.

On the other hand, let me be fair: Jung's well-known phrase, "fortunately I am Jung and not a Jungian", in this light sounds cynical and mocking. It is as if Jung is still fighting the ghost of the Oedipal father, and, thus, was not able to accept the positive component of being also a father, or even a follower. Such an attitude has been transmitted transgenerationally in Jungian movements, as the weight and depth of Jungian thought has largely been ignored by the institutional bodies that organise and diffuse science and culture, such as the academic and scientific communities. I think that this lack of interest in analytical psychology is not due only to Jung's highly complex thought and its non-reductive twentieth-century epistemology. I believe that a further reason is that, without a Father principle to encourage some level of institutionalisation, a Jungian "scientific" community has never been firmly established, so that Jung's work has been left in a limbo of misinterpretation and new-age-like vulgarisation.

It goes without saying that, in the interplay of the opposites, such a fluid Jungian *ecclesia* has spared the Jungian community from many painful schisms and splits, but, by often encompassing and absorbing conflicting points of view, it has also slowed a fruitful advancement of analytical psychology.

As we did for Freud, also for Jung we can ask what might have been the goal for which his unconscious had set up his relationship with Freud.[2] A possible answer is the following: as we know, Jung considered the Oedipal–infantile transference situation as a first phase of an analysis in preparation for the possibility of further work, in which the meaning of regression cannot be understood in terms of a reactivation of the structures of infantile complexes, but as completely new models of potential individuative reorientation. It is for this reason that Jung considered transference as much "the alpha and omega of the analytic method" as an impediment to it.

Thus, it seems possible that a certain part of the emphasis that Jung puts on the concept of individuation, opposed to the risk of the regressive undifferentiation into the collective, may represent the constructive part of the legacy of the ancient struggle against a father who never could become a friend. Like his patients, Jung also struggled to free himself from the infantile Oedipal aetiology and so enable the libido to flow towards its intrinsic ends of adulthood and individuation. This is the "transformation" that Jung called the fourth stage of analysis.

If I am right in thinking that a part of what we, as analysts, have been through in our history derives from the two masters' unresolved Oedipal conflict, I also must emphasise that such a vicissitude deserves the definition of a *felix culpa*. As a matter of fact, without such an unresolved conflict, we could not pose ourselves these fundamental questions: does the Oedipal complex have a goal? Can it transform and transcend itself because of its own nature?

My answers are: yes, I believe this is possible. I believe that the elaboration of Oedipal conflicts and their transcendence leads us to the transformation of love into friendship. To understand this observation, let us return to the theme of betrayal: Jung felt that Freud wanted him to be and to remain a son forever, always second, and he felt betrayed by this. Freud could not accept that his psychoanalytical creation should undergo attacks and defections, and he, too, felt betrayed. All of the vocabulary used in those years was military or religious: "conquer new followers"; "destroy the enemies"; "convert new initiates". In short, nothing close to an objective or scientific attitude.[3]

Then, in 1910, after the first signs of crisis between the two, Jung writes a letter to Freud in which he quotes Nietzsche:

> One repays a teacher badly if one remains only a pupil.
> And why, then, should you not pluck at my laurels?
> You respect me; but how if one day your respect should tumble?
> Take care that a falling statue does not strike you dead!
> You had not yet sought yourselves when you found me,
> Thus do all believers -.
> Now I bid you lose me and find yourselves;
> And only when you have all denied me will I return to you.
> (Nietzsche, 1883–1885, I, 3)

One can agree wholeheartedly with this, even if, again, it shows clearly how Jung projected the image of the father on to Freud.

Here, it is Nietzsche who can show us the way to a definition of friendship and to shed light on the path that neither Freud nor Jung had been able to follow.

I believe that both Freud and Jung could have accepted the possibility of rethinking the nature of their relationship through Nietzsche's philosophy, as he was so significant for both: for Freud, who avoided reading him too much, so as not to be too influenced by him (Lehrer, 1996), and for Jung, for whom Nietzsche's thought had an absolutely pervasive influence.

In the libidinal love that is central to psychoanalytical theory and practice (and, I believe, fundamental to analytical psychology as well), the object is desired as a possession (whether anaclitic or narcissistic) at the risk of unmournable loss, while in friendship the object is desired for the destiny it is called upon to accomplish for itself.

In *The Gay Science*, Nietzsche writes,

The lust of property, and love: what different associations each of these ideas evokes! and yet it might be the same impulse twice named: on the one occasion disparaged from the standpoint of those already possessing (in whom the impulse has attained something of repose, who are now apprehensive for the safety of their 'possession'); on the other occasion viewed from the standpoint of the unsatisfied and thirsty, and therefore glorified as 'good.' Our love of our neighbor, is it not a striving after new property? . . .

There is, of course, here and there on this terrestrial sphere a kind of sequel to love, in which that covetous longing of two persons for one another has yielded to a new desire and covetousness, to a common, higher thirst for a superior ideal standing above them: but who knows this love? Who has experienced it? Its right name—friendship. (Nietzsche, 1882, par. 14)

Within the projective identification between Freud and Jung, it seems clear that each was more worried for himself and only accepted the other in the measure in which the other corresponded to his own individual aims. The son and the father met one *against* the other, and the intense love was a love springing from a state of narcissistic dependency.

In contrast, in *Thus Spake Zarathustra*, Nietzsche wrote that friendship represents a common "longing for the *Übermensch*" (Nietzsche, 1883–1885, volume 1, par. 14), which means that friendship is seen as the fundamental—and interpersonal—way by which one transcends his own nature.

For Nietzsche, the "love for one's neighbour" (as in *The Antichrist* (1895)), which we could here define as a projective ambivalent idealising of the object—that kind of love that Jung and Freud shared before the catastrophic end of their relationship—actually is the escape route for two still immature human beings, neither of whom has yet learnt how to stand on his own, or to find his own meaning within himself.

While love yearns for the object as a possession, friendship makes the other *free* by wishing him to *become* himself, thus paradoxically promoting separation and solitude. In the first case, one does not fall ill by solitude, but, as Nietzsche wrote, by *multitude*.

Freud desired loyalty from Jung. He dreamed of and created a Son who was supposed to perpetuate his creation and his own life, so overcoming his relationship with his own father, Jacob. Jung, for his part, created a Father who could idealise him and support him on his path towards separation, almost as if granting him permission. Yet, nothing that one owns may be given by concession: everything that is most precious for us must be *taken*, must be, as with Hermes or Prometheus, *stolen*. The catastrophe was not due to the nature of their relationship, but to the non-transformability of its nature.

But how can one transform, or transcend the erotic, mimetic, and acquisitive Oedipal relationship? To look for a possible answer, let us return to Nietzsche, who, in *Zarathustra*, writes,

> If, however, you have a suffering friend, then be a resting place for his suffering; like a hard bed, however, a camp bed: thus will you serve him best. And if a friend does you wrong, then say: 'I forgive you what you have done to me; that you have done it to yourself, however—how could I forgive that! (Nietzsche, 1883–1885, volume 2, par. 26)

Now, the "hard bed" Nietzsche is referring to is precisely what neither Freud nor Jung had ever been able to accept, or, in other words, to demand: *the voluntary betrayal of the friend* to induce him into solitude and, in so doing, fulfil himself. It is along these lines that Nietzsche wrote in *Zarathustra* and later took up again in *Ecce Homo*, his last book—almost a testament before falling into madness—"The man of knowledge must be able not only to love his enemies but also to hate his friends" (Nietzsche, 1889, Preface).

This is a truly significant phrase. It is the key to understanding how much friendship is different from love, as the latter is, after all, always based upon the possession of the object. Friendship transcends love because, through its betrayal, it promotes and presupposes the necessary solitude through which the subject becomes rooted within himself in order to become himself.

I am much indebted to Hillman's view of sacrifice and betrayal, as he describes them in his classic book *Senex and Puer* (2005). Nevertheless, I do not fully agree with him, because I think that his view of the sacrifice necessary to reach adulthood envisions betrayal as an intrinsically *violent and shocking experience happening against the Puer*. My idea is that such a rupture belongs to an environment based on a classical Oedipal constellation founded on a polarisation between father and son, desire and fear, and in which betrayal and sacrifice play the same role that Freud attributed to castration anxiety. It seems to me that, in Hillman's view, betrayal is something that the *Puer* must suffer *against* his will, against his original desire. By this the superego would be created as a collective agency to which the *Puer* sacrifices his original impulses. What I would add here is that there might be a *second* way to reach adulthood, a way similar to Winnicott's idea of the transformation of the sense of guilt into a genuine preoccupation for the destiny of the depressive object. In the view I am here expressing, the sacrifice, the break that is indispensable for growing out of infantile acquisitive love, might not be *imposed* just by fear and menace, but also *embraced* by a *higher form of love*.

At this point, we are ready to move finally to the "analytic situation". The patient should find in it a *temenos* that is adequate, a "holding" space for the original trust in the analytic relationship. It is evident that in every analysis a founding condition of safety is essential. In this space of safety and absolute trust, the patient cannot but regress and give himself up to the reactivation of constellations that come from the mythical galaxy of the infantile universe.

This relationship, however, is, in truth, but a partial relationship; the ghosts that govern it prevent the patient access to a complete relationship with the object, a relationship in which, unlike a libidinal investment, love is orientated not towards possession, but towards the liberation of the object from oneself. I believe that the very expedient used by the psychoanalytic situation, ruled by anonymity, abstinence, and the neutrality of the analyst, promoted a constellation within the transference neurosis which is bound to the inherently ambivalent nature of the Oedipal complex in which dependence and longing alternate with hatred, envy, and inevitable disappointment. It calls forth ambivalent sons and daughters who depend upon and envy the parental rival they must overthrow and the parent they cannot possess, rather than sons and daughters that can identify themselves with the parental ability to foster difference, or, rather, to foster that transcendental function—love—that makes us fully human.

Now, I believe that the Oedipal complex, deeply rooted in the analytical situation, does not have only a cause (mythical–infantile), but also a goal: the goal is the preparation, after the initial trust, of a space for betrayal. A condition, that is to say, in which the patient is finally abandoned to himself. It is clear that here we prefigure two types of solitude, the negative type that is full of resentment, and a positive type, in which the betrayal signals the patient's final taking leave of his infantile condition and "the initiation to the tragedy of the adult" (Hillman, 2005).

To grow up is not enough: a cut is necessary, a caesura. What is necessary is a betrayal of illusions, of the phantasmic theories, of the delirium that governs the burning infantile desire for the mother, in which everything exists to satisfy the infant's needs and desires. At the height of his passion, Christ voices his loudest cry: "*Eloì, Eloì, lamà sabactanì?*" ("My God, why hast thou forsaken me?"), and at that moment becomes man. Suddenly, he is alone, in order to promote the same destiny in everyone of us: the potential destiny of self-transcendence, the appropriation of one's own life and of the supreme love in which the love of one's Self, as well as the love of the Other for his own Self, is objectively stronger than my desire for possession. This love that is stronger than love, which does not want the object but demands only freedom from it, is called, in a word, friendship.

These observations lead one, I believe, to ennoble in an absolutely key way the role and the value of the therapeutic alliance. In fact, far from representing a relationship transacted between the centres of consciousness, from which this meaning of alliance could not differentiate itself more clearly,[4] the capacity of the analyst to keep firm in himself the therapeutic alliance (friendship) with the central self of the patient, is thus revealed as an absolute essential condition for analysis, as well as a measure of the essential difference that exists between patient and analyst. Rooted in the calm centre of the ambivalent hurricane, crossed by sometimes furious, misdirected, and destructive passions, is the psychological ability of the analyst to guarantee the therapeutic alliance that gives analysis the possibility to remain in a psychic space of calm and self-centring from which the relationship with the patient radiates. In the raging of ambivalence, hate, and love, in the throes of the Dionysiac impact that such impulses entail in the patient (but also, in the ordeal of co- and countertransference, within the analyst as well), it is exactly the capacity of the analyst not to divert from the self of the patient a gaze that is at once "friendly", tranquil, and firm, and that can redeem the individuative nature of the process.

As the intrinsic nature of any human encounter is unique, it is impossible to put forward any generalisation. This means that the need to support and guarantee the betrayal I am describing here may be fundamental for some (many, I think) patients, but not necessarily for all of them. As a matter of fact, for some patients, the difficult task might be *not to break relationships, but hold them within a sense of stable continuity*.

Nevertheless, there are at least three frequently occurring categories in which what I am describing here might be significant in order to support the process of growing out of a libidinal, infantile, acquisitive, narcissistic relationship.

The first of these categories has to do with an inner experience of libidinal dependency on an idealised lost object, which must be abandoned in order to find it again at a transformed level.

L, a forty-five-year-old woman, came into analysis with me after a long analysis with a colleague, which had ended six years before. She came because, at the end of a marriage based mainly on a general unconscious pact of compensation, which had slowly poisoned all areas of their relationship, she had developed a very strong ambivalent bond with a man. His presence, but also the fear of losing him, literally drove her crazy. She would act out rage, pain, and anger, regardless of any situation in which she found herself. She spent nights and days crying, or extremely angry, and feeling utterly confused and hopeless. I will not go into detail about this complex story, but, at a certain point, she mentioned almost casually that, when she was a baby, her nanny had the habit of trying to feed her by holding her upside down. The sadistic nanny was fired when my patient was two years old. This idea immediately made deep sense to her, and being held right side up *vs.* upside down became our main metaphor, providing an integrative image within which some important thoughts could take a clear form.

The most important of these thoughts was that she could feel right side up when she could see this man as a frail human being (as he was, not being completely physically healthy himself). Such a realisation enabled L to hold in mind the *perception* of this man as a separate entity. Thanks to this perception—at first very frail and intermittent— L suddenly understood that the only way to have him was to let him go, and that there are situations in which love is expressed within a paradox by *choosing an abstinent distance*. This realisation was the beginning of a new, long, and painstaking phase, as she was called not to accept an Oedipal defeat before a competitive mother, but an autonomous self-sacrifice to free this man from her own intense, narcissistic, libidinal love in order to rescue and find, on the other side of the tunnel, "just" a man, a man who could once again say the words: *Ecce homo*, and whose imperfect love and presence she could bear.

In the second category fall some of those analytical processes that have reached a point of stagnation. In such situations, the cause of stagnation might be the postponement of the necessary betrayal and sacrifice of a once fruitful analytical relationship, which is now turning into a deadly *putrefatio*. In some cases, what we are called to do is to decisively promote *the end*. A true end: an end that should be forever.

I have experienced such a situation more than once, always with patients with whom I had a very "positive" and constructive relationship throughout the analytical process. This was the case with G, a fifty-year-old woman. Towards the end of a long and successful analysis, there was a period of stagnation and growing confusion lasting a few months. A dream announced the need to part.

> In this dream, G arrives at my office, but finds it empty. I am dead. She is shocked. The concierge hands her a picture that I had left for her—a picture of a garden.

Through the telling of this dream, a flood of feelings of loss and fear of being left came into the session, together with the sudden realisation that everything must pass.

G associated the picture of the garden with a beautiful place to find an introverted sense of peace and beauty, after having lived a life of very painful relationships of dependency on persons who did not love her (including her mother and husband), and whom she had felt to be absolutely right in every respect, especially when their opinions were dismissive and critical of her. The fact that, during her analysis with me, G suffered from a cancer, and that her life had been spared, made it clearer that the garden was the ultimate gift of our voyage together: the preciousness of life itself, superior to any other's acceptance or permission, a place of introverted centredness. We decided that it was time to finish, and to bear the sacrifice of our relationship as the final holder of G's old dependent way of life. The last three months of work together became once again intense and meaningful for both.

The third category deals with the process of growing out of analysis as such, and of leaving the identifications with (or the counterphobic identifications against) one's analyst. No need to underline how much such a process might prove relevant for the very identity of the analytical communities, often marked by the belonging, if not a sort of identification, to one's personal or training analyst.

In fact, analysis itself can be completed only with the constellation of the resolution of that essential difference that distinguishes the patient from the analyst on whom he depended just a moment before. This heralds the possibility that the asymmetry between the friendship of the second and the acquisitive, ambivalent love of the first is transformed into a common friendship. Yet, this can happen only through the betrayal of the illusions of omnipotence and at the end of analysis.

I believe that in the analytical relationship, we are called to do what Jung and Freud were not able to do. We are called to prepare the betrayal of our patient's idealisations in order to surrender them to the embrace of their own life. It is a tragic duty that constitutes the measure of the final act of every analysis; the act that completes analysis is the end of analysis.

If, instead, we avoid this sacrifice, if we postpone the end, if we sweeten it, if we fragment it, if we do not allow the patient to enter into the last room, which is that of solitude, the one in which the analyst who is the most trusted, finally abandons him, we will remain narcissistically children: the patient as well as the analyst. When the idealised transference relationship is ready for its end but this is not promoted, sacrificing it to the unanalysed life, then the process gets bogged down and rots in a time that is destined to be never-ending. It is the acceptance of solitude that marks the true end of analysis: its being terminable. It is through the acceptance of the definitive absence of the analyst in the patient's life that the analyst can disappear as a father in order to be transformed into a guarantor, a sort of friend *in absentia*. As with the transitional object, the analytical function can become diffused in the environment as an ethical search for the truth, as method and attitude of life towards the unconscious. If the process has been completed, if the betrayal has been accomplished, the patient can no longer go back to an infantile trust based on maternal projections. If, instead, we indulge the infantile projections of the patient and we hand him over to them, the missed betrayal of the patient's desire for the analyst's presence will be transformed into an acting-out through which, as Jack London wrote about the fate of his hero Martin Eden, in the moment that the patient will know, he will cease to know.[5]

In the most important moment of the end and of the betrayal, to continue to comply with the desire to possess the object—and satisfy the desire to return to an unconditional trust—would signal the annihilation of the meaning of the analytical process itself. Conversely, only through the end-process of analysis can both the analyst and analysis itself, finally de-idealised, come to occupy a potential space. The experience of being separated will by no means destroy them. On the contrary, they will transcend their own natures, given that the patient will be called upon to become conscious that he will never possess the analyst for himself, exactly because now the analyst obliges the patient to realise his desires *without* him—constrained by now within his own solitude. "You didn't desire me, but instead something more difficult and necessary: to become yourself by living."

This is the highest among the analytical functions: that of being a *friend*—albeit an absent one—of the patient: something that neither Freud nor Jung was able to be. This friendship, which sacrifices its own presence, opens the patient up to the possibility of entering into the world of this earthly life, this temporalised and transient life that is given to us precisely thanks to the sacrifice of the passionate and acquisitive relationship with the analyst and its transcendence into a *stellar friendship*:

> Stellar Friendship. We were friends, and have become strangers to each other. But perhaps this is as it ought to be—and we do not want either to conceal or obscure the fact as if we had to be ashamed. We are two ships each of which has its own goal and course. Our paths may cross and we may celebrate a feast together, as we did—and then the good ships rested so quietly in one harbor and in one sunshine that it may have looked as if they had reached their goal and as if they had but one goal. But then the almighty force of our tasks drove us apart again into different seas and sunny zones. Perhaps we shall never see one another again, or perhaps we may meet again but fail to recognize one another: our exposure to different seas and suns has altered us! That we had to become strangers to one another is the law above us— by the same token we should also become more sacred to each other

and the memory of our former friendship more sacred. There is probably a tremendous but invisible stellar orbit in which our very different ways and goals may be included as small parts of this path—let us
rise up to this thought. But our life is too short and the power of our
vision too limited for us to be more than friends in the sense of this
sublime possibility. Let us then believe in our stellar friendship,
though we should have to be terrestrial enemies to one another.
(Nietzsche, 1882, par. 279)

Only through solitude and betrayal—hating thus the true friend—
is it possible to transform the transferential relationship. This transformation leads to another kind of relationship, which is, at the
same time, entirely symbolic (because it is founded on absence and
solitude) and completely human: friendship.

In this way, the patient will finally be ready to leave behind his
fantasies to become embodied and live outside in the world, out
where others, equal to himself, are real and alone. It is in the moment
in which one accepts this absence as the necessary condition for a true
existence that one can say of analysis what Goethe wrote in *Faust*'s
closing lines:

> Uns bleibt ein Erdenrest,
> Zu tragen peinlich.
> *(Earth remnants burden us*
> *To bear them is toil)*
> (Goethe, 1976, lines 954–957)

Outside the illusory space of acquisitive love, the other may differentiate itself from that object of Oedipal love that the child believed to
be his rightful possession. Within the potential space of friendship, no
one owes anyone anything. It is all a gift. As a result of the betrayal of
hedonistic maternal love, in which trust was once absolute and intact,
acquisitive love can be transformed into a true sentiment of the soul;
a sentiment moulded in the difficulties and harshness of life, but also
shaped by the admiration for those who—thanks to the firmness with
which I, their friend, force them—try to live with responsibility and
fullness the unique sense, both unalterable and fragile, of their own
existence, now finally, *necessarily*, made free.

It is precisely within such a space of spiritual freedom that, as
Montaigne thought, it is really possible to be friends. Friendship,

therefore, unlike all other forms of passion and desire, firmly intertwines itself with our will and choice, so as to make of these a perfect wreath to crown a better love that binds and frees two yet imperfect beings.

Friendship can never be portrayed as a force that enslaves its friends, as do love, fear, or hate, which burn and fade furiously, consuming their own time. Instead, it seems to consist in a faithful constant *attitude* towards its object, a precious attitude embedded and soaked in time through which one is constantly called to refine and transcend, over and over again, the hardship of life and our own imperfection. Only in friendship do freedom, will, and love form an harmonious whole, while we keep inhabiting this sub-lunar world. It is a truly *human* whole in which my friend at the same time *happens* to me, while he is incessantly *chosen* by me in such a way that, as Montaigne beautifully wrote:

> *Si on me presse, continue-t-il, de dire pourquoi je l'aimais, je sens que cela ne se peut exprimer qu'en répondant: parce que c'était lui; parce que c'était moi.*

> (If you press me to say why I loved him, I can say no more than it was because he was he, and I was I.)[6]

*   *   *

The title of this chapter is "Beyond Oedipus". Now, in closing this book, I ask myself whether this beyond might not just imply the end of the analytical journey. Here, I like to think of the word end with its double meaning of end of something, and end towards something, as I am convinced that the intrinsic finality of everything that exists in time, and supremely for us human beings, is moulded with the mournful experience of the transience within time. As a matter of fact, I believe that where there is no end, there can be no ends.

While the very experience of time intrinsically is the experience of an incessant passing away, yet this experience as such also marks an eternal blueprint of all that passes away, leaving behind an unexpected gift. This gift resembles what in the second century Chinese treatise *Huainanzi* is called *xin*, to indicate the resonance of the musical stone that the God hits, the resonance that, like the fragrance of the ever passing eternal rose, fills the world in waves. This gift, which permeates our most intense experiences, emanates precisely from what is no more: it is its most highly intensified presence; the expanding fragrance and resonance of the very life of what once had been, and that we now may very well call meaning-beauty.

In the previous pages, I wrote that the end of an analytical journey happens when the loss of the everlasting presence of the infantile objects is consumed through betrayal. I wrote that this may mark a passage through which the archetypal configurations of the child, as described by so many tragedies (Oedipus, Electra, Antigone, Orestes, Laius, to mention a few), give way to a whole new world: the world of finiteness and friendship. The death of our acquisitive love initiates us into a new dimension of life, where new intensities may be born from the very experience of our finiteness, our mortality, our wholly real presence in this world. As Klein understood in her own way, gratitude may then fill our psychological space, as the fragrance of the rose, or the music of the stone, fill the world.

In *Problems of Modern Psychotherapy* (1966), Jung explains the potential relationship between four different aspects of psychotherapy. From the initial confessio of the patient's secret to the analyst, the need may come about for clarification of the transference. In turn, such a clarification of the transferential (infantile) bonds may give rise to the need for education, that is, for the patient's need to take responsibility for his/her understandings. In some cases—and ideally it might be desirable in all—the "structural" fourth and final phase of psychotherapy—the intrinsic future of the whole process—will be that of transformation.

I like to think that the future of a cure, such as that of analytical psychology, may be a very particular way to attempt to realise the transformation that Girard (1987) pursues in his great vision: the possibility of finally taking responsibility for ourselves, of overcoming the need to project into a scapegoat a split Archetypal Shadow with all our demands, our responsibilities, our positive and negative hopes.

Overcoming such a dynamic, redeeming such a Shadow, and so unveiling the true nature of friendship, is a task for all humanity; a humanity too frightened by its biological frailty and unconscious of its enormous aggressiveness, so which, like Laius, passes on this archetypal conflict to its children, generation after generation, so condemning them to everlasting Oedipal status. Such a task, as universal as it is, can be contained only in the small, precious, laborious, refined vessel of a human relationship.

Notes

1. The specularity—the secret symmetry—between Jung and Freud is quite evident in the period immediately following their separation. The institution of psychoanalysis is reinforced by the split, while Jung leaves the house of the father, the psychoanalytic community, as he resigns from the editorial board of the *Jahrbuch* (1913) and the presidency of the International Psychoanalytical Society (20 April 1914). Furthermore, he resigns from the Burghölzli, the university hospital, almost as if trying to exit the scientific–cultural universe (the father's universe) in order to be reborn in a new world.
2. This way of interpreting neurosis, in that it is the fruit of an unconscious "arrangement", is inspired by Adler, and is well discussed in Giegerich (1998).
3. Here, I agree with the acute observations of Polanyi (1958) when he argues that it is *normal* that the scientist who advances a new vision of the world by means of a new paradigm cannot but live as the hero-founder of a realm where those who do not accept the new ground rules are excluded.
4. According to the exception that I propose here, the therapeutic alliance represents the deepest aspect and the most refined capability of the analyst without which no technical ability or scientific learning *palia est*.
5. *Martin Eden* is an American novel, written by Jack London in 1909, with Nietzschean and Spencerian undertones, in which a young autodidact struggles to become a writer. The words quoted here are the closing words of the novel, when the hero commits suicide by drowning.
6. M. de Montaigne, *Essays*, Book, 1, ch. 8.

References

Gay, P. (1988). *Freud, A Life for Our Time*. New York: Norton.
Giegerich, W. (1998). *The Soul's Logical Life. Towards a Rigorous Notion of Psychology*. New York: Lang.
Girard, R. (1987). *Things Hidden Since the Foundation of the World*. Stanford, CA: Stanford University Press.
Goethe, J. (1976). *Faust II*, W. Arndt (Trans.). New York: W. W. Norton.
Hillman, J. (2005). *Senex and Puer*. Putnam, CT: Spring
Jung, C. G. (1966). *General Problems of Psychotherapy. Problems of Modern Psychotherapy*, C.W., *16* (2nd edn). Princeton, NJ: Princeton University Press.

Lehrer, R. (1996). Freud's relationship to Nietzsche: some preliminary considerations. *Psychoanalytic Review, 83*: 363–394.

McGuire, W. (Ed.) (1974). *The Freud/Jung Letters: The Correspondence between Sigmund Freud and C. G. Jung*, R. Manheim & R. F. C. Hull (Trans.). Princeton, NJ: Princeton University Press.

Nietzsche, F. (1882). *The Gay Science*. Lexido Classics Edition, 2010.

Nietzsche, F. (1883–1885). *Thus Spake Zarathustra: A Book for Everyone and No-one*. Harmondsworth: Penguin Classics, 1961,

Nietzsche, F. (1895). *The Antichrist*. New York: Arno Press, 1972.

Nietzsche, F. (1889). *Ecce Homo*. Kindle Edition, 2011.

Polanyi, M. (1958). *Personal Knowledge*. Chicago, IL: University of Chicago Press.

INDEX